The House at Henley

by GERALD PARKHOUSE

Christ Church

OXFORD

Published in 2015 by Christ Church, Oxford OX1 1DP

ISBN: 978-0-9569755-1-5

British Library Cataloguing in Publication Data.
A catalogue record for this book is available from the British Library.

Cover and text designed and set by Baseline Arts Ltd, Oxford
Printed and bound by TJ International Ltd, Padstow, Cornwall

Cover image: *Dominic Harrod, cox of the Christ Church 1962 Ladies' Plate crew, walks across the boat enclosure at Henley. Henley Royal Regatta*

NOTE: The material contained in this book is set out in good faith for general guidance and no liability can be accepted for loss or expense incurred as a result of relying in particular circumstances on statements made in this book. Laws and regulations are complex and liable to change, and readers should check the current position with the relevant authorities before making personal arrangements.

Contents

Preface

In 1993 I spent an academic term at Christ Church researching the House's rowing results and the composition of its crews for events on the Isis and at Henley Royal Regatta in the nearly 50 years which had elapsed since the end of World War II. During the course of this project I became aware that there resided in the College Archives a small number of record books maintained by Presidents and Secretaries of the Christ Church Boat Club. In later transcribing and editing two of them, covering the period 1860-1909, it became apparent that Christ Church had had a long association with Henley Regatta, stretching well back into the 19th century. This was strengthened by an investigation of the life of W.A.L. Fletcher, the greatest 19th century Christ Church oarsman, who went on to become a leading Boat Race coach and rowing administrator. I set about the task, now completed, of writing Fletcher's biography.

The exposure gained in the course of the foregoing research investigations sowed in my mind the seed of creating as comprehensive as possible a record of the House's involvement with Henley Regatta, something which had never before been attempted, as far as I could ascertain, in respect of Christ Church or any other Oxford college. The task, spread over 10 years, seemed from the outset to represent a daunting challenge, and so it turned out. What period should the research seek to cover? Henley Regatta was held for the first time in 1839. Perhaps the first 50 years would be a sizeable initial target, or the first 100 years, maybe. The same problem had no doubt faced Richard Burnell when he came to write his 1989 history of *Henley Royal Regatta*. He had elected to go for *A Celebration of 150 Years*. That set the benchmark. The first 150 years of the Regatta's existence became the target for my own survey.

Gradually sources of information became known and were investigated. Pam Cole, of Regatta Headquarters, furnished me with the Regatta's dates for every year. I was able to use these, over time, to look up the race-by-race reports of *The Times* correspondents for years in which Christ Church was represented. Information regarding the latter could be gleaned from sources such as *Oxford Rowing* (1900) by W.E. Sherwood, a Christ Church man, which contained a section on *Henley and other Races.* Later I made the acquaintance of H.G. Steward's race-by-race *Records of Henley Royal Regatta....*

(1903) covering the years 1839 to 1902, and the two companion volumes bringing these records up to 1968. Rowing Reports in *Bell's Life* supplemented, for many of the years, those in *The Times.*

But as the year-by-year experiences of Christ Church crews unfolded, it was clear that something was missing. Had not Fletcher won the Grand for Leander three years running? Had not Jumbo Edwards won two Henley finals for London Rowing Club, as well as one for Christ Church, in a single day in 1931? How many such non-House crews had included Christ Church men? To find the answer was no easy matter, but in the end it was possible to identify over one hundred such crews with members drawn from Christ Church. No doubt certain of such cases have been inadvertently overlooked. But such a number serves to underline what the text will show to be the College's heavy and consistent commitment to Henley, from the very first year of the Regatta through the following century and a half of competition.

However, an account doing no more that chronicling the appearances of House crews and House men at Henley would fail to convey any of the flavour of the way the Regatta developed from its start, basically relying on Oxbridge college, club and university entries to give it momentum, to becoming the focal point of annual international competition which it is today. How and when new events were introduced into the calendar, how the rules – as regards entry qualification and the definition of amateur status, for example – evolved over the years, how the Regatta grew from a one-day to a five-day event, how the line of the course itself underwent modification, what part the railway and the motor car played to facilitate access to Henley for spectators, deserved mention. Such aspects, along with the recounting of a range of incidents involving crews, umpires' decisions, appeals (not necessarily involving Christ Church crews), and the like, would serve to convey the essence of the "culture" of the Regatta, and to make clear the importance of the Stewards and the Committee of Management in ensuring a smooth conduct of affairs, so helping to provide a setting against which the performance of crews could be more clearly judged.

I therefore endeavoured to weave such background elements into the story without losing track of the book's purpose – to be specific concerning Christ Church's involvement with the Regatta.

The principal sources I have drawn on, save one, are identified in the text as they occur. The exception, from which a number of comments by OUBC Presidents are drawn, is a series of handwritten record books maintained by successive Presidents and fortunately preserved in the Modern Papers Room of the Bodleian Library. There are eight such numbered volumes (1-8) covering the period 1839-1923.

Thanks are due to many people who have provided information, comments, and clarification during the course of the preparation of the book. The College Archivist, Judith Curthoys, patiently and with unfailing good humour responded to dozens of requests for the clearing up of details on points arising, and made available for inspection the several crew photo albums, including the Hodgkin Collection, stored in the Archives. Pam Cole (already mentioned) similarly handled a number of requests for information made of Regatta headquarters, and provided access to Minute Books covering Stewards' meetings, while Mike Sweeney, Daniel Grist and Edward Warner also gave useful input, the latter kindly providing copies of selected photographs of races originally taken by Bushells, the Henley photographer, which are now deposited with the Regatta authorities. Colin Harris, Superintendent of the Special Collections Reading Rooms at the Bodleian Library, provided access to the record books mentioned, and gave valuable assistance. Roger Hutchins of Magdalen helped unravel many a knot arising from uncertainties in the way in which rowing races on the Isis were organized in generations past, and kindly gave permission, on Magdalen's behalf, for the reproduction of a relevant article by Richard Burnell which originally appeared in the history of Magdalen College Boat Club, 1859-1993,

Well rowed, Magdalen! Peter Burnell, himself a rowing Blue and Magdalen man, generously gave permission to reproduce a photograph of the 1908 Olympic crews' members, and the maps of the Henley course, which appear at the end of the book, all of which originally appeared in his father's book, referred to above. Amy Terrière of the British Olympic Association provided helpful information on the 1908 Olympics. Dr. Stephen Coleman, Academic Dean of Elmira College in the U.S., kindly made available office space to facilitate the progress of the work to its completion.

Former members of the Christ Church Boat Club were generous with information and input. These included Bill Rathbone, David Edwards, Jonny Searle, and Jon Carley. Some - Dick Gould, Sir William Gladstone, Duncan Spencer, Francis Gladstone, Jonny Searle and David Edwards - consented to the inclusion of articles, recollections or interviews which give additional insight into the periods covered by several chapters of the book. It is saddening to need to record the death of Dick Gould in 2014.

With the exception of photographs held in the College Archives, the sources of photographs in the text are indicated along with the captions. Bill Rathbone, Will Watson, Sir William Gladstone and David Edwards made such material available. John Eade of thames.me.uk gave permission to reproduce the photo of the 1891 Leander Grand Challenge Cup crew. Some years ago I acquired a photo album put together by J.F. West, bow of the Christ Church 1908 Thames Challenge Cup crew. This contains many Christ Church rowing pictures from that era, several of which appear among the illustrations.

Valerie Parkhouse and Nancy Burch are owed thanks for their patient and painstaking typing, and re-typing, of my hand-written drafts.

For the willingness of the House to sponsor and finance the publishing of this book thanks are due to Simon Offen, Deputy Development Director, and, for the preparation of the book for publication and its execution, to Andrew Esson, the book's designer, and Jacob Ward, Christ Church Development Officer. Without the College's sponsorship of the project, and the support of the Christ Church Boat Club Society, the book could not have been produced in the elegant form now made possible.

I hope that the book will be of some interest to readers. It has certainly been rewarding to have been able to bring together the strands of the House's illustrious association with Henley, and so perhaps to promote interest in, and support for, the Christ Church Boat Club, while encouraging its future members to aspire to perpetuate the proud history of which they are heirs.

This book has principally been written with Christ Church readers in mind. For others kind enough to read it, unfamiliar with Oxford jargon, the term "the House" is the affectionate everyday name for the college used by its members, derived from its original Latin name, stemming from Henry VIII, *Aedes Christi*, House of Christ.

Gerald Parkhouse, April 2015.

The House at Henley
1839

THE ORIGINS OF HENLEY REGATTA are so well documented and commented on that it is unnecessary to repeat them in the present context. Suffice it is to say that the Henley reach of the Thames had, for its straightness and width, early attracted the attention of the increasing number of people engaged in aquatic sports (as they were termed in those days); for example in 1837 the Dean of Christ Church objected to the House competing on the Thames at Henley against St. John's, Cambridge, as C.C. Knollys recounts in *Oxford University Challenge Races*… (1873). Indeed Henley had been selected as the venue for the very first University Boat Race in 1829. Also, the holding of an annual Regatta was seen by local landowning dignitaries, and the principal townspeople, as a potential source of income for the town and its tradespeople.

On 26 March, 1839, then, a number of resolutions were passed at a meeting, calling for the purchase of 2 Cups as prizes for 2 events, an amateur race in eight-oared boats, open to all challengers, and a race for four-oared boats to be competed for by "*Henley amateur crews*". Six Stewards were appointed to regulate and manage the Regatta, they to be assisted by a Committee of 14 persons.

At a further meeting on 1 May the rules for the 100 guinea-value "Henley Grand Challenge Cup" (the eight-oared race) were established. (The cup itself bears the inscription "Henley Regatta Grand Challenge Cup 1839"). The rules provided, as to entry qualification

> *…that any crew composed of members of a College of either of the Universities of Oxford, Cambridge, or London, the Schools of Eton and Westminster, the officers of the two Brigades of Household Troops, or of members of a club established at least one year previous to the time of entering, be considered eligible.*

Insistence on the amateur status of any competitor was clear from the start; every coxswain had to be a member of the club whose crew was competing. (At that time the coaching of crews was often carried out by professional watermen steering in the coxswain's seat. R. Coombes, such a waterman, coached both Oxford and Cambridge.) Entries had to be made by 25 May. The course was determined as being *"about one mile and a half commencing near the* [Temple] *Island and terminating at the* [Henley] *bridge."* The Stewards were to choose an Umpire. If there were more than 3 entries for an event, there were to be heats (determined by the drawing of entrants' names from a hat). The competitors were to toss for stations.

The rules for the four-oared race, to be known as the Town Challenge Cup, were similarly drawn up, entry being restricted to clubs whose members resided within 5 miles of Henley-on-Thames. The Regatta was advertised to take place on 14 June.

Those familiar only with the tremendous scale (and reputation) of Henley Royal Regatta today need to be reminded of the extremely modest nature of its beginnings, As noted, there were only 2 official events. The Regatta took place on a single day, and, indeed, it was over and done with in 3 hours. The first race for the Grand Challenge Cup took place at 4 p.m., and the Final at 7 p.m. In between were the race for the Town Challenge Cup, and a race for professional watermen, which was not an official Regatta event.

Similarly, competitors were few. There were 4 entries for the Grand, and 3 for the Town Challenge Cup. For the former these were the Oxford Etonian Club, Wadham and Brasenose (BNC) Colleges, and Trinity College, Cambridge; for the latter The Wave, The Albion and The Dreadnought clubs.

In the Grand, following 2 heats, Trinity, Cambridge, defeated the Oxford Etonians in the Final by 1/2 a length. The latter crew, which had won its heat against BNC by 6 lengths, included no fewer than 5 members of the House. R. Elwes rowed at 3, W.J. Garnett at 4, E. Boscawen at 6, S.E. Maberly at stroke, while E. Clayton was cox. So Christ Church made its mark in no uncertain fashion, though without entering its own crew, at the very outset of the Henley saga.

The Umpire for this first Regatta was J.D. Bishop of Leander (at that time a London-based club). A later report, in 1846, describes him as being of the London Amateur Scullers' Club. Bishop rode on horseback *'a notice being posted requesting that no one else would ride on the towing path for fear of accidents'.*

(H.T. Steward *The Records of Henley Royal Regatta from its introduction in 1839 to 1902* (OUP 1903)).

As well as the Challenge Cups being presented at the ceremony following the end of the Regatta, silver medals were given to the winners.

The watermen's race, involving a row from Henley Bridge to Temple Island and back, took place on the initiative of members of Leander present, who subscribed to the prize of a cash purse.

1840–1849

1840

THIS YEAR THE REGATTA TOOK PLACE OVER 2 DAYS, Thursday and Friday, 2 and 3 July. The qualification for the Grand Challenge Cup was altered (the first of a series of amendments adopted over the years) so as to permit officers of the Army and Navy, and not just officers of the Brigades of Household Troops, to compete. Also a new four-oared event was added, the District Challenge Cup, open to amateur crews or clubs based in the towns of Maidenhead, Marlow, Wallingford and Henley.

Before the Regatta took place a difficulty arose over entries by certain Oxford crews, the heads of whose colleges objected to the college names being used to give the identity of the crews' entries. This was resolved by the entries being changed, in the case of the Wadham crew, to "The Admiral", of University College to "The John Cross", and of Brasenose to "The Childe of Hale" clubs. The Oxford Westminster Club also adopted the name "The Queen Bess". The course was described by *Bell's Life* more precisely in the following terms:

> *The course commenced opposite the Temple on the island, and extended for about a mile and 550 yards upstream, the finishing-point being within 50 or 60 yards of the bridge, which was an improvement on last year, when the boats had to proceed under the bridge to conclude the heat.*

Steward adds the following clarification:

> *Another paper gives the distance as some 10 yards. Probably the winning-post was in the same position that it occupied for so many years afterwards,*

viz. opposite the steps on the Lion lawn, which are some 40 yards from the bridge. The description as opposite the Temple on the island may have meant opposite the ditch in front of the Temple, the usual starting-place for many years. If so, and the winning-post was opposite the steps on the Lion lawn, the distance would be 1 mile 558 yards.

After 2 withdrawals (by BNC and the Cambridge Subscription Rooms) there were 7 entries this year for the Grand Challenge Cup, namely Wadham and University Colleges, Oxford, Trinity, Cambridge (who as the holders in a challenge event needed only to row in the Final), King's College, London, the Westminster Club and the Etonian Club, Oxford, and Leander.

The Etonian Club crew, who won their heat against King's College easily, once again included 4 House men. Maberly (who had been the second President of the OUBC between October 1839 and February 1840) again stroked, with Boscawen once more at 6, and with W.C. Rayer at 3 and R. Fort at 4. The Westminster Club crew included House men M.C.M. Swabey at bow, and E.V. Richards at 7.

The winners of the 3 heats, Etonian Club, Leander, and Wadham, next met each other in a 3-station race, Bucks, Centre, and Berks. Leander won without difficulty and in the Final met Trinity College, whom they also defeated.

1841

The Regatta was again a 2-day event, held on 24 and 25 June. A new race '... *open to amateur crews of all England in four-oared boats with the same qualifications as for the Grand Challenge Cup...*'. was instituted. Although only medals were awarded this year to the winners, it was decided that a cup should be designed, to be named "The Stewards Challenge Cup". Thus came into being the second of the still-surviving great Henley events. (The Cup was completed in 1842, and presented to the winners of the 1841 event).

J.D. Bishop acted as Umpire for the third year, now – for the second year – from a boat manned by 8 London watermen, who also competed for a purse in a four-oared race. This race, not part of the official programme of events, took place almost every succeeding year until, in 1869, the Umpire was conveyed in a steam launch.

No Christ Church crew entered for the Regatta, but S.E. Maberly stroked "The Midge", a London-based Oxford club, in the Stewards. In a 3-boat race

"The Midge" beat the Cambridge Subscription Rooms and the St. George's Club, both also London-based.

1842

This was again a 2-day event. The Grand Challenge Cup was won by the Cambridge Subscription Rooms, who in the Final beat the CUBC entry. It was an oddity of the time that, in the first heat rowed, T.S. Egan of Caius coxed the CUBC, whereas in the Final he coxed the Subscription Rooms. The Oxford Aquatic Club, stroked by Maberly, entered for the Grand Challenge Cup, but, having beaten the Oxford Etonians in their first heat, they were defeated by CUBC, by a yard, in their second. The OUBC had entered a crew for the event, but withdrew as soon as the draw for the heats was made, because it was known that if they beat CUBC in their first heat, several members of the latter crew would take the places of some of the Subscription Rooms' crew in order to strengthen it. To this the OUBC objected, but were overruled by the Stewards on the grounds that there was nothing in the rules to prevent such substitutions from being made; the rules were modified after the Regatta to prevent this happening again.

In the Stewards Challenge Cup Maberly again stroked "The Midge" crew to victory over the Dreadnought Club, Henley.

1843

Oxford University entered a crew for the Grand Challenge Cup; it won its 2 heats, against the Oxford Etonian Club and First Trinity, Cambridge, with a House man, E. Lowndes, at bow. The Final was to be rowed against the Cambridge Rooms, London, who had won the event the previous year. (The Oxford Etonian Club had Sir Francis Scott at bow, and was captained at stroke by H. Morgan – both of Christ Church, while the Oxford University Aquatic Club – another contestant in the Grand – was stroked and captained by Maberly.)

The Final of the Grand, rowed on the second day of the Regatta, produced high drama resulting in the need for the rules to be clarified, even before the race started. F.N. Menzies, the captain and stroke of the OUBC crew (he was President, for the second time, from March to November that year) had been taken unwell after arriving at Henley, Showing what was in Victorian times often referred to as "pluck", he deemed himself well enough on the day of the Final to take his place in the crew. While waiting to board the Oxford boat for the race, he was taken ill and fainted. Could a substitute be permitted to take his place? The Stewards decided against this, influenced by the decision that had been made the previous year, and conscious of the fact that the general public had bet heavily on the outcome of the race. Cambridge agreed to a 1 hour's postponement, but with Menzies' recovery in time a matter of doubt, Oxford decided to row with only 7 men. Cambridge now appealed to Lord Camoys, *'acting Steward'* (Cook) of the Regatta, not to allow this, but as there was no rule against it, and if Cambridge refused to row Oxford could row over and claim victory, he denied the appeal. This resulted in disagreement in the Cambridge boat as to what to do. Oxford re-arranged their seating order, putting the former 7 at stroke, bow (Lowndes) at 7, and rowing without a man at bow.

The race was rowed, with Cambridge winning the toss and claiming the Berkshire station, leaving Oxford on the Bucks side – protected from the wind by the boughs and foliage of the trees and bushes on that side of the river. Oxford established an early lead and won by nearly a length.

In the Stewards Challenge Cup, after King's College, Cambridge withdrew, only 2 entries remained, St. George's Club, London and the Oxford University Midge club, stroked by Maberly. Two other Fours from Oxford sought permission to compete as late entries, which the Stewards agreed to – no doubt because thereby the event would be more competitive and more interesting to spectators – provided neither St. George's nor The Midge objected. St. George's did object, no doubt concerned that, if the 2 Oxford crews were allowed to enter, others might want to do so as well, and that those who had already placed wagers on the outcome would be compromised if, after the fact, the field was opened up to new contenders. In the Final, St. George's won by 2 lengths.

There were 3 other events at Henley Regatta this year. The Town Challenge Cup was won easily by the Henley Albion Club, who also rowed over unchallenged for the District Challenge Cup. The final event was a race, for a purse of £10. between 2 Fours made up from the crack professional London watermen who had crewed the Umpire's cutter.

Bell's Life of 2 July, 1843, provides 2 interesting pictures of the scene at Henley in those very early days of the Regatta.

The various stands were well filled with company, and the one adjoining that erected for the especial accommodation of the stewards, &c., being under the control of the committee contained a large number of elegantly attired ladies, among whom we noticed Lady Camoys and family, and other highly influential residents in the county. The band of the 2nd Regiment of Life Guards were stationed opposite the Stewards stand, and greatly added to the enjoyment of the scene by the admirable manner in which they executed numerous difficult and popular pieces of music. The picturesque meadows on the Berkshire side of the river were crowded with spectators, and the bridge and parts adjacent lined with carriages and other vehicles. The "teams" from Oxford were particularly numerous, and we observed no fewer than five tandems entering the town at one time, and the "ribbons" were handled in a manner that at once proved that the parties were "masters of the art." Henley, in fact, never looked more gay, and when we take into consideration the attractive nature of the sport, and the beauty of the surrounding country, we are not at all surprised at the great influx of visitors.

After the sports on the water, the winning crews, the Oxford banners being very conspicuous, headed by the 2nd Life Guards band, proceeded to the Town Hall, amid immense cheering. The usual ceremony of presenting the cups then took place by Lord Camoys, in the presence of a large assemblage of beauty and fashion. Mr. Menzies, who managed to attend the meeting, signed the rules on the presentation of the Grand Cup. Lord Camoys, addressing the company, spoke of the flourishing state of the Henley Regatta, and the gallant manner in which the contest had been rowed, under the circumstances. The result could not fail to be most gratifying to the public, and he could not express the pleasure he felt in presenting the cup to Mr. Menzies, as the captain of the Oxford University boat. Mr. Menzies, who was evidently much excited, returned thanks, and concluded by stating that as long as Oxford could send crews they would do their best to keep the Henley Regatta live, and retain the cup. The other cups were also presented in due form. Thanks were also voted to the umpire, and Mr. Wood, in returning thanks, expressed his sincere wishes for the welfare of the Regatta, and begged to add his name to the subscription list as an annual subscriber. Three cheers were given for the ladies and the company departed, many no doubt wishing that a regatta would be held every month. Thanks are due to the committee appointed to superintend the erection of the visitors'

> *stand, and a general wish was expressed for it continuance hereafter. Better accommodation could not have been offered to the public.*

The convenience of the spectators in the Stewards' Stand was further enhanced, according to *Bell's Life*, by

> *The "Telegraph" . . . a new and excellent continuance,* [which] *presented the names of the Oxford University and Cambridge subscription rooms, London, Clubs, as the competitors in the Grand Heat for the 100 Guineas Challenge Cup.*

The way the "telegraph" worked is uncertain: Henley Regatta Headquarters can find no reference to it in its archive. It is safe to assume that it was a semaphore type of system, such as that – employing a series of relaying points visible one to another (from which the place name "Telegraph Hill" came into being) – used to flash news of Wellington's victory at Waterloo to London. From 1822 to 1847 such a semaphore telegraph system, with 15 stations, connected the Admiralty to Portsmouth Dockyard; there were many others in England, and in other countries. The first commercial electrical system had only come into use on the Great Western Railway, between Paddington and West Drayton, in July 1839.

Press reports did not uniformly, at this stage, refer to the Grand event by its official name. As well at the "100 Guineas Challenge Cup", as noted, it was also referred to, in another account, as the "Henley Cup".

Similar uncertainty surrounds the spelling of the Stewards Challenge Cup. As noted, when it was first introduced in 1841 no apostrophe was placed after "Stewards". But the Visitors' Challenge Cup, inaugurated in 1847, did – from the start – incorporate the apostrophe into its name.

The use of "Stewards'" quickly became common, as witnessed by *Bell's Life's* use of it in its July 2 1843 report on that year's Regatta, and that form remains in use to the present day.

At the end of the first day's racing there had been an incident of novelty entertainment, providing light relief to the spectators, and taking the following form.

As a finale to the afternoon's sport, three men in wherries started to catch the man in a canoe, who is so frequently seen at Hungerford, and various other parts of the river, displaying his dexterous tricks among the steam boats, &c. It was a laughable affair, and seemed to afford infinite amusement to the ladies, all attempts to catch him proving unsuccessful. At length, a sweet-tempered youth having got near the canoe, flung himself on board, completely on to it, but still could not lay hold of the whiskerandos, its owner, who adroitly slipped into the water and swam ashore. The canoe went to the bottom, but was subsequently fished up. (*Bell's Life*, 2 July, 1843).

A rowing race between professionals; wherries chasing a canoe weaving in and out of the small craft lining the course? Where might all this lead? The answer was, of course, to a grand and brilliant future, attained step by step, as the premier venue in the world for amateur rowing competition. The Thames Grand Regatta, inaugurated this year, and where Oxford University won the Gold Challenge Cup against among others, Leander and the Cambridge Rooms, London, was to prove to be no rival. With Prince Albert as Patron it became the Royal Thames Regatta. It was held on the Tideway between Chiswick and Putney. But its days ended in 1850.

1844

Despite the need for careful scheduling to avoid conflict with the Royal Thames Regatta, and the worry that entries for Henley might suffer accordingly, Henley Regatta this year well and truly got into its stride, as *Bell's Life* reported on 30 June, under the headline "*The Henley-on-Thames Grand Regatta*":

> *This is the sixth year of the regatta, and we are happy to be enabled to state that in each succeeding season its prosperity increases, a circumstance mainly attributable to its staunch patron, Lord Camoys; the Mayor of Henley; Lords Orkney and Parker; Sirs W, Clayton, Bart., and E.G. Clayton East, Bart.; W.P. Freeman, Esq., John Fane, Esq., C. Lane, Esq., Rev. C. Keene, and the rest of the stewards; the gentlemen of the committee, and to the indefatigable and praiseworthy exertions of the honorary secretaries, Messrs. Nash and Towsey, to all of whom the inhabitants of Henley, and the lovers of the exciting, but unobjectionable sport of rowing, are much indebted. Notwithstanding the rain* [sic] *descended throughout Tuesday in*

> *London, the weather was fine at Henley, and long before the race appointed for the day commenced, the bridge and places in its immediate vicinity, were crowded with carriages containing a galaxy of beauty and fashion, and in the meadows on the Berkshire side of the river there was a vast assemblage of spectators, especially on the second day, among whom were a great many ladies, who preferred promenading along the banks of the Thames to any other means of viewing the interesting proceedings. The Stewards Stand was as usual fitted up in excellent style, and in front were displayed the cups and other prizes, which attracted much attention. On both days it was crowded with distinguished and influential parties of ladies and gentlemen, and W.P. Freeman, Esq., one of the most active stewards, kindly threw open the delightful and extensive grounds at Phillis Court* [sic] *to the visitants of the stand in question. The large marquee of the Horticultural Society was erected for the occasion, numerous seats provided for the accommodation of the company, and the Henley band, stationed on the water opposite, to entertain them during the interval of the races.*
>
> *In front of the Stewards' Stand a barge was stationed for the band of the 1st Life Guards, who played a number of the most favourite pieces of music, in the most efficient manner, frequently calling forth the applause of all present. Several other stands were erected, and the scene both on the shore and on the water was one of the most picturesque and animating that can well be imagined, the weather, on the whole, being favourable, although it was remarked that the farmers had been long anxiously looking forward to the commencement of the regatta, as rain would assuredly fall on that occasion.*

As to the number of entries, '*the gentlemen of the University of Oxford . . . have kindly expressed an intention to promote as much as possible, the annual meetings on Henley's beautiful reach*', and the number of events was significantly extended by the inauguration of the "Diamond Sculls" event for amateurs, open to all England without restriction. The Presentation Prize for the event was certainly elegant:

> *At the top of a long gold pin are a pair of well-executed sculls crossed, and from these are suspended a valuable drop diamond. On the guard pin, attached to the other by a neat gold chain, are green stones representative of a wreath of laurel.* (Steward).

The new event attracted 11 entries, and for the first time Christ Church furnished competitors in its own right. H. Morgan and Sir Francis Scott, winners of the OUBC Sculls in 1842 and 1843 respectively, entered their names, though Scott withdrew.

The House was in a very strong position this year. They were Head of the River in Summer Eights. Morgan, as indicated, had won the OUBC Sculls, and M. Haggard and W.H. Milman the Pairs, using outriggers for the first time on the Isis. In addition, Morgan, Milman and F.M. Wilson had been members of the Oxford University crew which had won the Gold Challenge Cup at the Royal Thames Regatta the previous week, beating both Cambridge University and Leander.

The 1844 Henley Regatta took place on Tuesday and Wednesday, 25 and 26 June. For the Grand there were 2 entries, the Oxford Etonian Club and Caius College, Cambridge. In the Oxford Etonian boat Wilson rowed 5 and Morgan stroke; they won by 3 lengths.

In the Stewards' Challenge Cup there were 4 entries, but the Royal Academy Club, London, withdrew. In the heat the OUBC crew (drawn from the Thames Regatta crew), with Wilson at 3, easily beat the Oxford Subscription Rooms, London (another name for the Oxford Aquatic Club), with Haggard at bow. In the Final OUBC met the holders, St. George's Club, and beat them by 1¼ lengths.

The Diamond Sculls attracted a number of the finest scullers in England, with 4 from the Amateur Scullers Club, London, including A.A. Julius, winner of the London Silver Sculls some years before, and T.B. Bumpsted, winner of the Sculling Challenge Cup at the Thames Regatta. Morgan won his first heat against Ive of the Dreadnought Club, Henley, and was in the Final with Bumpsted and Conant of St. John's, Oxford. The race quickly became one between Bumpsted and Morgan, the advantage, and the race, going to the former when one of Morgan's sculls twisted in his hand. Bumpsted slipped ahead to win by 1 length.

As to the other events, Henley Aquatic Club won the Town Challenge Cup, while the District Challenge Cup went to the Eton and Windsor Club. A prize of £20 was rowed for by 2 Fours made up from the Umpire's watermen. These Fours were steered by the coxswains of the 2 crews entered for the Grand, Shadwell of Oxford and Egan of Cambridge. An additional prize of a Coat and Badge for scullers resident within 5 miles of Henley attracted 9 entries. This prize was not restricted to amateurs.

After 6 years, the Regatta's accounts showed an accumulated deficit of no more that £26.

1845

This year was marked by the inauguration of two new events. The "New Challenge Cup" for Eights was open to colleges and other amateur clubs '*except University Clubs, Subscription Rooms or Clubs similarly constituted.*' (Steward). The following year this event was given the name by which it has since been known, The Ladies' Challenge Plate. An event for amateur Pairs, open to all England, was for presentation prizes of Silver Wherries, one to each member of each winning Pair.

These awards were described thus by *Bell's Life*:

> *The Silver Wherries are perfect gems of the kind, being about nine inches long, and have been made from one of Searle's models of pair-oared racing-boats. These, standing on gilt supports, are fixed on black stands covered with velvet, with, under the boat, a silver shield engraved "Henley Regatta 1845", and the whole covered with glass shades.*

So now there were two amateur events for Eights, 1 for Fours, 1 for Pairs, and 1 for Sculls, in addition to the other, lesser races earlier mentioned, though the Coat and Badge event for Scullers did not take place due to an insufficient number of entries.

The Regatta took place on Friday and Saturday, 6 and 7 June. The Grand Challenge Cup was contested between crews from the OUBC and the CUBC. Milman and Wilson (now President of the OUBC) rowed 3 and stroke in the former crew, which lost by more than 2 lengths. Four crews entered for the New Challenge Cup, namely St. George's, London, Trinity, Cambridge, Lady Margaret Boat Club (St. John's, Cambridge) and St. John's, Oxford, who withdrew before competing. The race was started 3 abreast, with Lady Margaret in the centre between St. George's (Berks station) and Trinity (Bucks station). It turned out to be a contest between St. George's and Trinity, the former winning by 2 feet.

For the first year of the Silver Wherries there were 6 entries, Caius and Trinity, Cambridge, Oriel, Oxford, Peacock and Chapman (Amateur Scullers

Club and Crescent Club – both of London) and Christ Church, represented by Milman and Haggard, who had again won the OUBC Pairs, this time in an out-rigged boat with the cox positioned between the 2 men. Merton College, Oxford entered but did not race.. In their 3-boat heat, the House men came second to Caius, who met Peacock and Chapman in the Final. Caius won by about 2 lengths.

Milman and Wilson rowed 2 and stroke in the Oxford University crew which beat St. George's in the Final of the Stewards' Challenge Cup. The race was the closest yet recorded at Henley. The Umpire judging the finish, Forest, reported to the Stewards that *'he could not determine by an inch which had won, and therefore declared it a dead heat!'* That was not the end of the matter, however, for J.D. Bishop, the race Umpire, who claimed that he had deliberately positioned himself to observe the finish, realizing how close the result would be, informed the Stewards that Oxford had won. The Stewards, in their wisdom, favoured Bishop's version of the outcome. If the weight attached to Bishop's verdict should appear to have been excessive, it may be noted that the following year there was no Umpire judging the finish, and the race Umpire – again Bishop – was the only official in a position to judge the result of another close-fought race. (At the Thames Regatta, 1845, which followed Henley, Oxford University again beat St. George's by 1½ lengths.)

In the Diamond Sculls, with 7 competitors, the success of J.W. Conant, of St. John's, who had beaten Sir Francis Scott in the Final of the OUBC Sculls, attracted considerable attention for his choice of an out-rigged boat. In his heat Conant was up against the redoubtable T.B. Bumpsted. *Bell's Life* described the race thus:

> *In a few strokes Mr. Conant led by over a length, showing in an extraordinary manner the superiority of the outrigging boat over the others, for such an advantage could not be accounted for in any other way. Mr. Bumpsted fairly turned round on his thwart to see what had become of Mr. Conant, and then set to work in the hopeless struggle to reduce the lead his opponent had gained.*

(No other competitor in the Diamonds used an out-rigger.) In the Final, however, Conant and Chapman – mentioned earlier – were beaten by S. Wallace of Leander.

Henley Aquatic Club won the Town and District Challenge Cups.

A new event, which was to be dropped after a few years, was for the prize of a Coat and Badge, the event being open to apprentices of Thames watermen who had served 5 but less than 7 years of their apprenticeship.

In terms of success and victory, the House's earliest appearances at Henley in 1844 and 1845 were in no way spectacular, but they were significant, in that the College entered for the Diamonds and the Silver Wherries (in 1850 renamed the Silver Goblets) in the years in which these events were inaugurated, and had also provided the stroke of the Oxford crew which won the Stewards in its first year, 1841.

1846

The Regatta took place on Thursday and Friday, 25 and 26 June. There was one new event, the Local Amateur Scullers' Race, for entrants from Henley; this attracted 10 competitors. As was now traditional, the Regatta was heavily supported by spectators and, despite mixed weather, attracted a high level of support from the "great and good" of society; the Marquis of Devonshire, the Earl of Falmouth, and Lord Kilmorey consented to their names being added to the list of Stewards. Earl Kilmorey (b. 1787), known as "Black Jack", was the backer of T.L. Jenkins, the only Etonian in the crew, who rowed 5 in the Leander boat which had defeated the Etonian Club, Oxford, in the Final of the Grand in 1840. That year Kilmorey had been one of those who subscribed the purse rowed for by the professional watermen in a scullers' match. His presence in a Four, '*Lord Kilmorey and his crew*', had been noted in 1840 by *Bell's Life*. Kilmorey's grandson, Lord Newry, who became the third Earl in 1880, stroked the Christ Church Torpid in 1860.

In 1846 Oxford and Cambridge undergraduates were present in large numbers to support their various crews, and the "riff-raff" generally stayed away. As Milman, now President of the OUBC, noted in the OUBC record book:

> *The sport at the Regatta's* [sic] *was . . . very superior the place being full of Oxford and Cambridge men and no more cads than absolutely necessary.'*

Due to the diligence of J. Nash, the Regatta Honorary Secretary, a good deal of information about the events and past results was included, along with the customary display of prizes, at the Stewards' stand:

> *... we noticed the very useful map of the regatta course, by Mr. Allnatt, which we have alluded to in a former number, and a chart, in the form of a volute or shell, in which every event connected with the regatta since its establishment in 1839 is shown at one view; it is divided into sections, each section representing the events of a year. The smaller semicircles are appointed to the various regatta prizes on their respective colours, and show the names of the clubs who have from time to time been the holders of the various challenge cups, and the names of the winners of the presentation prize. In the larger white spaces between the smaller series of semicircles appear the appointments of stewards" committee, dates of entrance days, and regattas, number of entrances for each prize, the names of the winning crews, the amount of every year's subscription, entrance fees, expenses, and, in fact, forming a perfect record of every incident interesting to the parties connected with the regatta.* (*Bell's Life*).

The Grand Challenge Cup was won by The Thames Club, London, who beat First Trinity, Cambridge, entered under the name "The Black Prince", and "Eton and Westminster, Oxford", old boys of these schools, now undergraduates, including 3 House men, Milman at stroke, Wilson at 4, and E.C. Burton at 2. These three crews, the only entries, raced in the Final with no heat taking place. (The Thames Club, along with other rowing clubs on the Thames, including Wandle, Argonaut and St. George's, was involved in a move to amalgamate into one club, which would be better able to compete at Henley with Oxford and Cambridge crews. The amalgamation resulted in the formation of the London Rowing Club in 1856. In 1860 a re-formation of the City of London Rowing Club resulted in a name change to Thames Rowing Club.)

In the Final of the Ladies' Plate, First Trinity, Cambridge beat Lady Margaret Boat Club. In the trial heat of the Stewards' the Dreadnought Club, Henley, met Guy's Club, London (representing Guy's Hospital). Bad luck almost ruined this race; the Dreadnought stroke, Page, had not been in the boat for 10 days due to an indisposition, while the Guy's stroke, Cooper, injured his back surmounting a 5 foot obstacle and might have been precluded from rowing. However, the crews raced. Bishop, the race Umpire, declared a dead heat, making a re-row – scheduled for the following day – necessary. The Dreadnought crew, believing that they had won, refused to race again, and so Guy's met Oxford University, the holders from the previous year, in the Final. (As mentioned earlier, in a Challenge event, the holder did not participate before the Final.) Milman and Wilson rowed in the Oxford boat, which Haggard coxed. Oxford won easily.

There were 9 entries for the Silver Wherries event, of which 6 were composite crews formed from members of different colleges or clubs. In the second heat Milman and Haggard, again entered for Christ Church, took on a Pair from Trinity, Cambridge, and a composite crew drawn from Queen's and Magdalen Hall, Oxford. (Magdalen Hall and Hart Hall later merged to form Hertford College.) In a close race,

> *The Oxonians and Cantabs ran in shoals along the path in the meadow, and by shouts, amounting frequently to screams, urged their respective friends to increased exertion.* (*Bell's Life*).

The House crew prevailed by ½ a length. The Queen's and Magdalen Hall men had fouled the Trinity Pair, and the race, between the 2 surviving crews, had been re-started. In the 3-boat third heat Wilson paired W.U. Heygate of Merton, and came second.

In the Final Milman and Haggard met the Fellows brothers (Leander and Exeter, Oxford), and George and Maule, another Pair from Trinity, Cambridge. Milman and Haggard won by 2 lengths, thus putting the name of Christ Church as an event winner in the Henley record book for the very first time.

The Final of the Diamond Sculls was won this year by E.G. Moon of Magdalen, Oxford, who took on T.H. Fellows of Leander (one of the two brothers just named). In their heats Fellows' opponent had broken his stretcher, while Moon had been fouled by E.G. Peacock. Moon won the Final easily.

A new Scullers' Race for local amateurs, with a presentation prize of a Silver Wherry, was won easily by H. Sargeant. Dreadnought again won the Town Challenge Cup, but the District Challenge Cup had no entries this year, and it was re-allocated in 1847. E.C. Burton won the Amateur Sculls event at the Thames Grand Regatta.

1847

This year the Regatta took place on Thursday and Friday, 17 and 18 June. The growing interest in the event, on the part both of ordinary spectators and of elements of the aristocracy, was heightened even more than by now had become customary by a fever of excitement among Oxford and Cambridge men, for the two universities were to meet each other in the heat of the Grand Challenge Cup. Due to a disagreement between the two over Oxford's proposal that professional watermen not be used to train the Boat Race crews, there had been no Boat Race this year, and Henley was the venue for their only encounter in 1847. (The Thames Club, as holders, was, as earlier noted, privileged to appear only in the Final.)

Two new events were introduced this year. The first was the Visitors' Challenge Cup, the former District Challenge Cup being re-assigned as the trophy; this event was open to any amateur Four. The second was a cup given by Mr. Donkin of Wyfold Court, Henley, named by the Stewards as the Wyfold Challenge Cup, to be awarded to the winner of the challenge heat (or heats) of the Grand Challenge Cup.

The race Umpire this year was Henry Wood of Leander. Interestingly, given past uncertainty over the judging of the finish of the races, two finish judges were appointed, A. Shadwell and T. Egan, who had coxed the two crews for the Grand in 1844. In accordance with their practice the Stewards and Committee met at Henley Town Hall on Wednesday morning – the day before the Regatta – to make the draw for the composition of the heats of the first day's racing. On Thursday they met again to finally decide on the order of racing. This having been done the Secretary of The Thames Club chose to raise verbally a matter which the Stewards had already settled the previous Saturday, based on written submissions. This was whether Thames was entitled to enter for the Ladies' Plate. Representatives of Oxford University had objected to this proposal – the event was restricted to *'college and other amateur clubs'*. Since The Thames Club was open to any amateur who chose to join it, it was in a class with organizations specifically excluded from participating in the event, namely, *'University Clubs, Subscription Rooms, or Clubs similarly constituted'*. The Stewards had denied The Thames Club the right to compete.

The Thames Club representative was joined in his protest by a legally-qualified St. George's Club spokesman. The Stewards' original decision was not seriously challenged by the arguments, and it was felt – certainly by the *Bell's Life* correspondent – that the objections had been, at the least, discourteous to the Stewards; the use of language, in the heat of the moment, such as "unfair" or "unfair decision" was highly inappropriate. Moreover the Stewards should stick to their own rules and not waver and should '*let their yea be yea, and their nay also adhered to*'.

It may have been partly to palliate St. George's, whose entry for the Stewards' Challenge Cup had, through a mistake, been received too late, that at the last minute the Stewards offered the Visitors' Challenge Cup as a new event for Fours.

In considering its own prospects for Henley Christ Church had every reason to be optimistic. They were Head of the River again and had won the OUBC Fours and the Pairs (coxless for the first time), while Burton had won the OUBC Sculls, against a field of 14 competitors which included 7 House men. Not surprisingly they decided to enter for several events though, for reasons not known, they chose not to try for the Ladies' Plate.

In the heat of the Grand the OUBC crew, including Haggard (2) and Burton (stroke), beat Cambridge by 2+ lengths in a record time of 8 min. 4 sec. As winners of the heat the crew was awarded the new Wyfold Challenge Cup. To the delight of their supporters they then won a hard-fought Final against The Thames Club by the comfortable margin of 3 lengths, and in a new record time of 8 minutes. (They thus won 2 trophies in 1 event).

In the Stewards' Challenge Cup, Christ Church (A. Mansfield bow, Haggard 2, Burton 3 and H.W. Richards stroke, with R.W. Cotton as cox,) rowed over to win the event, Worcester College, Oxford, having entered but then withdrawn. Christ Church and St. George's both entered for the Visitors' Challenge Cup. For this event A. Milman came into the Four at bow, and W.H. Milman at stroke (the Milmans were brothers), and Richards moved to cox. St. George's was beaten by a length in the record time, for Fours, of 9 minutes.

In 1860, Arthur Milman, by then a distinguished barrister, played a key part (as Judith Curthoys tells us in *The Cardinal's College*) in the process which resulted in the Governing Body of Christ Church being expanded to give the Students – for the first time – a role in the governance of the House, hitherto the exclusive privilege of the Dean and Chapter.

The Ladies' was won by BNC once more rowing as "The Childe of Hale Boat Club", against First Trinity, Cambridge. The Silver Wherries went to

Falls and Coulthard of St. George's on appeal. The Diamond Sculls were won by W. Maule of Trinity, Cambridge, and the Local Amateur Scullers' Race, for the Silver Wherry prize, again by H. Sargeant. Unchallenged, the Henley Dreadnought Club rowed over for the Town Challenge Cup. Finally the London watermen made up 2 Fours for the professional race for a money prize.

The Regatta was regarded as a great success, the OUBC President, Royds of BNC, being delighted at bringing back no fewer than five cups. His pleasure, though, may have been slightly soured by the exuberance of some of the Oxford supporters. Thus *Bell's Life:*

It is with regret that some Oxonians, elated with the success of the University beat [boat] *in the trial heat, overstepped the bounds of prudence on Thursday night, to the great annoyance of many respectable inhabitants, especially to some of the most staunch and liberal supporters of the regatta. Let us hope such unbecoming proceedings will be avoided in future, for there is really not wit or fun in wrenching off knockers or playing similar hankey pankey tricks.*

Such behaviour being then, as now, unknown at the House, one may be sure that Milman & Co. returned to Oxford with the 2 Christ Church trophies to a quiet and very sober celebration!

1848

In the light of the dispute the previous year regarding the right of The Thames Club to participate in The Ladies' Challenge Plate, the rules were amended by the Stewards for 1848 to provide the following very detailed statement of eligibility for this event, which now also applied in the case of the Visitors' Challenge Cup:

> *The clubs of Colleges and other public Establishments and such other amateur clubs (University clubs and Subscription Rooms excepted) as shall have been established one year previous to the time of entering, and are restricted in the selection of their members to one particular profession, or class of persons, or to any particular county town or place (distant at least seven miles from Westminster Bridge) shall be eligible to contend for these prizes, provided*

> *that each of the crew shall at the time of entering be a* bonâ fide *member of such club, and shall not then be a member of any other rowing club; but such restriction shall not apply to the connection of a member of a College club with his University club. If any College or Establishment having a rowing club shall include among its members persons who are not also members of such College, &c., it shall not on account of such combination be considered to be disqualified, provided that that the crew be composed of members of such College or Establishment. Any amateur club professing to be the club of a particular town, and selecting its members from that town or neighbourhood, shall be allowed a circuit of five miles for that purpose, provided that in such case the spirit of the above rule shall not in any respect be infringed thereby.*

At Oxford the House had once more done well in OUBC events. They were Head of the River for the second year running, and were in the Finals of the OUBC Fours, Pairs and Sculls, though losing in all three events. When it came to selecting an OUBC crew to defend the Grand at Henley, no fewer than 5 Christ Church men were chosen. W.G. Rich was at bow, Haggard at 2, Mansfield at 6, W.H. Milman at 7, and Burton (President of the OUBC since October 1847), at stroke. According to Knollys '*. . . the Cambridge term ended early, and in consequence they could not send any crews.*' (The Regatta took place on Thursday and Friday, 6 and 7 July).

This year Christ Church decided to enter for the Ladies' Plate, the Stewards' and Visitors' Cups, and the Silver Wherries. The greatest success was winning the Ladies' at the first attempt, the crew being:

		st. lb.
Bow	H.W.P. Richards	10. 4
2	M. Haggard	10. 4
3	J. Rich	10. 4
4	J.E. Henderson	10. 7
5	A. Mansfield	11. 10
6	E.C. Burton	11. 0
7	W.H. Milman	11. 0
Str	W.G. Rich	10. 1
Cox	J. Greenwood	7. 9

(J. Rich was the younger brother of W.G.) Both Balliol and Worcester entered for this event, but the former withdrew. The single heat was also the Final, between the House and Worcester. *Bell's Life* gave the following report on the race:

This was a very exciting race, and a vast number of "undergraduates" ran along the meadows to witness it. The Christ Church crew was on the Bucks shore station, and they started off well together and at a rattling pace, and with an apparent determination "to do or die." For about a quarter of a mile there was no perceptible difference, but then the Christ Church boat drew slightly ahead, gradually increased their advantage to an extent as to be enabled to take their opponent's water, coming out their own boat's length clear at Poplar Point. The race was continued with praiseworthy perseverance and spirit, and the exertions of each kept up with no apparent diminution to the end, the Worcester opposite the Grand Stand, being in-shore, the stem of their cutter overlapping, although only in a trifling degree, the stern of the leading boat, but were unable to get any nearer to them, and Christ Church won with their own length clear and barely a yard. Both crews were loudly cheered at the finish.

In both the Stewards' and the Visitors', Christ Church was the only entrant. Consequently the House, represented in each event by the same crew, as below, rowed over twice to claim 2 further victories:

Bow	A. Milman
2	M. Haggard
3	E.C. Burton
Str	W.H. Milman
Cox	R.W. Cotton

For the Silver Wherries event Haggard and W.H. Milman were the House crew. There were three entries, but one withdrew, and only The Thames Club and Christ Church competed in the only race, the Final. Because of a foul by Thames soon after the start, they were disqualified, and the Christ Church men won. Interestingly, for reasons not known, Haggard and Milman had chosen to enter under the assumed names "A, Thompson" and "B. Thompson". (A similar deception on the part of Oxford competitors will be noted under the commentary on Henley Regatta 1851.)

As usual, the greatest interest, and the heaviest level of betting (in those days an important feature of the Regatta) centred on the Grand Challenge Cup, competed for on the second day. There were only two entries, the OUBC and The Thames Club, the latter keen to redeem their honour besmirched by their loss (as holders) to the OUBC in 1847. Both crews spent two days practising over the Henley course. Oxford achieved a time, against some wind, of 8 min. 5 sec., while Thames, in a complete calm, recorded a practice time of 7 min. 55 sec.; Oxford supporters maintained that Thames' '*chronometer had been influenced by some undue leaning*'. (*Bell's Life*). The crews looked so close that "evens" were the odds offered on each.

On the day of the race a gale was blowing from the Bucks side of the course, but instead of selecting that station Thames – who had the choice – picked the Berks station. From the start of a fierce contest Oxford began to lead, and were clear of Thames before reaching Remenham, winning, accord to *Bell's* '*without apparent fatigue*', by 20 seconds against a strong wind. Thames' bow had broken his stretcher at the start, but this was not judged to have had any influence on the outcome of the race, the official verdict on which was a win '*Easily*'.

The other Henley events, including the watermen's race, took place, the Diamond Sculls being won – notwithstanding the previously mentioned comment by Knollys – by W.L. Bagshawe of Trinity, Cambridge, who beat W. Wilberforce, representing the OUBC. The qualification for the Local Amateur Scullers' Race was modified this year to permit entries from those resident within 12 miles (previously 5 miles) of Henley.

With wins in 4 events, on top of 2 the previous year, and not counting its contribution to two successful OUBC wins in the Grand, the House was now beginning to make its mark in a serious way as a major competitor at Henley Regatta, which had just celebrated its tenth year. Milman and Haggard had succeeding in winning five events out of five entered for at the Regatta. While 2 of these victories were uncontested, and the number of entries was small compared to the fierce competition to take place in years to come, their success nevertheless constitutes a record for Henley, never since matched by any other competitors. (For confirmation of this, see Burnell, p. 157.)

With Henley now well established, and with only 2 of the events which were to feature on its calendar of major events until 1939 remaining to be instituted, the practice, largely followed hitherto, of giving the full title of each event, will be discontinued, and events will be referred to by the names – "the Grand", etc. – by which they are known to regular supporters of the Regatta. Similarly, the names of Oxbridge colleges will be given in forms well known to oarsmen readers. Finally, the minor Regatta events will no longer be reviewed, save where they are of interest.

1849

The House did not make an appearance at Henley this year, even though they had been Head of the River for the third successive year. Wadham and Oriel, however, entered for the Grand, along with Second Trinity, Cambridge, Head of the River on the Cam. Wadham entered as "The St. John of Malta" and Oriel as "An OBC", this in order '*to escape the wrath of their heads of colleges*', according to Burnell. In the Final (there was no separate heat) Second Trinity finished ahead of Wadham, but were disqualified on a foul. Wadham accordingly won the Grand, and were awarded the Wyfold Cup also. In the Ladies' they again beat Second Trinity. So they came away with three trophies won in just two races.

Second Trinity lost the Stewards' to Leander, but rowed over to win the Visitors'. An Oriel Pair lost the Final of the Silver Wherries to a Thames Club Pair. The Diamonds were won by T.R. Bone of "London" (he was described the following year as representing the Meteor Club, Hammersmith). In 1848 Bone had been beaten in a heat by that year's winner, Bagshawe.

1850–1859

1850

THE PICTURE PRESENTED THUS FAR OF THE EARLY YEARS OF THE REGATTA has been one of increasing momentum from year to year, with excellent administrative arrangements, a smoothly-operated schedule of races, with support from the aristocracy, the gentry, and ordinary spectators, and with great interest and involvement on the part of Oxford and Cambridge college men. This nascent dominance of the English rowing scene was not, however, without threats. Conflict with other sporting events could undermine attendance, and participation was affected by the willingness and ability (or otherwise) of the Oxford and Cambridge University Boat Clubs, and of individual colleges, to put together, and keep together, crews in training between the end of the May Races and Summer Eights until the starting dates of the Regatta, well after the end of the Universities' terms.

In 1850 the Henley Stewards were faced with a difficult choice. Not only did they not want to conflict with the Royal Thames Regatta, but term ended at Cambridge on 1 June, but at Oxford not until 12 June, while 13 June was a big day at the Ascot summer race meeting. The Stewards decided that 14 and 15 June would be the best days on which to hold the Regatta, and advertised it accordingly, but there was so little interest on the part of prospective competitors that, in the event, the Regatta was a 1-day affair, taking place on Friday, 14 June. Illness and the unavailability of key crew members were factors limiting the response of Oxford and Cambridge colleges to the invitation to submit entries, the deadline for which was extended by the Stewards in the hope of gaining more competitors. Despite these difficulties, however, spectator attendance on the day was at its customary high level, the aristocracy and gentry being as usual well represented, and the band of the Life Guards once again providing light entertainment.

In preparation for the Regatta the Stewards had adopted the "Laws of Boat-racing" as approved by Oxford and Cambridge and the principal London boat clubs. These clarified in some detail matters such as the right of the Umpire to determine, upon appeal, whether a foul had take place, and to disqualify an offender, what constituted a "straight and true" course for a competing boat, and when it was in order for one crew to take another's water. Two changes had also been made regarding 2 of the events. The race for Pairs, hitherto known as "The Silver Wherries", was from now on to be called "The Silver Goblets", presentation goblets in future being the presentation prizes. The Diamond Sculls event, for which there had been presentation prizes but no trophy, was now renamed "The Diamond Challenge Sculls". The trophy was described thus:

> *The sculls are models of about six inches in length, formed of frosted and bright silver, the handles are filled gold, the sculls crossed and corded gold, the cord appearing in the centre of a wreath of green enamel set with rubies and brilliants and tied with gold, the end of the tie sustaining a brilliant drop.*

From 1850 on the winner of the Diamonds was presented with a silver-gilt "pineapple" cup in place of the original diamond scarf-pin. These cups continued to be presented until the 1970s, when their cost became too prohibitive.

The difficulty in finding competitors was reflected in the 1850 results. The OUBC crew (with W.G. Rich – OUBC President – stroking, and R.W. Cotton coxing) rowed over for the Grand, and also collected the Wyfold Cup. Lincoln, Oxford rowed over to win the Ladies', and the OUBC Four, with Rich as Cox, to win the Stewards'. (CUBC withdrew after entering). The Silver Goblets were won easily by Horne of BNC and Chitty of Balliol, who beat a scratch crew which only entered for the event to provide some semblance of competition. The House won the Visitors' against Lincoln, the crew being:

Bow	J. Rich
2	Hon. A.A.B. Hanbury
3	H.B. Arnaud
Str	W.G. Rich
Cox	R.W. Cotton

The Diamonds was won easily by the previous year's winner, Bone, over J.E. Clarke of Wadham.

This year T.S. Egan (3 times a winning Cambridge cox) officiated as race Umpire and Burton and Haggard as Judges at the finish.

1851

This year saw a huge boost to Henley Regatta's reputation and fortunes, for Prince Albert had agreed to become Patron, and henceforward its title was to be "Henley Royal Regatta". The popularity of the event remained undiminished, and it was estimated that on the first day there were 7,000 spectators on the Berkshire bank between Henley Bridge and Temple Island. The Regatta reverted to a 2-day length, taking place on Tuesday and Wednesday, 17 and 18 June.

Though not part of the official Regatta programme, a 4-oared race on the first day '*open to the world*', and with a first prize of 100 sovereigns, attracted much attention. The entrants included R. Coombes Crew, stroked by the great Bob Coombes, (whose name was mentioned in the commentary on Henley 1839), the "Champion [waterman] of the Thames", and coach of the Cambridge Boat Race crews in 1846, 1849 and 1852, as well as of Oxford in 1840, and Clasper's Crew. The latter were members of the Clasper family of Newcastle, with the redoubtable Harry Clasper at stroke. Clasper, a Tynesider, had invented the outrigger, adopted by both Universities in 1846, and had in 1847 built the keelless Four, referred to later, in which the OUBC was to win the Stewards in 1852, as well as a keelless Eight in 1849. Harry Clasper and his son, Jack, were to build many successful racing Eights over many years.

These 2 crews met in the second heat. However, bow of Clasper's boat *"broke his thowl"* (*Bell's Life,* 1851 report) and the Coombes boat rowed on to a leisurely win. In the final of this event Coombes fouled MacKenny's Richmond crew at Poplar Point. (The match between Coombes and Clasper was re-rowed as a separate private event the next day with a prize of £40, Clasper winning by a margin of 2 or 3 yards).

As to the formal Regatta events, the 2 contestants in the Grand were the OUBC and the CUBC – W.G. Rich rowed bow for the former, with E.C. Burton, who had returned to Oxford to coach the crew, at cox. In a second thole pin mishap, that of the Cambridge 3 broke 300 yards from the start, and the OUBC won by 6 lengths in the record time of 7 min. 45 sec. At the time of the accident to the Cambridge boat it was estimated by the Umpire that Oxford were between 2 and 3 lengths ahead.

Three clubs entered for the Ladies' Plate, BNC and Christ Church, and First Trinity, Cambridge. The House was in sixth place in Summer Eights this year. It appears that at Oxford at this time the heads of various colleges continued to view participation at Henley with disfavour. BNC again entered as "The Childe of Hale", and Ballliol missed their heat of the Stewards' '*in consequence of the Head not allowing them out*', according to *Bell's Life* as quoted by Steward. Another source, Knollys, states however that because of this restriction Balliol did row, but under assumed names. The likely presence of the Balliol crew at Henley is borne out by the fact that, as will be seen, Chitty of Balliol undoubtedly won the Silver Goblets.

For its part, the House entered as "Westminster and Eton Club, Oxford", and with the crew under assumed names, it being known that Dean Gaisford would not grant the necessary leave. However, a newspaper reporter at the Regatta ascertained the correct names and published them as being those of Christ Church men; the upshot was that those concerned were punished by '*losing a term*'.

The Ladies' race was rowed 3 abreast. BNC won, with the House second, and First Trinity (Head of the Cam) third. The Christ Church crew – giving the correct names – was:

Bow	J. Rich
2	H.B.H Blundell
3	Hon. A.A.B. Hanbury
4	H.B. Arnaud
5	J.W. Malcolm
6	P.W. Nind
7	W.G. Rich
Str	H.R. Barker
Cox	R.W. Cotton

The House also entered for the Visitors' against BNC, Balliol, and First Trinity. The latter won the 3-boat heat, and met Christ Church (the holders) in the Final. The House won a close race, '*with the stern of the Cambridge boat nearly touching the other's rudder at the finish*'. (*Bell's Life*, 1851 report.) The crew was:

Bow	W.G. Rich
2	E.C. Burton
3	B. Arnaud
Str	H.R. Barker
Cox	R.W. Cotton

Bell's Life published Burton's and Barker's names as "Thompson" and "Johnson" – the pseudonyms used by Milman and Haggard in 1848 – and Cotton's as "Collins".

In the Diamonds Arnaud entered as "Mr. Box" and Blundell as "Mr. Cox", both acknowledging nevertheless their affiliation with Christ Church; both were eliminated in the heats. ("Box and Cox" was the title of an 1842 farce by J.J. Morton, the basis for Sir Arthur Sullivan's later successful comic opera of the same name.) In the Silver Goblets J.Aitken (Christ Church) teamed up with Chitty of Balliol using the assumed name "Guess". In a 3-boat Final (there were only 3 entries) they beat a Leander Pair and Clarke of Worcester and Vaughan of Oriel. The last-named resourcefully adopted the name of the Head of his College, and entered as "Hawkins". Dr. Edward Hawkins was the Provost of Oriel.

Harmless deceptions such as these paled before the downright duplicity of Cambridge in the Stewards'. W.G. Rich was still President of the OUBC, and he took the opportunity to explain the circumstances in the customary report in the OUBC President's record book:

> *In regard to the University Qualification!!!* [Cambridge had entered as "Cambridge, (University qualification)"] *the Cantabs treated us wroughley* [sic] *on the Sat*dy*. evening previous to the Regatta a verbal message was given to our Sec*ty*. that "Cambridge were thinking of putting on a Scratch University Four (Scratch meaning simply that they had not practiced quite as much as was necessary) – would we like, to meet them for the Stewards Cup. We having only on*[e] *day for practice (Monday) the Regatta being on Tuesday, of course could not do so, with the disadvantage of rowing unpractised against a crew at least partially fit – our Surprise then was great when not having had time even to reply to the Cambridge message, on our arrival at Henley we found the Cambridge University Four entered for the Stewards Cup as the Cambridge (University Qualification) Four and though it may be said*

> *"what's in a name" in this case the Cantabs provided a disgraceful shelter in the event of their being defeated by a college crew. With a "Pot hunting" spirit they entered – for no glory could attach to victory – with a sneaking spirit they chose a name which might screen them in defeat.*

Bell's Life, in reporting on the same incident, referred to a report that Cambridge entered – First Trinity having withdrawn at the last minute on the day before the Regatta – in order to create at least a degree of competition for the event. However, the *Bell's* correspondent said,

> *'that he had heard of their exploits several days previous to the regatta, and saw them practising several times over the course; it was comprised, too, of the stroke and three others of the university crew.'*

In the first heat of the Stewards' the Cambridge University crew beat the House Four (the same crew as the Visitors', with the same pseudonyms) in a race which was neck and neck as far as the Poplars. Here Cambridge, with the advantage of the inside bend, pulled ahead to win by a length and a half. In the Final they comfortably beat BNC, who had rowed over in their heat, Balliol, as suggested, having failed to arrive in time for the race.

Bell's Life provided a description of the natural course of the stream on the Henley reach. H.T. Steward considered it '*so close that it is worth recording*'.

> *The natural course of the stream is direct from the bridge upon the projecting wall of Phyllis Court grounds, nearly opposite to Poplar Point (not upon the Point itself, as so many have supposed); thence it flows obliquely towards the gate below the Point, and then it proceeds still more obliquely and more quietly to the boughs near Fawley Court, leaving comparatively dead water for some distance below the grounds of Phyllis Court. The stream becomes stronger as it approaches the channels on either side of the Island, but is much sharper on the Buckinghamshire side than on the barge channel or Berks side, while at the head of the Temple Island are the remains of a small 'eyot' or 'ait' or island, which acts as a breakwater.*

1852

This was a poor year for competition, Cambridge University crews being unable to enter, the dates fixed, Friday and Saturday, 25 and 26 June, '*being too late for them*' according to the OUBC President's report. In consequence with only the OUBC (the holders) entered for the Grand (the Oxford term ended around 20 June) they would have rowed over to win the event. However, Lord Camoys, Vice-President and acting Steward of the Regatta, intervened, asking the OUBC President, R. Greenall of BNC, to make up 2 crews for the sake of making it a race.

Accordingly, 2 Oxford crews were put together, it being agreed that whichever one won would be called the "Oxford University Boat Club", and the losing boat the "Oxford Aquatic Club". H.B.H. Blundell rowed 2, and H.R. Barker 7, in 1 crew, stroked by Greenall, and J.W. Malcolm and P.H. Nind 5 and 6 in the other, stroked by W.O. Meade-King of Pembroke. Greenall's crew won the race, and so went into the records as being the OUBC crew. H.T. Steward notes, however, that technically '*the winning crew, though they received the medals, cannot be considered as an Oxford University Boat Club crew*'. The Oxford Aquatic Club (the only challenger) was awarded the Wyfold Cup.

For the Ladies' Plate the House, fourth on the River this year, entered but withdrew, as did University, leaving the only other entry, Pembroke, Oxford, to row over to win. In the Stewards' Barker and Nind rowed 2 and 3 in the OUBC Four who beat Argonaut Club, London, and The Thames Club, by 2-3 lengths. T.S. Egan coached the Cambridge Blue Boat for several years between 1836 and 1868, and in 1852 he had also coached Oxford, as he was to do again in 1856. He also coached the OUBC Four at Henley, where, incidentally, he once more umpired. Egan persuaded the OUBC to use (for the first time at Oxford) a keelless outrigged Clasper boat, as mentioned earlier. This was described by Greenall as '*certainly one of the fastest lightweight fours ever tried out*'. It had been built by Clasper in 1847 for a Clasper/Coombes encounter.

As holders, Christ Church entered for the Visitors', the crew being:

Bow	Blundell
2	Nind
3	Malcolm
Str	Barker
Cox	H. Barnes

The Argonaut and The Thames Club with the same crews as for the Stewards', competed in a heat, which Argonaut won. In the Final they beat the House.

Christ Church had not won the Silver Goblets event since Haggard and Milman's second win in the Silver Wherries in 1848. In 1852, however, Barker and Nind entered, as did a Pair from the Wandle Club, and 2 composite Pairs, Short of New College and Irving of Balliol, and Blundell (of the House) and Denne of Univ. In the first heat Barker and Nind beat the last-named Pair easily, while in the second Short and Irving beat Wandle on a foul. Unfortunately, however, Irving was unable to row in the Final, in which Barker and Nind rowed over to win.

As has been seen, the House had not in any way to date excelled in the Diamonds, and 1852 was no exception. Blundell entered, but was beaten easily by E. Macnaughten of Trinity, Cambridge, who defeated E.G. Peacock in the Final, thus reversing the outcome of the previous year's encounter.

Two of a small number of changes in the rules this year were the opening up of the Town Cup to amateur clubs belonging to towns located on the banks of the Thames from Windsor to Oxford (but excluding, naturally, any with undergraduate associations with Oxford University), and the interesting rule that '*Judges at the winning-post shall be appointed by the Umpire*'. In quoting this provision made by the Stewards, H.T. Steward adds the note:

> *This had practically been the case for some four years, and the rule was doubtless intended not only to give the Umpire the power, but to make it incumbent upon him, to appoint the Judges.*

The weight which the Stewards had placed on Bishop's view, as Umpire, that Oxford had won the Stewards' in 1845, is more understandable in the light of this comment.

1853

This was not a year of great significance for the House. The OUBC, with Nind at 6, won the Grand against the CUBC by 18 inches, and the Stewards' (Nind at 2) against the Argonaut Club by 2½ lengths. First Trinity, Cambridge, won the Ladies', Argonaut the Visitors', and Christ's, Cambridge, the Goblets. It appears that Pembroke was the only Oxford college to enter crews – for the Ladies' and the Visitors'.

1854

This year the Regatta was held on Thursday and Friday, 29 and 30 June. Now in its sixteenth year, it had cemented its position as England's premier showcase for rowing, '*. . . the oarsman who has not shown his quality there, can never hope to have a name among the great*' (*Bell's Life*, 9 July, 1854). There was the usual gathering of the socially prominent, and '*never was there a greater concourse of spectators drawn together in any previous year*'. Messrs Breakspear and Brooks (Mayor of Henley) provided '*their annual "spread" where the champagne flowed freely*', while Mr. P.B. Cooper followed his normal practice of accommodating competitors' boats from Cambridge and London in the garden of his house at the foot of the bridge, he also providing '*creature comforts*' for the oarsmen and their friends. (Mr. Cooper was Treasurer of the Regatta from its inception). The band of the Blues serenaded those on the bridge and in the stands, and the Umpire's professional watermen, stroked yet again by Dick Coombes, put on their usual immaculate display of rowing, that '*precise and even dip in which they alone are perfect*'. The appearance of the Eton Eight, '*in their uniform of light blue*' also added grace to the occasion; they were not yet competitors, but played a part in the proceedings – '*in one of the heats they good-naturedly carried the umpire*'.

Despite their difficulty in keeping a crew together so long after the end of term, First Trinity, Cambridge, entered for the Grand where their sole opponent was Wadham, who had risen from ninth to fifth on the River and were game enough to keep the Oxford flag flying, there being no other Oxford crew able or willing to enter. (The House had risen one place, to third, this year in Summer Eights). Wadham and First Trinity had met in the Grand in 1839. This year Wadham established a small lead from the start, but First Trinity drew steadily ahead and won by 2 lengths. The same crews had earlier in the day raced for the Ladies' Plate, First Trinity again being the winners.

In the Stewards' Pembroke, Oxford, beat Lady Margaret by 1 length, but, the same crews entering for the Visitors', here the finishing order was reversed, Lady Margaret winning by 2 lengths.

C. Cadogan of Christ Church and W.F. Short of New College, the winners of the OUBC Pairs for a second successive year, entered for the Silver Goblets. They beat a Pair from the Wandle Club in the first Heat. Craven and Swaine of St. John's, Oxford, rowed over in the second heat. (Two other Oxford Pairs had entered, but withdrew.) In the Final Cadogan and Short won very easily, '*their opponents* (Craven and Swaine) *not having a shadow of a chance from the first, and rowing as if they were quite aware of it*'. *(Bell's Life)*.

The Diamonds were won by Playford of the Wandle Club, he having been a member of the Pair defeated by Christ Church in the Goblets. The Town Challenge Cup was competed for (there had been no entries for the previous 3 years), and the Watermen's race again took place, with Coombes' crew victorious.

1855-1859

For a number of years from 1855 no House crew was entered for Henley. Indeed, the third place on the River in Summer Eights which was achieved in 1855 was not matched until 1871. Head of River in 1849-1851, Christ Church never again held that position during the balance of the century.

In 1855 Nind rowed 6 in the Oxford University crew which lost to Cambridge in the Grand. E. Cadogan partnered by W.F. Short of New College, was beaten for the Silver Goblets. Balliol won the Ladies'. This year the Wyfolds became an event for coxed Fours, Oxford and Cambridge crews composed of resident members not being allowed, however, to compete.

In 1856 Exeter was the only Oxford college at Henley, entered, without success, for the Ladies'. The qualification for this event was modified this year, being narrowed to admit only Oxford and Cambridge college crews, and crews from Eton and Westminster.

In 1857 (from this year the OUBC Pairs were rowed in the Summer, not in October) Exeter, Head of the River, won the Ladies' and Pembroke, Oxford, the Visitors' and the Wyfolds, the qualification for which was now relaxed to permit any amateur crew to enter, with the exception of past or present entrants for the Stewards'. Edmond Warre, of Balliol, partnered by A.P. Lonsdale, won the Silver Goblets. (Warre was to go on to be the inspiration for rowing at Eton, and later Head Master. His Henley successes included winning the Ladies' and the Goblets twice. He had been in the 1855 Balliol Ladies' crew. He rowed for Oxford in the Boat Race in 1857 and 1858, winning in the first of these years).

The 1857 Boat Race crew, including R. Martin of Christ Church, but in a different rowing order, was beaten in the Grand by London Rowing Club, which had been founded the previous year. 1857 was also the year in which the Great Western Railway opened the extension from Twyford to Henley.

In 1858 Balliol, with Warre at 6, won the Ladies'.

In 1859 Warre, with Arkell of Pembroke, won the Goblets for the second time. An OUBC crew, with C.G. Lane of the House, (and with Warre at 4), lost to London Rowing Club, who again won the Grand.

1860–1869

THE HOUSE DID NOT SEND A CREW TO HENLEY DURING THIS DECADE, fifth place on the River in Summer Eights being the best result achieved.

In 1860 no Oxford crews went to Henley, and indeed there were no entries at all for the Ladies' or the Visitors'.

In 1861 Trinity, Cambridge, won the Grand (as Holders), the Ladies', the Stewards' and the Visitors'. Eton and Radley for the first time entered for the Ladies'. Hopkins and Norsworthy of Magdalen won the District Goblets for Pairs; the Local Amateur Scullers' Race had been re-designated under this name in 1857. The District Goblets had been restricted to amateurs residing within 25 miles of Henley, but excluding the universities and the public schools. In 1861 this restriction was removed; the event was discontinued in 1867.

In 1862 W.B. Woodgate of Brasenose, who won the Goblets with W. Champneys, dead-heated against E.D. Brickwood for the Diamonds, and lost the re-row. He went on, however, to win the Wingfield Sculls, and so became the first Oxford University Amateur Champion of the Thames and Great Britain. The Wingfields had been established in 1830, taking place in August on the birthday of Henry Wingfield, the founder of the event. Initially the course was from Westminster to Putney. In 1849 it was changed from Putney to Kew, and from 1861 it was from Putney to Mortlake. (In October 1831 a Championship of the Thames for professional scullers had been instituted).

For the Final of the 1863 Visitors', the Umpire's boat was crewed by past university oarsmen, instead of London Watermen; P.H. Nind rowed at 6 in this crew. This year saw Univ. win the Grand, the Ladies' and the Stewards', and BNC the Visitors'. Woodgate, this time with R. Shepherd, again won the Goblets. Parker, of Univ., won the Wingfields.

In 1864 Univ. rowed over for the Visitors', and Woodgate won the Diamonds.

1865 was a year in which no Oxford University crews entered for Henley, though E.B. Mitchell of Magdalen, one of 2 or 3 Oxford individual entrants, won the Diamonds.

In 1866 the Oxford Etonians entered a crew for the Grand. H.P. Senhouse of Christ Church rowed 3, the cox being C.R.W. Tottenham, also of the House. The Oxford Etonians won the event. Univ. won the Stewards' and the Visitors', and Michell the Diamonds' for the second year in a row. Two Exeter men won the District Goblets. The Oxford Etonians, with Senhouse and Tottenham in the crew, were beaten for the Wyfolds.

Tottenham, deserves special mention, for he created a never-equalled record for a cox by winning the Boat Race 5 years in a row between 1864 and 1868.

1867 saw the Oxford Etonians, with Tottenham again coxing, win the Grand for a second year, while University won the Stewards' and W.C. Crofts of BNC the Diamonds.

Another special note needs to be made, namely of the entry for a House man in the latter event. At first sight it appears unremarkable. W.G. Edwards had won his first heat of the OUBC Sculls in 1865, but lost his second heat. In 1866 he won the race for second place in a field of 10 competitors, but in 1867 again lost his heat. In the 1867 Diamonds he lost his heat to Stout of London Rowing Club in an exciting race. What is interesting is that Edwards (later Canon Edwards) ever got to handle an oar or a scull at all while at Oxford. He had come up to the House

> '. . . *in the days when the social status of noblemen, and the fine distinction between 'armigeri' and 'generosi' among gentlemen-commoners, were duly noted in the books, Edwards was a mere 'servitor', one of a group of students whose menial duties, in days not so long gone, had included waiting at table upon their undergraduate betters, in return for their education. Having an interest in rowing, Edwards sought out the Etonian President of the Boat Club, Senhouse, and was permitted to join the Boat Club in 1846. He quickly made his mark, stroking the Torpid, and the Eight, in 1866, rowing in ten crews in all.*'
>
> (*Christ Church, Oxford, A Portrait of the House*, Ed Christopher Butler, p. 128-9).

1867 was also the year of the Paris Exhibition, Emperor Louis Napoleon III's Exposition Universelle, and a Grand International Regatta was held, supported mainly by Oxford crews. In the Fours, Tottenham coxed a scratch crew of Oxford Etonians in an event for which crews from Canada, Hamburg, Boulogne, Tours and Paris, as well as London Rowing Club, were also entered. The Etonians came third. The winners, the Western Club of New Brunswick, were allowed to start without a cox, and in addition caused much unhappiness because they were not amateurs. In an event for Coxed Pairs an OUBC crew, coxed by Tottenham, was unsuccessful against 5 continental crews.

A further Regatta, the British Regatta at Paris, managed by an English Committee, and open to the world, took place. The Oxford Etonian Club, with 1 change from the Paris Regatta crew, but with Tottenham coxing, beat London Rowing Club by 1 length in the first heat of the Fours. Three French crews, and Worcester, Oxford, also entered. The Etonians met Worcester in the Final and won easily.

The Eight Oar Race was entered for by 4 crews, the Oxford Etonians, Worcester and Corpus Christi, Oxford, and London Rowing Club. Tottenham coxed the Etonians, who won by ½ a length in a race rowed 4 abreast.

1868 once more saw no House representation at Henley, though Univ. won the Visitors', Crofts and Woodgate of BNC the Silver Goblets and Pembroke, Oxford, a new event, the "New Challenge Cup", officially named the Thames Challenge Cup. This was the third-ranking event for Eights, coming after the Grand and the Ladies'. For the first time composite crews (for example one made up of members of more than 1 Oxford or Cambridge college) were barred from entering. Nor could any crew contain individuals who had rowed in, or were entered for, the Grand or the Stewards', or who had been in a Head of the River crew at Oxford or Cambridge. This qualification was quickly changed for 1869, however, barring entry to the Thames for any crew or individual entered for the Grand or the Stewards' at the same regatta.

In 1869 a new event for coxless Fours was instituted, with the name of "The Presentation Cup for Fours without Coxwain". It was won by the Oxford Radleian Club, stroked by T.H.A. Houblon of Christ Church. The event came into being because in 1869 BNC, competing in the Stewards', had made their cox jump overboard at the start. For this they were disqualified. This action, however, drew attention to the absence of any coxless Fours at Henley, and the 1869 invitation was to serve to fill this gap. It had only a short life, however. In 1873 the Stewards' became a coxless Four event (as did the OUBC Fours the same year) and the new cup was not competed for after 1872.

In 1869 Univ. won the Visitors'. The Oxford Radleian crew was beaten for the Stewards'. The rule for the Wyfolds was tightened so that no crew, or individual member could enter both for this event, and for the Stewards', at the same Regatta.

1870–1879

1870-1873

THIS DECADE STARTED WITH THE OXFORD ETONIANS (with no Christ Church crew members) winning the Grand and the Stewards'. Univ., who were Head of the River, entered the same Four for the Visitors' as had won the event in 1869, but they were beaten by Trinity College, Dublin. Houblon again stroked the Oxford Radleians, without success, in the Stewards'.

In 1871 Christ Church, who had won the OUBC Fours by beating Balliol, entered for the Stewards' and the Visitors', but won neither event. In Eights Week the House had risen from 6th place to 3rd, and Pembroke from 8th to 4th. Pembroke had rowed over behind the House for the last 2 nights of racing.

Bovill, President of the Christ Church Boat Club, made these comments in the *Christ Church Boat Club Captain's Private Log Book 1860–1909:*

Owing to our success in the Eights and our having the same crew which in last Michaelmas term showed some promise in their untrained state as a four, we determined to send a crew to Henley which was as follows:

Bow	*J.G. Brymer*	*11.7*	*Radley*
2	*E. Giles*	*12.4*	*Westminster*
3	*E.C. Bovill*	*12.0*	*Westminster*
Stroke	*T.H.A. Houblon*	*10.4*	*Radley*
(cox)	*E.O. Hopwood*	*8.0*	*Manchester*

The crew began to practise about the end of the first week in June, but owing to the temptation of the commemoration week and the engagements of the

> *crew at the end of term, practise was altogether interrupted till our arrival at Henley, which owing to the late fixture of the Regatta we were obliged to put off till the week after commemoration week. On our arrival there we practised and trained steadily but without a word of advice until the arrival of Mr. Woodgate (B.N.C.) who had promised us his services and whom we had expected to be there with us from the first day we got there. As he only came a day or two before the Regatta his good intentions of improving our style were rendered rather useless owing to the very short time he had to do it in, and the result of the racing (which may be seen in the Secretary's book) was a disappointment not only to ourselves, but to the whole of the Oxford party at Henley. I have little to say about the crew, and were it not that one should endeavour to take warning by defeat as well as example from success, would with pleasure forget our unprofitable journey to Henley. Our practise* [sic] *was very short, but as many crews have gone from Oxford and done well with the same amounts of practise* [sic], *I cannot attribute our want of success to this alone, and I fancy that we may have got into careless habits in the spurting and hurry of the summer races. And having no one to look after us and set us straight during our practice, we made not the least progress towards improvement, but were probably slower and certainly more unsteady than the first day we got into our boat.*

The Christ Church Boat Club's *Secretary's Book 1860-1874* also commented on this crew's performance in the following entry:

> *Though our eight had been successful, yet as Pembroke, who were faster than us, were going to send theirs to Henley it was useless to think of putting on an eight. We thought however that we might get a four which would represent us respectably and accordingly a meeting of the Boat Club was held which was largely attended and at which it was decided to put on a four for the Visitors' Cup. This crew after a short practice at Oxford left for Henley 10 days before the Regatta. We were unfortunate in having no one to coach us, until about 3 days before the Regatta when Mr. Woodgate of B.N.C. took us in hand. His efforts to correct our faults at so late a period served only to unsettle us and we came to the post most certainly in worse form that when we first entered our light boat at Oxford. The first race we had was against 1st Tri coll Cambridge who had the following crew:*

Bow	*G.L. Roves*	*10.42*
2	*C.S.G. Read*	*12.5*
3	*James B. Close*	*10.9*
Stroke	*John B. Close*	*11.8*
Cox	*H.G. Gordon*	*8.5*

We got a very bad start and never got together for a single stroke, towards the Poplars we came up a little but fell astern again and were beaten by 2 ½ lengths. Time 10 m 9 sec a strong wind blowing right down stream.

After this failure we were persuaded much against our will to start for the Stewards for w[h] we had entered. We had to compete ag[st] an L.R.C four and a four from Tynemouth, both boats of a far superior calibre than that which had defeated us. Consequently though we started much better we were outpaced all the way and did not pass the post.

The great lesson to be learnt from this Henley expedition is never to allow a crew to row without some one constantly to look after them.

Bell's Life's comment on the Stewards heat was that, '*Christ Church finished a bad third, several lengths astern of the north country four*'.

The House, after the experience of the previous year, chose not to enter for Henley in 1872, even though they had got to the Final of the OUBC Fours, and J.B. Little had won the race for second place in the OUBC Sculls. Pembroke, Oxford won the Visitors', and C.C. Knollys of Magdalen the Diamonds, going on to win the Wingfield Sculls also.

Similarly, in 1873 there was no House entry for Henley Regatta. None of the Oxford college crews which participated won any of the 4 events for which they entered, and Knollys was beaten in the Diamonds. In 1873 the Stewards, as perviously noted, became a coxless Fours event, followed the next year by the Visitors' and the Wyfolds. The Visitors' continued to be an event restricted to college crews.

In 1872 sliding seats had been introduced to Henley, London Rowing Club using them in winning both the Grand and the Stewards'. In 1873 sliding seats were used by both crews in the Boat Race.

1874-1877

Between 1874 and 1877 Oxford college representation at Henley was, with one exception, confined to crews from BNC and Univ. The latter won the Visitors' in 1876, and the following year T.C. Edwards-Moss of BNC won the Diamonds.

1878-1879

In 1878 W.A. Ellison of the House, partnered by T.C. Edwards-Moss, won the Silver Goblets for the Oxford Etonians; Edwards-Moss won the Diamonds for the second time. Thames Rowing Club won the Grand, defeating Jesus, Cambridge, who, with the same crew, beat Eton in the Final of the Ladies'. London Rowing Club won the Thames. Dublin University rowed in the first heat of the Stewards' against Columbia College Boat Club from New York, and a crew from the Shoe-wae-cae-mette Boat Club, also of the U.S.A. London Rowing Club won the Final against the last-named crew. In the Visitors' Columbia College, with the same crew as for the Stewards', won the Final against Hertford, Oxford. In his heat of the Diamonds Edwards-Moss beat G.W. Lee of New Jersey, U.S.A. (1 of 2 American competitors).

The following year, 1879, J. Lowndes, of Hertford, whom Edwards-Moss had beaten the year before, himself won the Final of the Diamonds.

1880–1889

1880

THIS WAS A BAD YEAR FOR HOUSE ROWING. The Eight fell 6 places to 13th, its lowest ever in the history of Summer Eights.

1888, however, saw the first entry since 1867 by a member of the House in the Diamond Sculls. C.E. Adam (who had come fourth in Lower Boy Sculling at Eton in 1874, and third in School Pulling in 1877), in a field of 4 won his heat easily against C. Vigers of Kingston and F.L. Croft of Leander, but lost the Final against Lowndes, (now of Derby R.C.), an easy winner.

Charles Elphinstone Adam had come up to Christ Church in October 1877, aged 18. His father – said to have been the model for Scud East in '*Tom Brown's Schooldays*' – served in India as Private Secretary to Lord Elphinstone, governor of Bombay. After returning home, he served as a Liberal M.P. for 21 years, and was a Chief Whip and Privy Councillor. He was appointed Governor of Madras in 1880 and died the next year. One year later, in 1882, his son Charles was created a baronet in recognition of his father's public service. (Adam had stroked the 1879 Torpid, and rowed 7 in the House Eight in 1879 and 1880. He had lost the Final of the OUBC Sculls in 1879 to Lowndes.)

The only other Oxford entry at Henley in 1880 was by Exeter in the Ladies'. L.R. West, stroke of the Oxford crew and the House Eight that year, rowed 2 in the Leander crew which won the Grand. West also stroked Oxford in 1881 and 1883, and achieved wins in each of his 3 years in the Blue Boat.

The qualifications for 3 events were modified for the 1880 Regatta. That for the Wyfolds stated that it should be the same as for the Stewards' but no former winner of the Stewards' could enter for the Wyfolds and the Stewards' at the same Regatta. It was no longer possible for anyone to enter for the

Ladies' who had exceeded 4 years from taking up residence at Oxford or Cambridge. Entry in the Thames was forbidden to anyone who had rowed in a winning Grand or Stewards' crew.

1881

The House was bumped on each of the first 4 nights of Eights, and finished in 17th place – again its lowest ever in the 19th century – having lost 10 places in just 2 years.

It would seem that Adam was not a great team man. In 1881 he was put at stroke of the Eight but – the words are those of The Boat Club President, W.R. Pidgeon – he

> *. . . was unable to stroke a boat at a very slow stroke, 32 or under, and consequently did himself no justice and fell into all manner of faults. Finding the boat go very badly, I changed him from stroke to 7, and finally to 3, meaning this last to be only a temporary change. However he came to me and said that he was unable to row as he had his final schools close at hand, and that I was not to suppose it was from 'pique' that he refused to row. He had thought, he said, that was worth the sacrifice of some of his work to stroke the Eight, but that men could be found as useful as himself for 7 or 3.*

1882

Christ Church rose 3 places in Summer Eights, to 14th on the River.

Adam this year again entered for the Diamonds. He won his first heat very easily against E.B. Martin of Evesham, but in his second heat he was outmatched by A. Lein, of Cercle Nautique de Paris, who lost the Final to Lowndes, who won the event for the fourth year in a row. The Grand, the Stewards', the Visitors' and the Goblets were all won by Oxford college crews.

An amendment to the qualification for the Ladies' and the Visitors' was made to limit entries to crews from colleges and schools *'in the United Kingdom'*. This was because the previous year it had been agreed that an American University was in fact a college and, therefore, entitled to enter.

Also for 1882 it was decided that boats used by crews entered for the Public Schools College Cup for Fours (an event started in 1879 which had a life of only 6 years) should have seats of no greater distance, front to back, that 6 inches. The rules prohibited the use of sliding seats, but in 1880 the wide seats of the Bedford Grammar School Boat had been well greased, thus giving the crew what was regarded as an unfair, or, at least, an ungentlemanly, advantage.

Exeter won the Grand, the first success in this event for an Oxford college since 1863.

1883

This year, in Summer Eights, the House gained 2 places, (making 5 bumps but losing 3 places due to an "an accident"), but still ended only in 12th place on the River. The unimpressive performance suggested by these words, however, far from reflected the reality of what actually happened. Unexpected occurrences robbed A.B. Shaw, the President of the Christ Church Boat Club, of the services of 3 experienced men expected to be in the Eight, and men from the Torpid had to be brought in to make up the crew. Nevertheless, in practice the crew was the second fastest on the Isis.

On the first night of Summer Eights the House bumped Balliol, and so moved up behind Trinity. On the second night, in the words of W.E. Sherwood in his *Oxford Rowing. A history of boat-racing at Oxford from the earliest times with a Record of the Races* (1900):

> *Christ Church close on Trinity when they* [Trinity] *made their bump. They could not get clear and Worcester rowed past and bumped them over two places.*

The House therefore lost 3 places. For each of the next 4 nights, however, they made a bump, so they achieved 5 bumps in 6 nights of racing. It was success of this magnitude which provided the incentive to go to Henley, and entries were accordingly made for the Ladies' and the Visitors', with Adam also choosing to enter for the Diamonds for his third attempt.

In the first heat of the Ladies' Christ Church led Trinity Hall, Cambridge, by 1½ lengths at the halfway point, and held on against pressure from Trinity

Hall, who had the advantage, on the Berks station, of the bend at Poplar Point, to win by just over a length. In the Final the House met Eton, who had beaten Radley in the second heat. *The Times* reported on the race:

> *The Eton crew, rowing the faster stroke of the two, soon drew in front, and were about a third of a length in advance at Remenham. Nearing Fawley Court boathouse the Christ Church men gained a bit, and reduced their opponents' lead a little. The Eton boys, however, again drew away, and at the half mile post were once more half a length in front, and this they increased to a length at the horse barrier. Christ Church, spurting in the slack water below Poplar Point, drew level with the Etonians opposite Phyllis Court, and, leaving them very fast, won a good race by a bare length, the boys rowing badly when once headed. Time, 7m. 50sec.*

In his book *Eton in the Eighties* (published in 1914) Eric Parker provides information on a misfortune affecting the Eton crew at the start of the race:

> *Eton drew the bad station against Christ Church in the final, and in paddling up to the start No. 5 broke his stretcher. It was patched up while Christ Church waited at the post, but broke at the first stroke of the race: yet even so, Eton were only beaten by a little more that a length in 7min. 51 sec – only a second longer time than the final heat of the Grand Challenge Cup.*

Indeed the results given by Richard Burnell in his *Henley Royal Regatta, a Celebration*... show the winners' time for both the Grand (won by London R.C.) and the Ladies', both rowed on the same afternoon, as the same – 7 min. 51 sec.

Bell's Life spoke highly of Christ Church's instinctive decision in reacting to Eton's misfortune:

> *The paddle down to the post for the Ladies' Plate was unlucky for Eton. No. 5's stretcher gave way, all to pieces. A new one was sent for, while the crew went to the bank. Christ Church magnanimously agreed to wait for the repair so long as the umpire could postpone the race. Fortunately there was a margin of some twenty minutes to spare between each race, besides the time to be consumed by the actual race. The damage was repaired by 3:17 p.m., and there was still a margin to spare. We must give Christ Church all*

credit for their sportsmanlike conduct. Some crews would have insisted on their full rights, and on a start to the minute, under such circumstances. It is a pleasure to see crews who recognize that a race is nothing without honour and fair play.

The House Henley crews were as noted on a following page.

In the Visitors' the House's opponents in the first heats were again Trinity Hall. Christ Church – this time on the Berks station – had a lead of nearly a length at the halfway point, but Trinity Hall came back nearly level. The House then drew away, and won by 3 lengths. In the second heat Caius, Cambridge, beat Third Trinity, who were disqualified. In the Final the House met Caius, who had the Berks station. *The Times* reported:

An exciting race was rowed between Caius and Christ Church to the White-house, where the last-named went in front, and led at the Horse barrier by three-quarters of a length. Caius in the slack water then drew up, and led by a length at Phyllis Court, but they unfortunately ran into the bank at Poplar Point, and Christ Church, passing them, won easily, Caius stopping short of the post.

Adam rowed over to win the first heat of the Diamonds, his 2 scheduled opponents not coming to the post. There were 2 other heats, so the Final was a 3-boat race between the heat winners. Adam was pitted against Lowndes (now rowing for Twickenham Rowing Club) and Achilles Wild of Frankfurt, Germany. Soon after the start Adam was fouled by Lowndes, and his boat was upset. The race was re-started, and Adam was quickly left behind by the other 2 scullers. Lowndes won comfortably by 6 lengths, Adam having given up at Fawley Court. The incident involving Lowndes was clarified by *Bell's Life;* Adam had been seriously disadvantaged:

He [Lowndes] *was in the wrong, fouling Adam, and if the latter had claimed the foul we fancy the Umpire would have had no choice but to send Lowndes home and leave Adam to fight for England. Adam particularly declined to claim, and pluckily started again in his wet clothes (procuring a dry jersey, but the rest of his raiment being unchanged). Of course in such a state any chance he had was crippled.*

Shaw commented in detail on the Henley experience in the *Captain's Private Log Book.*

> *The action of the officers and others in sending 2 boats to Henley was fully justified. . . The long-looked-for drive arrived at last, and the crew became a fast one. The opinion of Woodgate as expressed in the St. James's Gazette, was that we owed our victory to life, dash, a long stroke, and a clean feather, an opinion which added to the other pleasures of Henley, since those were the very points which we all had felt were needed, and which it had been the aim of our coach to instill. My personal opinion is that of these four points, a clean finish (that is one where the oar is held square till it comes out of the water, instead of beginning to turn under water after it has got past the rigger in the stroke) is at once the rarest and most valuable accomplishment that a crew can have. Not a few people, and I regret to say ex-presidents among the number, in criticizing the crew asked why we scarcely feathered our oars at all. Such a question, if not put just to test our knowledge, certainly seems to betray a want of thorough acquaintance with the theory of the finish. A late president of the O.U.B.C., Mr. Kindersley, in coaching the Trials last year, urged the importance of this square finish and assured his listeners that it was to attention to this point more than to anything else that our many victories over Cambridge of late years are due. Such an opinion from as good a coach stands in need of no corroboration, and in saying that our own experience at Henley exactly fell in with this view, we only express our satisfaction that we find ourselves in agreement with a competent authority. As regards our non-feathering, in case this finish over which we ourselves had labored as hard should fail to become a tradition in the club, I venture to append a few remarks. If it were, in any proper sense of the words, a matter of opinion whether the style we have striven after was or was not the correct one, I should not presume to inflict on future presidents personal opinions. It is only the conviction that a square finish must commend itself to reason as absolutely the only correct one, that induces me to write anything at all.*
>
> *Our experience is that at Oxford even among eights men not one in twenty keeps his blade square to the end. To do this it is necessary that directly the arms begin to bend and the elbows to drop, the wrists should, relatively to the rest of the forearm rise, in reality remain at the same height.*

Nearly everyone drops the wrists when the elbow drops and so turns the blade under water; there is not anything like the same resistance against the blade. Such a finish also looks much prettier to an outsider who regards only the body and hands.

But it is no less plain that such is wrong. The reason why the right finish is not more generally adopted is l) that it causes so much awkwardness at first,being a cramped and unnatural position of the wrists, as any one can discover for himself at any time, 2) that it causes for a long time a very dirty finish, (not more so than before, only more obviously dirty,). 3) It tends to knock a man over at first since he is exposing the full surface of the blade to the full action of the water when his body is in its most strained position. 4) That it is a very great trouble, without immediate recompense; and since the reasons which make it the correct and therefore the necessary finish are not sometimes made clear to a beginner, it calls for more faith in the coach than unfortunately some people are willing to place.

In concluding these remarks on this point, one ought to say that Exeter Coll., certainly the best college eight seen for many years, owe their success as much as anything to attention to this point. Individually, like ourselves they were rough and clumsy, but as a crew they were very good. Without doubt the ill-success of Cambridge at the late Henley Regatta was attributable to their feather under water more than to any other fault.

That we had our fair share of luck, and perhaps a little more, at Henley is plain. Success at Henley is almost impossible without luck. But it is satisfactory to hear and read that we were the best of the entries for the Ladies' Plate, and could, not impossibly, have won in the final even if Eton had had the better station (Woodgate's opinion), which is equivalent to saying that we were about a length and a half better than Eton. Nevertheless we were sincerely glad not to be called on to make the experiment, as Eton were by general confession 'one of the best crews ever turned out from that famous nursery of rowing', (Brickwood in the 'Field'). As to our racing for the Visitors' Cup, we were undoubtedly very lucky, not, as most people thought, by our opponents getting on the bank in the final heat, for that was their bad watermanship steering and no more a piece of luck for us than if they had rowed badly, but by Third Trinity throwing away their Trial Heat by a most stupid foul. But in justice to ourselves we ought to say l) that the four weakest men in the crew had to be selected to row in the four and do doubly duty, so that we were within two stone of our adversaries in weight (Trinity Hall were 21 pounds a man heavier); 2) that on the second day (when we had to race against a fresh crew who had only entered for the one event), owing to an accident to Eton, we had to row the two races within two hours. 3) That having won the Ladies' we cared very little about winning the Visitors'. 4) That we used an old and borrowed boat. 5) That we had had very little practice, only having entered ourselves for the fours when it seemed probable the eight would have to be taken off, and so making it quite subservient to the interest of the eight.

Finally I would say that while no one would wish to call our eight elegant, no one could deny that it was fast. It would, I think, be nearly impossible to meet with a crew keener on winning or one more ready to sacrifice its comfort and even opinions to the necessities of training. D.J. Cowles Esq. coached us every day till we left Oxford, and it is only stating a fact to say that, without him, we should not have gone at all to Henley, and, going, should not have won. Of thanks he would have none, declaring repeatedly that he would be more than repaid if we succeeded, and reminding us, with much effect, that to be beaten would leave us in his debt. At Henley, where we spent five days before the regatta, we were coached by the Rev. E.H. Walters, who came down from town every morning to do so. Our fastest time up at Oxford was from the lock gates to the post above the Folly Bridge end of Salter's raft 7.35, dead calm, a faint breeze just at the end against us, water so low that we had to come up the wrong side for a great part of the course; only one boat got in our way, stroke 36–38. Compared with our times in the practice for the May races (for a course from the white willow to the top of Salter's raft), the fastest of which was 6.47, a careful calculation showed us to have improved 15 secs., i.e. reckoning the extra distance traversed to have been equal to 63 secs., not too liberal a calculation. 7.35 was twice done by us on successive nights, the first time with a good wind behind us, the second time as described above. Exeter Coll. on this latter occasion rowed over the shorter course in 6.28, a fastest on record, though when they rowed there was a slight wind behind, which had entirely dropped when we went down to the lock. They, however, rowed to the post above Salter's, twenty yards farther than our short course, so that we calculated ourselves to be six seconds behind them. Our boat was a new one by Clasper, and our oars, a beautiful set, were by Ayling. The four was an old boat by Halford hired by us from Magdalen Coll. with 8 inch slides. The slides in the eight were 10 inches. The oars for the four were built by Norris of Wandsworth, and were very bad, being too large, and made of unseasoned wood. The eight was composed of:

Bow	*A.J.Newsom*	*(Christ's Hospital)*	*9.7*
2	*C.K.Bowes*	*(Epsom)*	*10.12*
3	*E.P. Whethered*	*(Charterhouse)*	*11.5*
4	*F.O. Wethered*	*(Eton)*	*11.10*
5	*Lord Pakenham*	*(Winchester)*	*12.4*
6	*E.H Kempson*	*(Rugby)*	*10.13*
7	*A.G. Shortt*	*(Private)*	*10.12*
Str.	*A.B. Shaw*	*(Christ's Hospital)*	*9.7*
Cox	*R.G. Rawstorne*	*(Winchester)*	*8.1*

The four was composed of

Bow	*A.J. Newsom (steerer)*
2	*E.H. Kempson*
3	*A.G. Shortt*
Str.	*A.B. Shaw*

1883 was the first year since 1848 that the House had won 2 events at Henley, and the first time since 1852 that any event had been won. The 2 wins represented the only Oxford successes at Henley that year.

1884

The House was well placed for the start of Eights Week, for the whole of the winning Henley crew of the previous year was available to row. An overbump on the first night gave warning of the crew's power and determination, and was followed by a bump on each of the following four nights; only Keble on the last night was able to hold them off. Six bumps brought the House up to 6th place on the River, the best position since 1875. It seemed a foregone conclusion that Christ Church would return to Henley to defend, and perhaps repeat, the 2 victories of 1883, but, as discussed below, the decision was not one easy to make.

The Regatta organizers were faced with the need to address 2 problems. One was – bearing in mind the fact that the boats started level – the disadvantage to the crew on the Bucks station, and the corresponding advantage to the Berks station crew, of the bend in the course at Poplar Point. Let Steward develop the issue:

> *The unfairness of the course by reason of the advantage gained by the inside boat at Poplar Point had long been the subject of complaint, and much correspondence in the newspapers had taken place for some years, in which cutting off Poplar Point, among other remedies, had been suggested. A Sub-Committee were appointed in March to report generally upon the subject, and in May presented their report, which after discussing the question in all its bearings concluded by stating that, in the opinion of the majority, "having regard to the probable cost of cutting off the Point and that after all it would only remove to a limited extent the unfairness of the present course, the Sub-committee do not feel justified in recommending the Stewards to undertake the work." But they added to their report that another proposed alteration of the course had been under consideration, viz. to start the races below the Island and to place the winning-post opposite the upper end of Phyllis Court wall. This some of the Sub-committee proposed, should be adopted.*
>
> *The full Committee, however, declined to adopt this recommendation, and decided that the course should remain as heretofore, but that the bays on the Berks side should be piled off so that the competitors could not take advantage of the slack water in them, and this scheme was tried at the Regatta this year, and again in 1885; but it did not meet the objection as to the unfairness of the course, though it afforded a haven of refuge for the pleasure boats.*

The second problem was that of a difference in the definition of amateur status between British and foreign entrants.

1878 had seen the start of what was to become a regular, and increasing number of foreign entries for Henley events, in the form of 2 entries for the Diamonds from the United States, 2 Fours from the U.S.A. and another from Ireland. The Shoe-wae-cae-mette Boat Club of Monroe, U.S.A. had entered for the Stewards', losing the Final – as has been noted – to London Rowing

Club, and G.W. Lee, of Triton Boat Club, New Jersey, U.S.A. and G. Lee of Boston, had rowed in a heats of the Diamonds. Columbia College had won the Visitors'. Objections were raised to such non-amateurs, as perceived from the British point of view, being allowed to compete, and in 1879 the Henley Stewards laid down the following definition of an amateur, adopting the one agreed the previous year between the representatives of the 2 universities and of the principal rowing clubs:

> *No person shall be considered an amateur oarsman or sculler, or coxswain:*
> 1. *Who has ever competed in any open competition for a stake, money, or entrance fee. (Not to apply to foreign crews.)*
> 2. *Who has ever competed with or against a professional for any prize.*
> 3. *Who has ever taught, pursued or assisted in the practice of athletic exercises of any kind as a means of gaining a livelihood.*
> 4. *Who has been employed in or about boars for money or wages.*
> 5. *Who is or has been by trade or employment for wages a mechanic, artisan or labourer.*
>
> (Quoted by Burnell).

Now, in 1884, the dispensation in favour of foreign crews (the words in parentheses at the end of section 1 above) was ended. The definition of amateur status was the same whatever the country of origin of a competitor.

To revert to the matter of the decision of the Christ Church Boat Club on competing at Henley in 1884, these are the developments as described by Shaw in the *Captain's Private Log Book*.

> *F.O. Wethered having failed to regain his strength during the training for the Eight, was advised by the doctors not to attempt Henley training, and it was therefore felt best to abandon all idea of Henley, as Buckley, who rowed in the "8" last year, was not available to take his place.* [Wethered had been in the winning Trial Eight in 1883, but had then fallen ill during the Christmas Vacation. Though not fully recovered, he had rowed in the Eight in Eights Week 1884. He was to row in the Oxford boat, however, for the 3 years 1885-1887, and to become President of the OUBC]. *Eventually, however, we determined to go to Henley since we held the cups, even though we did not expect a repetition of last year's success.*

It is only right to say that the majority of the crew thought the decision to go to Henley a mistake, seeing that we could not do ourselves justice, but Cowles's opinion, that it was better to go and be beaten than not to go at all, prevailed, considering the circumstance that we held 2 cups. We went, and were beaten; for the Ladies' Plate by Radley in the lst heat, they having the inside station, and for the Visitors' Cup by 3rd Trinity in the final, we having beaten Caius on the first day. In every race we had the outside station. The cause of our failure was palpably our weakness. All the men were much down in weight. It was indeed impossible that the case should have been otherwise. To begin with, bow, 7, and stroke, the 3 most important places in the boat, were all much put down by schools, and Shortt in addition had been training ever since October for Fours, Trials, Varsity, Eights and Pairs.

And what was worst of all, he was in the schools for eight days in the middle of training, when of course we could do no hard work. So that our overtraining was in no way due to too much work, for we never went a long course, and did not even go over the short course every night, whereas last year we rowed the long course twice, every-single night rowed over from the lock, having nearly always rowed over from the raft in the first journey. We were in fact suffering from too little work, i.e. we had never really got hard; and so the rowing at fast strokes in the heat of Henley pulled us all down. Of course we were very careful not to do too much at Henley, and so we only rowed over the course once, instead of as last year 3 times. But all our caution was in vain. We had not been able to do enough work in the early days of training, and so we ran down instead of running up at the finish.

That it was our condition which made us so slow was manifest, for most people, e.g. Brickwood in the "Field", remarked how good was our time, and how level our all round appearance. This was only as it should have been, for all the men took wonderful pains to improve their form, and in most cases succeeded. I think this was a very praiseworthy effort considering how long the men had been rowing. For most men, after rowing in many crews, get slack about improvement and are content to row in their old form, whereas at least four of our men displayed better form than they had ever done before, tho' want of condition prevented individual excellence producing excellence in the crew as a whole. In my opinion then our journey to Henley was full of instruction. The men rowed well as long as they could, and in the races certainly did better than they ever did in practice. This helped to make

> *me think that another week's practice at the slow stroke would have made a real difference to us. It was not till the day before the race that the boat showed any tendency to lift well and go fast. However, that is a matter of small importance now. The point of interest is that it was condition and not style of rowing that stood in our way.*

The House crews were as follows:

LADIES' CHALLENGE PLATE			VISITORS' CHALLENGE CUP		
Bow	A.J. Newsom	10. 0	*Bow*	A.J. Newsom	10. 0
2	R.H. Williams	10. 5	*2*	C.K. Bowes	10. 8
3	E.P. Wethered	10. 6	*3*	A.G.Shortt	11. 10
4	C.K. Bowes	10. 8	*Str*	A.B. Shaw	9. 8
5	Lord Pakenham	12. 1			
6	E.H. Kempson	11. 3			
7	A.G. Shortt	11. 0			
Str	A.B. Shaw	9. 8			
Cox	R.E. Rawstorne	9. 0			

It appears that, in the first heat of the Visitors', Caius, Cambridge, had been at a great disadvantage, though in no way was the House crew responsible. As *Bell's Life* (July 1884), tells it:

> *Caius were sorely handicapped through two collisions. A couple of popular actors gave their boat one knock, and the umpire's launch also damaged them. On their form in practice they could hardly expect to beat Christ Church, and with a boat hurriedly patched, they had no chance whatsoever.*

In the Final the House '*who pulled slowly and went slowly*' *(Bell's Life)* were easily outclassed by Third Trinity, Cambridge.

The Eight were similarly outclassed in the first heat of the Ladies' by Radley College, who were, at that period, after Eton the most pre-eminent rowing school. The Final of the Ladies' this year was between these 2 schools; Eton won the event for the eighth time.

In 1884 the qualification for the Ladies' was widened to permit the entry of '*Non-Collegiate Boat Clubs of the Universities*'.

1885-1888

Although the House maintained its very respectable position in Summer Eights, rising to 4th place on the River in 1888, there does not appear to have been an exceptional crew on any of these years, and there is no mention in the *Captain's Private Log Book* of any consideration being given to entering for Henley. F.O. Wethered did, however, row 5 for the Oxford Etonians who were defeated for the Grand in 1886.

In 1885 it was determined that henceforth the Stewards of Henley Royal Regatta would elect, annually, from their own number, a Committee of Management which would exercise control over the Regatta in all matters except the Rules of the Regatta and their application. Over time, the number of rowing men on the Committee increased, and the influence of local Henley people who were Stewards declined.

In terms of the organization of the Regatta, the most important development – arising out of the investigation made in 1884 – was the decision to re-align the course; in 1886 what was known as the "New Course" (superseding the "Old Course") came into being. Moving the start to just below the end of Temple Island (on the Bucks side) permitted the finish to be moved to Poplar Point, preserving the original length of the course. The bend at Poplar Point was thus eliminated, there remaining 2 slight bends in the early part of the course, which were compensated for by means of a staggered start. At the same time the course, 150 feet wide, was piled. Unfortunately, the re-alignment of the course favoured the Bucks station, because the boat on that side of the river had even greater protection (afforded by shrubs and trees) from a "Bushes Wind" blowing across the course. The solution, over time, was to push the course further to the centre of the river, by narrowing its width, ultimately to 100 feet. At the same time the number of crews competing in any race was reduced to 2, which meant that the Regatta had to be lengthened from 2 days to 3 to accommodate the need for more heats.

In 1886 also, the qualification for the Thames was amended, making it the same as for the Grand, but with the proviso that no one could enter for, and row for, this event and for the Stewards' at the same Regatta.

The qualification for the Ladies' was amended to exclude anyone who had exceeded 4 years from the date of first coming into residence at the university, while each member of a public school crew had to be a bonâ fide member *in statu pupillari* of such school. The new rule for the Wyfolds prevented anyone from entering for this event and the Stewards' at the same Regatta.

This year, also, the rules in force at Henley were adopted by the Amateur Rowing Association, which issued its General Rules for Regattas which had country-wide effect. An agreed revised definition of an amateur now debarred anyone *'engaged in any menial duty'* from competing.

1889

This year, the House having retained its Summer Eight place at 4th on the River, the matter of going to Henley was brought up. As Frederick Fell reported in the *Captain's Private Log Book*:

> *I summoned a meeting of the Eight to find whether everyone was willing to put on, and finding that they were I summoned a B.C. meeting in the J.C.R. where the matter was discussed with but little opposition, and all the details which I had previously investigated were laid before the house. Here it was agreed to take the Barge to Henley; I thought it best to put on for both the Thames Chall. and the Ladies' Plate, the latter being the race we had set our hearts on because if we were beaten in the Ladies' the enormous expenses of Henley would not at once be thrown away as we should then have a try at the Thames. At the Wood Wharf I succeeded in getting a good position for the Barge for £10. The Wharf being above the winning post I did not have to correspond with the Thames Conservancy. From our Barge (the 3rd from the winning post end of the Wharf) we could see nearly the whole course, while the 2 barges below us paid more, but owing to the shape of the wharf could see less.*
>
> *At the meeting of the B.C. £40 was guaranteed from the B.C. funds and a subscription list was put up in the J.C.R. where we collected . . . .* [no figure is given]. *I went to Henley myself to secure a place for the Barge and to secure a House. We took Belmont House – New Street. It has a nice little garden at the back and was altogether satisfactory. For this House we paid £22 for a week. We went there on the Sat. before the races which began on the following Wed. I let the landlady cater for us as far as ordering what I told her. When there was anything over in the shape of chops or cold meat I had it minced or hashed for luncheon. The butcher's bill came to £7, but having been warned that these people need to be closely watched, I took care to note what I had ordered.*

The catering for barge luncheons and teas was done by Cockburn of King Edward St. at the rate of 5/– a head for luncheons and . . . [no figure is given] *a head for tea. I had written to Morris of Reading to do it but after waiting several days and receiving no answer was compelled to take immediate steps and give the contract to someone close at hand. I guaranteed, after due enquiry as to what other Colleges did, 50 people to lunch the first day and 70 the next 2 days. However, the number which came was so far below the estimate that a deficit of about £30 had to be made good to Cockburn. One day when we had 25 to lunch New Coll. had 100! In fact this part of the proceedings collapsed thro' want of support from the men; Cockburn had to send his goods by rail, which properly speaking should have gone to Henley with the barge, which added to the expense; but the Barge had already started while I was waiting for Morris' reply to my letter offering him the contract.*

We had to pay Thames Conservancy £4 for moving the Barge at all. The cost of taking the Barge up was £ . . . [no figure appears].
The Eight was made up as follows:

T.G.R. Blunt	*Bow*
J. Richards	*2*
E.F.B. Fell	*3*
C.E. Blakeway	*4*
R.H. Harvey	*5*
P. Elford	*6*
W.A.L. Fletcher	*7*
F.W. Douglass	*Str*
H.H. Houldsworth	*Cox*
J.F. Ure	*Sub.*

The reason of our great improvement on our performances during the Eights races may in great measure be attributed to the Revd. Sherwood, formerly of Ch:Ch:, who undertook the sole charge of the coaching.

I attended the committee meeting which met to arrange the times of the races day by day, and always succeeded in getting the Ladies' put before the Thames.

The Christ Church Eight, winners of the Ladies', at the Christ Church barge at Oxford, Eights Week 1889.
Christ Church Archives

> *About half an hour before the race we used each to take a couple of tea spoonfuls of Brand's essence mixed with bread crumbs. Each man had to go to bed for an hour between the races. The decoration of the barge cost £5 for illuminating it on the last night.*

W.E. Sherwood, who gave great service to the Boat Club as coach over several years, was a member of the House who had twice rowed for Oxford, in 1873 and 1874. He was Treasurer of the OUBC from October 1874 to February 1877, and in the latter year coached the Oxford Blue Boat. He resumed as OUBC Treasurer in January 1890. In 1900 he published, as earlier indicated, his monumental *Oxford Rowing*, which gave a history of rowing at Oxford and detailed listings of the results of all OUBC events, and of the performance of Oxford crews in the Boat Race, at Henley and other important regattas, up to 1899.

The 1889 Henley Eight was a strong crew, including 7 members of the Summer Eights crew and 5 of the Eight from 1888. One of the newcomers to the Eights in 1889 was W.A.L. Fletcher, who had rowed in the Eton Eight the previous year. He had come up to the House in January 1889 and, though he had never stroked an eight before, was made stroke of the First Torpid.

In the Thames the House's first race was against First Trinity, Cambridge, whom they beat by 1¾ lengths in the opening heat of the first day. In their second race they easily defeated Jesus, Cambridge, who had earlier beaten Keble. In the Final they met London Rowing Club, who had earlier beaten Thames R.C. London were leading at the ¼ mile mark when

> *the bow man's oar got fouled of some young swans and ran down deeply into the water. This gave Christ Church a lead of three or four lengths, and although London went on in pursuit, the Oxonians won by four lengths in 7 min. 16 secs.*
> (*The Times,* 6 July, 1889).

In the Ladies' Christ Church met Eton, who had won the event in 1884 and 1885. Eton had previously beaten Radley. The race was close-fought. Eric Parker commented in *Eton in the Eighties* that the Eton

> *crew owing to some accident started badly, so that their opponents were clear at Fawley Court; then Eton spurted again and again, crept up and up, and lost on the post by a third of a length.*

In the Final the House again met First Trinity, Cambridge, achieving at the top of the Island a small lead of ¼ of a length, which was lost at Remenham. Christ Church then began to pull away, and won by 1½ lengths.

Following the crew's return to Oxford after the double victory at Henley, there was a little tidying-up to do, as reported by J. Richards, who succeeded Fell as President of the Christ Church Boat Club.

> *Coming into office as I did directly after Henley, on 6th July, I found many matters connected with this Regatta, ever glorious to the House Boat Club, which required attention and completion, and notable among others the collecting of subscriptions due from, and promised by, members of the House towards the Henley fund. This task, however, was not too burdensome, tho' it of course entailed a good deal of writing, and before the commencement of the Michaelmas Term I was able to forward a cheque to the Treasurer for the amount of all subscriptions previously unpaid.*

> *The actual expenditure incurred by sending the VIII to Henley, £150, would have been fully met by the voluntary subscriptions of members of the House, together with the sum £45 contributed by the Boat Club, but for an unfortunate arrangement with the caterers who supplied lunch etc. on our Barge at Henley, contracted as it was on terms most advantageous to these persons, and most disadvantageous to the Boat Club; those actually present at the lunches supplied fell far short of the numbers guaranteed, so that the deficit amounting to £30 had to be handed over to the caterers, Messrs. Cockburn and Co. To raise this amount I had to start a "Henley Deficit Fund", but this I did privately not wishing again to ask those members of the Boat club for a subscription who had so generously come forward last term; in fact the Boat Club has to thank those of its members who won honours at Henley both in /83 and /89. for the blotting out of this debt; Cross, the 'House' valuer, designed and executed cases for the Henley cups, "Ladies'" and "Thames", and these with the cups were placed in the Junior Common Room during term; in the vacation they were deposited for security in the Old Bank. On Sundays I allowed the cups to grace High Table, a move which was, I think, appreciated by the Dons, who had liberally given to the Henley Fund.*

The decade of the 1880s had proven most fruitful for the House. They had won the Ladies' twice and the Thames and the Visitors' once each. There was every reason to hope that this run of success could be maintained.

1890–1899

1890

CHRIST CHURCH'S PROSPECTS FOR HENLEY LOOKED VERY GOOD. As noted below, the Eight performed well in Summer Eights, repeatedly hounding Magdalen, who were ahead of them in 3rd place, while not achieving a bump. By then W.A.L. Fletcher had emerged as a major factor in Oxford rowing. He was, for his day, physically a giant, standing 6 feet 3 inches tall, and with a weight which, from his 11 stone 8 pounds in the 1888 Eton crew, increased to 13 stone by March 1890, when he was 20 years of age. (His weight was to increase by a further 8 pounds by 1893.) His giant size was to earn him the popular nickname "Flea". He developed into an extremely powerful oar.

Fletcher had stroked the House Four in the OUBC Fours in Michaelmas Term 1889, and had come to the notice of G.O. (Guy) Nickalls, who had become President of the OUBC in May that year. Nickalls had already rowed for Oxford 3 times in 1887-1889; Cambridge had won the Boat Race 4 years in a row since 1886. Although unable, on account of an accident, to take part in the Trial Eights in 1889, and not included in the Oxford crew which started training on 20 January, 1890, Fletcher was brought into the Blue Boat a week later by Nickalls, and, surprisingly, given his weight, was put as stroke. (In the previous 30 years Oxford strokes had weighed 12 stone or more on only 7 occasions). But Nickalls had his reasons, as noted in the record book maintained by successive OUBC Presidents:

> *'… I may say I chose him at stroke because I believe in a heavy stroke, and because one day I noticed him stroking a light four in a Race.'*

Nickalls' judgment proved excellent. The Oxford crew, which was in poor shape, pulled itself together at the last minute. A nail-bitingly close race, in which, according to Nickalls, *'the boats were never practically speaking clear of each other for four miles'*, ended with an Oxford win by 1 length. Fletcher's contribution to the victory, as stroke, was beyond question: *'He is the finest oar for his age and experience that I have ever seen.'* (Nickalls). Fletcher became a member of the OUBC Committee in October the same year.

Not surprisingly, Fletcher was the stroke of the House crew in Eights Week. Richards describes preparation and performance in these words:

> *According to custom the VIll came up to commence practice on the Monday. before term, and operations were begun by tub pair exercise on 21st April. The first difficulty which presented itself was the selection of a stroke; those thought likely to fill that thwart were J.D. Ure, J. Richards, and W.A.L. Fletcher who stroked the 'Varsity to victory at Putney; however, this difficulty soon resolved itself as J.F. Ure was forbidden to row on account of schools in June, and J. Richards was incapacitated by illness, in fact only being able to enter the boat a few days before the races; therefore, W.A.L. Fletcher was put stroke, tho' weighing nearly 13 st.*
>
> *The Revd. W.E. Sherwood, who so successfully coached the Henley VIII last year, was again good enough to give a helping hand whenever he could; the thanks of the Boat Club is due to him, also to the Revd. W.O. Burrows for his exertions on the bank, and to A.B. Shaw who expressly came from Town to impart his thorough knowledge of the art. Practice was carried on this year under exceptionally favourable circumstances, and many fast times were done in consequence, in fact throughout the Varsity the times were very good; St. John's, who were 5th on the river, the House starting 4th, perhaps excelling all in point of swiftness and celerity, according to their own particular time piece, the accuracy of which machine may however be questioned, judging by their performance in the races: the House VIII usually got over the full course in about 6.45.*
>
> *The nightly struggle which was carried on last year between the House and Magdalen was destined to be continued also this year, and the crew after six nights' hard racing were compelled to remain where they started on the river.*

The VIII was composed as follows:

Bow	*W. P. Blencowe*	*10.1*	*Eton*
2	*J. Richards*	*10.11½*	*Radley*
3	*H. Pilkington*	*11.1*	*Shrewsbury*
4	*B.R Collins*	*11.5½*	*Eton*
5	*C.E. Blakeway*	*12.13*	*Shrewsbury*
6	*F.B. Gunnery*	*11.4*	
7	*R.H. Harvey*	*13.0*	*Radley*
Str	*W.A.L. Fletcher*	*12.13*	*Eton*
Cox	*H.H. Houldsworth*	*8.4½*	*Eton*

> *On the first night of the races, at the crossing only a yard separated the two boats, and had the stroke been quicker, success would have crowned our efforts; on the second night we had a bad start, Magdalen well away: on the third night, Saturday, the crew made a determined effort to catch Magdalen, but only managed to get within two yards of them; on the last three nights we gained but never came so near as we did on the first and third nights. St. John's, who rowed behind us,* [and] *were not dangerous, used to gain at first, but were always a respectful distance away at the end of the course. The fault throughout the races was the inability to row a fast stroke; the crew used to come over in the races at about 36, when they ought to have been striking 39 or 40.*

After Summer Eights were over Fletcher teamed up with F. Wilkinson of BNC to enter for the OUBC Pairs. They were narrowly beaten by Guy Nickalls and Lord Ampthill, who went on to win the Goblets at Henley.

The decision to enter for Henley, and the run-up to the races, is described by Richards in the *Captain's Log*:

> *A general meeting of the Boat Club was summoned on 4th June in the Junior Common Room to discuss the advisability of representing the House at Henley Regatta again this year; it was unanimously decided to enter the VIII In the "Thames Challenge Cup" and "Ladies' Challenge Plate", the Boat Club promising a donation of £25 towards the Henley expenses, and the House pledging to subscribe the rest. The VIII was admitted to have been one of the fastest boats on in the "Eights", and this, combined with the fact*

that we were the holders of both the "Cups", justified our again entering the lists. Practice for Henley was at once commenced, the Revd. W.E. Sherwood took the crew in hand and advised a change of strokes, as it was thought that W.A.L. Fletcher would not be able to set a fast enough stroke for the Henley Course; Guy Nickalls, Pres. O.U.B.C., saw the crew and thought the change would be beneficial, so J. Richards went stroke.
The VIII was constituted as follows:

Bow	*B.R. Collins*	*11.4*	*Eton*
2	*W.P. Blencowe*	*10.0*	*Eton*
3	*H. Pilkington*	*11.2*	*Shrewsbury*
4	*F.B. Gunnery*	*11.2*	
5	*C.E. Blakeway*	*12.7*	*Shrewsbury*
6	*W.A.L. Fletcher*	*12.12*	*Eton*
7	*R.H.Harvey*	*12.13*	*Radley*
Str	*J. Richards*	*10.8*	*Radley*
Cox	*H.H. Houldsworth*	*8.3*	*Eton*

The same house as last year was again secured, Belmont House, New Street, conveniently situated near river and town; the crew took up their quarters there on the Friday before the Regatta, which was fixed for 9th, 10th, 11th July. All went well until the afternoon before the race when R.H. Harvey became suddenly ill. He had rowed 7 in the last winning Trial VIII, was now occupying the same thwart in the "House" VIII, and had been chosen to fill the post of 9th man for this year's 'Varsity crew, so that his loss was a great one.

Harvey's place was taken by J.P. Ure, who had been a member of the Eight in 1889 and a substitute for the Henley Eight that year. Ure now rowed at 3 and Pilkington took Harvey's place at 7.

On the first day of the Regatta the House were required to race 3 times. They met Eton in the Ladies' Plate. Eton took a quick lead, which was reduced to 3 feet at Fawley. At the mile mark Christ Church were level; they nosed in front at the lower end of Phyllis Court and won by $^1/_3$ of a length.

In the Thames they first met Univ. Another close race ensued. The House led at Remenham by a foot or two, and Univ. by a similar amount at Fawley.

After ¾ of a mile the crews were level, but the House pulled ahead to win by ½ a length. The third race (again in the Thames) was against the second crew of Trinity Hall, Cambridge, whose first crew was entered for the Grand and the Ladies'. Christ Church established a slight early lead, hung on to it, and increased it to ¾ of a length at the mile mark to win by 1¼ lengths.

The next day they met Molesey Boat Club in the seventh heat of the Thames. According to *The Times* report of Thursday, 10 July, Molesey were ½ a length in front at Remenham Rectory. They increased this to a length at Fawley, were 1¾ lengths ahead after a mile, and won by 2½ lengths. *Bell's Life*, however, had a different story to tell. Christ Church were just in front at the top of the Island, and a little more than a canvas ahead at Renenham Rectory.

> *At Fawley they still led, but by no more than a quarter of a length …*
>
> *Again going the faster they had an advantage of half a length at the three-quarter-mile post . . . Molesey, now drew up fast and . . . led by a canvas at the mile. A crab in the boat sent them all abroad, so that Christ Church was again a trifle in front at the horse barrier above the White House. Molesey had, however, again forced the nose of their boat in front at the Isthmian and drew away once more. Christ Church, however, spurted in the most determined manner, and after all seemed likely to win. They were their canvas behind passing the Press Stand, and going fast, Molesey won a splendid race by three feet only in 7min. 35sec. . . .*

The *Bell's Life* account was preferred by John Richards (it being reproduced, undated, in the *Captain's Private Log*), by Steward, and by Ampthill, now President of the OUBC, in his report on Henley. In his *Captain's Private Log* report on the race Richards added that . . .'*in the race against Molesey B.C, we had the misfortune to lose our "fin", a misfortune which effected* [sic] *both steerer and crew.*' Molesey lost the Final of the event to Thames Rowing Club.

The House's next, and final, race was against the first boat of Trinity Hall in the 6th heat of the Ladies'. Trinity Hall led by ½ a length at Remenham Rectory, by a length at Fawley, and won by 2½ lengths in the fastest time of the day, 7min. 11sec. Trinity Hall lost the Final to Balliol.

Bell's Life commented that '*Christ Church were naturally tired with their previous exertions during the day*'. Ampthill also noted that, in the race against Molesey '*Christ Church's severe efforts of the previous day with an untrained man in the boat had naturally told on them*', and he added, commenting on the race with Trinity Hall, that '*Christ Church* [were] *now quite exhausted . . .*'.

At a meeting of the Christ Church Boat Club, held on the last Thursday of Trinity Term, Fletcher had been elected President of the Club for the ensuing year, to come into office after Henley Regatta. Technically, holding the office of President carried with it the responsibility of recording the activities and progress of the Boat Club in the *Captain's Private Log*. There are, unfortunately, no entries from the end of Richards' report on Henley in 1890 to the first entry of C.R.M. Workman as President, in 1898:

This Log Book was unearthed in a packing case in the Lent [Hilary] *Term of 1898 and sent to me by W.A.L. Fletcher, who was coaching the Cambridge Eight.*

It is possible, nevertheless, to piece together from other sources the story of the House's association with Henley Regatta in the intervening period. Although no Christ Church crew went to Henley after 1890, until 1896, the House continued to feature prominently in Regatta events through the personal successes of Fletcher.

1891–1895

In 1891 Fletcher won his Blue for the second year running, rowing at 7 for Oxford in a crew whose members included not only Guy Nickalls and Lord Ampthill (now President of the OUBC) but Nickalls' younger brother Vivian, who had rowed in the Eton Eight against Christ Church in 1890, and had now come up to join his brother at Magdalen. After a ding-dong battle, Oxford won the Boat Race by ½ a length. At the start of Trinity Term Fletcher became Secretary of the OUBC.

After Eights Week the penultimate OUBC event of the academic year, the Pairs, took place. Fletcher teamed up again with his partner from the previous year, Wilkinson of BNC, who had rowed behind him in the Blue Boat at 5, and was, like Fletcher, a very heavy man, weighing 13 stone 8 lbs. to Fletcher's 13 stone 2 lbs. Only 2 crews entered for the event, the other being V. Nickalls and H.B. Cotton (who was to win his Blue the following year), with a weight disadvantage of 2½ stone per man, despite which they won by 2 lengths.

Fletcher was recruited to row at 6 in the Leander crew, competing in the Grand. All the crew were OUBC men, past or future Blues, and including

The Leander Club Crew, 1891. Top Row: R.P.P.Rowe(7); Lord Ampthill(4); V.Nickalls(3); J.A.Ford(2); W.F.C.Holland (Captain, Bow). Lower Row: G.Nickalls(5); W.A.L.Fletcher(6); L.S.Williams(Cox); C.W.Kent(Stroke); H.B.Cotton(reserve); F.Wilkinson (reserve); R.C.Lehmann(Coach). John Eade, thames.me.uk

the Nickalls brothers and Ampthill. In the first heat Leander met Thames Rowing Club, the race ending, most unusually, in a dead heat. In a re-row the following day Leander were easy winners, and so qualified for the Final. Here they met London Rowing Club, the 1890 winners. Leander won by 1 length in the time of 6 min. 51 sec., which remained a course record until 1934.

In the Silver Goblets Fletcher and Wilkinson entered (for the OUBC) as did Ampthill and Guy Nickalls (for Leander). The 2 Pairs met in the Final, which Ampthill and Nickalls won by the tiny margin of 1 foot.

The 1892 Oxford Boat Race crew again included Fletcher, now rowing at 6, as well as Vivian Nickalls. Oxford had a lead of 3 lengths at Barnes Bridge, and won the race by 2¼ lengths in a new record time. The OUBC President, R.P.P. Rowe, a 4-time Blue, described Fletcher as '*the finest oar it has been my lot to see*'. Perhaps it was no surprise that Fletcher was elected President of the OUBC to succeed Rowe.

After Eights Week, in which the House held its position at 4th on the River, Fletcher formed a new partnership, with Vivian Nickalls, for the OUBC Pairs, which they won. Based on this success they entered (as Oxford University) for the Goblets, and won the Final by 5 lengths against a Thames

Rowing Club Pair. Fletcher was invited, for the second year running, to join an all-Oxford Blue Leander crew competing in the Grand. They beat First Trinity, Cambridge by a length in the second heat, and in the Final met Thames Rowing Club, who had beaten London Rowing Club in the first heat. Leander were a length up at Remenham Rectory, and 4 lengths ahead at the mile post. Paddling, they won easily by 3 lengths.

Fletcher now had 5 Henley wins, and 3 Boat Race wins, to his credit.

In preparing the Oxford crew for the 1893 Boat Race Fletcher was fortunate in having 4 Old Blues, beside himself, potentially available. These were all included in the final crew, 6 of whom were Etonians. Once again, the race turned out to be a close-fought affair. At Hammersmith Bridge Oxford led by ½ a length, and at Chiswick Church, after 2½ miles, Cambridge were only a length behind. At the finish Oxford led by 1 length at 4 feet, the time for the race (18 min. 25 sec.) not being bettered until 1911.

Fletcher had accomplished 4 Boat Race wins, a feat only twice before accomplished, by Willan of Oxford in 1866-9 and by Muttlebury of Cambridge in 1886-9.

By the time Henley came around, he had handed over the Presidency of the OUBC to his successor. He was once again invited to join the Leander crew for the Grand, this time composed of 5 Oxonians and 3 Cambridge men, and rowed (for the third time) at 6. Fletcher also again competed for the Goblets with Vivian Nickalls as his partner in an OUBC entry.

In the Grand, Leander defeated first Magdalen, Oxford, and next Trinity College, Dublin, to reach the Final, where they met London Rowing Club. Leander led by a length at Fawley and won by 1¾ lengths. One of the entries for the Grand was a French crew from Société Nautique de Basse-Seine; French entries were also made for the Thames, the Stewards', the Goblets, and the Diamonds. These foreign entries were facilitated by a change in the Regatta rules, made following representations by the Amateur Rowing Association. Entries by French clubs affiliated to the Union des Sociétés Françaises de Sports Athletiques would be exempted from the general rules for foreign entries, provided that the Secretary of the Union made a written guarantee to the effect that each person entering had never broken any of the specific rules defining an amateur. (In the following 6 years similar exceptions were made to cover entries guaranteed by the National Rowing Associations of Germany, the Netherlands, and Belgium).

In the Goblets Fletcher (stroke) and Nickalls first met W.F.C. Holland and J.A. Ford, both Oxford Blues, Ford having rowed in the 1892 and 1893 Blue Boats. They were entered for Leander. Fletcher and Nickalls established a lead of 1 ½ lengths at Fawley, and went on to win easily by 3 lengths. In the Final they met R.O. Kerrison and T.G. Lewis, Cambridge Blues in 1893 – and again in 1894 – rowing for Trinity, Cambridge. *The Times* (Saturday, 8 July) reported that

> *Nickalls and Fletcher led out and rowed right away from their opponents, the Cambridge pair steering a very erratic course and going into the piles on the Bucks side.*

Fletcher did not compete at Henley again after 1893. His total of 7 events won, plus his 4 Boat Race victories, had established him as a leading force in rowing. He was to further enhance his reputation as a Boat Race coach, while he also became an important figure, as will be seen, in the organizing and running of Henley Regatta.

The names of the Nickalls brothers, both Magdalen men, have been mentioned several times, and it is only proper to make reference to their amazing, and unequalled, success as competitors in Henley Regatta events. Between 1885 and 1907 G. (Guy) Nickalls won no fewer than 22 "open events" (see Burnell footnote [2], page 158) at Henley in 70 races, of which he won 60. V. (Vivian) won 10 events between 1888 and 1896, winning 27 of 32 races. Between them they rowed 7 times for Oxford, and won the Diamonds 6 times.

In 1894 and 1895, rowing together, they won the Silver Goblets. In celebration of these 2 successive wins their father, Tom Nickalls, donated the Nickalls Challenge Cup in 1895. From this year on the event carried the title "The Silver Goblets and Nickalls Challenge Cup". (The brothers won the event for the third time in 1895).

No Christ Church crew entered for Henley in 1894 or 1895. In 1893 Regatta entries had reach a record 53, and there was a proposal in 1894 to make the Regatta a 4-day event. The Stewards' decision to run preliminary races, if necessary, before the start of the Regatta, obviated the need to extend the length of the Regatta. In 1894 the definition of an amateur was amended to exclude any person disqualified as an amateur in any other branch of sport.

1896

During the years preceding the House had become unlucky in Summer Eights. From 1888 to 1893 they had been in 4th place on the River, but had then slipped, first to 5th, then to 8th, and in 1895, to 11th place. They held on to that position during Eights Week 1896. For whatever reason they then decided to enter a Four in the Wyfolds. The crew was :

		st. lb
Bow	H.J.G. Blaauw *(steers)*	10. 10
2	C.R.M. Workman	12. 6
3	W.J. Oakley	13. 2
Str	C.L. Bryden	10. 9

In the third heat they met London Rowing Club. *The Field's* report (11 July, 1896) reads as follows:

> *Christ Church started at 20 and 38 stroked in the opening half and full minute, London pulling 22 and 42, and in a very short time the latter were ahead. They steered for the piles on the Bucks shore, but discovered their danger in time, and led by half a length at the upper end of the Island, and by three-quarters at the Rectory. They were no farther in front at the half-mile post, where they came out from the neighbourhood of the piles, which they had been dangerously close to again. Before reaching Fawley Boathouse they were clear, and they led by a length and a quarter there. The time to that point was 3min. 50sec., and then they steadily gained, winning with something in hand by two lengths in 8min. 3 sec.*

London met Trinity Oxford in the Final; Trinity won a hard race by ⅓ of a length.

1896 saw the first visit to Henley of Yale University, who entered for the Grand. (Cornell had come in 1895). Though defeated by Leander in the third heat by 1¾ lengths, Yale fought hard, such that '. . .*two of the crew on going ashore utterly collapsed*'. (*The Field*). Although they lacked a long body swing, they were remarkable for their uniformity of action. As much as anything else the Americans were admired for their modesty and sportsmanship. This was in contrast to the, as widely perceived, un-sportsmanship of the Cornell crew the previous year, who, in a heat of the Grand, had rowed on the command "Go" despite the hands of their Leander opponents being raised to show that they were not ready. '*It is said that the umpire believed Leander had made a bad start. But it was Cornell rather than the umpire who attracted the wrath of the crowd*'. (Burnell, p. 111).

1897-1899

1897 year saw Christ Church's last visit of the decade to Henley. They gained 5 places in Eights Week, rising to 6th, and entered for the Ladies' and the Thames.

A slight adjustment to the course was necessitated this year on account of a large tree having fallen into the river from Temple Island. The starting line was, therefore, brought 35 yards upstream, and the finishing line moved upstream 35 yards above the end of the Phyllis Court wall.

The Field (17 July, 1897 reported on the increasingly unruly behaviour of occupants of pleasure boats observing the races.

> *One cluster encroached upon the course from the Oxfordshire side of the river just opposite the crew's inclosure, and interfered with the London Rowing Club's Grand Challenge Cup eight at a critical moment in a hard race with Trinity Hall, causing a disaster. Possibly the result of the struggle might have been the same in any case, but it was no certainty until the mishap took place. The umpire's launch had the greatest difficulty in making its way down the course, and one canoe containing a lady and gentleman was upset. Some people appeared to take a pleasure in obstructing the passage of the launch, and on one occasion a mob, who, from the appearances of the individuals, should have known better, most disgracefully abused the umpire at the start. It has been getting clearer every year that, if the regatta is to continue, there is but one of two courses to take – either the river must be kept entirely clear of pleasure boats, or the course should be boarded in from pile to pile, so that they cannot get on to it, being confined behind the piles. In either case ferry places would have to be provided at certain points, under the charge of officials.*

On the first day of the Regatta, the House met Trinity, Oxford in the second heat of the Ladies'. Trinity were 3rd on the River in Summer Eights – 3 places ahead of the House. The general risk of disruption resulting from pleasure boats invading the course, could have affected the outcome of this race, as *The Field* also reported:

> *This was a hard race in which Christ Church always held a slight advantage. They nearly fouled a skiff which deliberately came on to the course right in front of them just at the start, but led by a quarter of a length at the upper end of the Island. Their rate of stroke was 20 and 39, and that of Trinity 19 and 38, in the first half and full minute. Steadily gaining, Christ Church were three-quarters of a length ahead at Fawley, reached in 3min. 20 sec. All the way up from there, Trinity spurted again and again, but whenever they drew up a little, Christ Church responded, and in the end won a desperate race by three-quarters of a length, the boats never having been clear of each other from first to last.*

The crew (the same for both events entered for) was:

Bow	H.T.G. Blaauw
2	G.H. Woodard
3	S.W. Warner
4	L.V. Bagshawe
5	C. ff. Eliot
6	C.R.M. Workman
7	A.W. Rickards
Str	E.J.H. Rudge
Cox	B.T. Holland

Towards the end of the day Christ Church met London Rowing Club in the fourth heat of the Thames.

> *Christchurch* [sic], *although they rowed only 18 and 36 strokes in the opening half and full minute to the 20 and 39 of London at once led, and were a quarter of a length ahead at the end of the time. They drew clear at the Rectory, and were three lengths ahead at Fawley Boathouse, reached in*

> *3min. 32sec., and from there they did as they liked, and paddled home very easy winners in 7min. 29sec.*
>
> (*The Field*)

On the second day of the Regatta the House were obliged to race twice with only 2 other races separating the 2 outings. In the Ladies' they met Emmanuel, Cambridge, who had lost their heat of the Thames the previous day. This was, in the opinion of *The Field* '*a really splendid race*'.

> *. . . Christchurch* [sic] *went away very smartly, and were half a length ahead at the upper end of Temple Island, and three-quarters at Remenham Rectory. They could not gain anything more, however, and at the Farm, Emmanuel began to creep up, so that they were but a quarter of a length astern at Fawley Court Boathouse, the time to which was 3min. 16sec. Continuing to go the faster, Emmanuel drew level at Bushey Gate, and were just ahead passing it, having an advantage of the length of their own canvas at the mile. Christchurch spurted, but Emmanuel were able to keep their lead, and at the lower end of Phyllis Court drew away, leading by half a length at the inclosure and winning a splendid race by three-quarters of a length, in 7min. 5sec.*

Emmanuel lost the Final of the Ladies' to Eton, who thus achieved the fifth of 7 consecutive victories between 1893 and 1899.

The second race was against King's, Cambridge, in the Thames. The House led from start to finish, and won by 2 lengths, thus qualifying for the Final, which was rowed on the third and last day of the Regatta against Kingston Rowing Club.

> *Both crews pulled 20 and 39 strokes in the first half and full minute, Christchurch leading at once by a little, and being their canvas in front at the upper end of Temple Island, but no further ahead at the quarter mile. Then Kingston drew up and got level at Remenham Rectory; but Christchurch were once more in front at the cottages above the Farm, and they reached the Fawley Boathouse in 3min. 21sec. with a trifling lead. From there to the mile post it was impossible to tell from the umpire's launch which was leading, first one and then the other appearing to show in front. Passing*

> *the mile mark Kingston were just ahead, and then gained fast, leading by a length at the Isthmian Club. Christchurch spurted at the lower end of the inclosure, but could make no impression upon Kingston, who gained still further, and won by three-quarters of a length in 7min. 9sec.*
>
> (*The Field*)

The President of the OUBC, C.K. Philips, commented in his report that

> *Christ Church improved extraordinarily with Mr. Fletcher's coaching, individually they were nothing, but they turned into a really good crew to race.*

In line with frequent practice at that time, the Christ Church barge was taken from Oxford to Henley so as to be available there for the use of members of the House and their guests during the Regatta. Photographs of the notice advertising the cost of tickets for meals on the barge, and of the record of the total cost of taking the crew's boat and the barge to Henley, of accommodating the crew there, of the entry fee for the event, and of other expenses, as written up in the Secretary's Book by F. Haverfield, are included in the illustrations accompanying this text.

The Secretary's Book also records that in 1897, in time for Henley,

> *To celebrate the Five Bumps we obtained leave from the President of the Varsity to adopt a very smart uniform consisting of white cap with House crest trimmed with blue white blazer & cashmere scarf. White shoes.*

While it may be assumed that uniforms such as this were intended for use on dry land, it was also the case, in the early 1900s at least, that they were worn by certain crews on the water. For example three occasions are known when Christ Church Head of the River crews (Eights and Torpids) wore such uniforms (with shorts substituting for trousers) down to the start of races. At the starting raft they then removed caps, blazers and scarves and raced in their normal rowing gear. Two photographs from 1908 which illustrate this are included. It is assumed that the privilege of going to the start in such uniforms was accorded, subject to rules, by the OUBC. On the other hand it is possible that this "dressing up for the occasion" was done in order to impress

Christ Church B. C.

THE House Eight has been entered for the Ladies' Challenge Plate and Thames Challenge Cup at this year's Henley Regatta, July 14th, 15th, and 16th, and arrangements have been made to send the Barge to Henley for the convenience of Past and Present Members of the House and their friends.

Tickets for all the three days, or any single day, may be had by Past or Present Members of the College, for themselves and friends at fixed daily charges: (*a*) 10*s*. each ticket for Luncheon and Tea and use of the Barge, (*b*) 3*s*. for Tea and use of the Barge after 3 p.m. Application to be made to either of the undersigned.

It would be a great convenience if gentlemen would obtain their tickets before the Eight leave for Henley on July the 1st, after which all communications should be addressed to

H. T. G. BLAAUW, *President*.

C. R. M. WORKMAN, *Secretary*.

Sargasso House, Henley-on-Thames.

June 1897.

Printed notice regarding the cost of meals at Henley, 1897. Ch.Ch.B.C. Secretary's Book 1875–1898.

the admiring young ladies adorning the upper deck of the barge on race days, such creatures being rare objects of attention for young men restricted, in term time at least, to an environment of male-dominated college life. Departing from the barge dressed in blazer and cap etc., would serve to make crews more worthy of the interest of the opposite sex than other, lesser, mortals, males present but not dressed in such vestments of sporting manliness.

Below and right: Henley Expenses for 1897, as listed by the Secretary of the Boat Club in his report. Christ Church Boat Club Secretary's Book 1875–1898

Henley Expenses 1897 .(viii with cox + spare man)

Expenses of VIII.

		£	s	d
House Rent – 'Sargasso' (Littlewood)		57	10	0
(1) Fruit + vegetables (Littlewood)	13 . 9 . 4 .			
(1) Bread (Gill, 95 Bell st.)	1 7 6			
(1) Milk, butter, eggs (Henley Dairy Co)	4 14 9			
(1) Butcher (Lester, Market place)	17 0 3½			
(1) Groceries (A. Austin)	7 8 10½			
(1) Fish (Collins, 43 King's Road)	16 14 4	75	17	1
(1) Wine + beer (Breakspear, the Brewery)	15 2 0			
Newspapers (Higgins, Hart St)			7	3
Washing (Hawkes) 1/8/9 +8/9		1	17	6
(2) Melville (scout – wages, excl. of board + lodging)		5	5	0
(2) Gardiner (scout boy " " ")		2	2	0
Railway tickets to Henley from Oxford, 10 tickets		1	10	10
Cabs + omnibus + Melville's fares		1	2	2
... during Regatta, to the starts		2	10	0
Races. Entries for Ladies + Thames		10	10	0
(3) Oars (Ayling + Norris – 2 sets)		16	5	0
Horsehire Heddaly (9s a day, by contract)		7	4	0
Taking boat to start + small repairs (per Gibbs)		1	14	3

25/- 9/3

Christ Church did not enter for any event at Henley in 1898 or 1899.

The problem of encroachment on to the course by pleasure boats was solved in 1899 when booms were put out to connect with the piles lining the course. This also enabled races to take place with shorter intervals separating them.

In 1899 Fletcher was elected a Steward of the Regatta, the first House oarsman to be so honoured.

Henley (contd)

	£	s	d
Gibbs: wages at Henley 17 days	8	10	0
Carriage of oars: 2 sets		11	7
Polishing viii (Plum)	2	0	0
Taking viii to Henley & back: Talboys	4	0	0
Barge. Registration with Thames Conservancy	14	2	0
(4) Flowers on barge + luncheon tables: Johnson	12	0	0
Talboys: taking barge to Henley & back	21	12	6
" : making new awning (½ paid by BC £10.0.0)	20	10	0
" : ferry skiff (? written wrong) — not paid —	4	10	0
" : small alterations inside barge &c	1	7	0
Gibbs: pair oar gig hired & extra man 4 days at 10/-	4	0	0
(5) Whiteley: deficit on sale of tickets for luncheons &c on barge; supper after races of viii &c.	34	3	11
New flag (Edgington)	1	5	0
(6) General. Printing notices & tickets Baxter	2	8	4
Stamps & telegrams: cheque book (2/6):	0	15	0
Firework Fund at Henley	1	0	0

F Haverfield
30 Oct 1897

1900–1909

1900-1901

THE HOUSE DID NOT ENTER A CREW FOR HENLEY IN EITHER 1900 OR 1901; in the former year they were bumped in each of the 6 nights of racing, and in the latter were bumped 3 times. However, in 1900 Lord Grimston, (later the Earl of Verulam), who rowed in the House Eight in 1900 and 1901, was a member, at 3, of the Leander Eight entered for the Grand. This crew beat the Club Nautique de Gand in a heat, and Trinity, Cambridge, in the Final.

In December W.A.L. Fletcher was elected to the Regatta's Committee of Management, to which he was re-elected annually up to the time of his death. He had coached winning Oxford crews in 1894 and 1897. In 1898 he had been asked, most unusually, to coach Cambridge, who had lost the previous 8 encounters. In 1899, his second and last year of coaching the CUBC Blue Boat, the crew achieved a 3¼ length victory over Oxford, their first for 10 years.

In November 1901 the Stewards considered a motion to ban foreign entries from the Regatta. This was triggered by increasing concern over the true amateur status of entries from the United States. Though the proposal was not approved, the following year a motion was passed providing that

> *No eight – or four – oared or pair-oared crew could compete if in the four weeks prior to the Regatta the crew had in any way been coached, controlled or directed in this training by any person not considered an amateur oarsman, sculler, or coxswain, under the general rules.*

This restriction did not, however, apply to scullers entered for the Regatta.

1902

For this year's Regatta Fletcher was appointed as one of 2 Umpires, joining F.I. Pitman, and succeeding Col. F. Willan, who had served for 19 consecutive years. Fletcher was to remain an Umpire until 1914.

In Summer Eights, 1902, following a final week's coaching by Fletcher *('his advice'*, reported the *Captain's Log, 'was invaluable')* the House made 5 bumps, and decided to enter for the Ladies' Plate. The crew was:

Bow L.H. Barnes
2 H.D. Seale
3 A.G.B. Priestley
4 E.D. Hay-Currie
5 J.D.F. Woodhouse
6 H.W. Jelf
7 J. Holt
Str J.G. Priestley
Cox H.R. Kirby

Christ Church was drawn against Eton in the third heat. *The Field* (5 July, 1902) reported on the race thus:

> *Eton went off at 18 and 37 strokes in the opening half and full minute, Christ Church taking 20 and 39 and at once leading. They were half a length ahead at the quarter mile, when Eton held them to the Farm, and then began to draw up. This they did so rapidly that at Fawley Court Boathouse they were half a length in front. They were well together and continued to gain very fast, Christ Church being quite done with, and rowing without any life. Eton were two lengths ahead at Bushey Gate, and gaining with every stroke, they won easily by four or five lengths in 7 min. 29 sec.*

Eton moved on to the Final, but lost it to Univ. The President of the OUBC, A. de L. Long commented:

Christchurch [sic] *sent an eight to Henley for the Ladies' Challenge Plate W.A.L. Fletcher coached them and turned them into a fairly decent crew, they were beaten in the 1st round by four or five lengths!*

The Christ Church Boat Club President, J.G. Priestley, added, in the *Captain's Private Log:*

> *As regards Henley that division of the work connected with the Crew, Barge, etc., tended to cause confusion and delay. Everything connected with moving the Barge should, if possible, be in the hands of one firm. Unnecessary expense was incurred by our being obliged to divide the work connected with the Barge among several firms owing to the cantankerous behaviour of Talboys.*
>
> *Despite the misfortune which attended our visit to Henley, I feel sure that it was of benefit to House rowing.*

1903–1904

Flooding interfered with practice for Summer Eights in 1903, and what looked like a promising House crew fell into the bad habits of lack of rhythm and slowness at the start and finish of the stroke. Fletcher, however, came to the rescue and a great improvement took place. Unfortunately, on the Friday before the races L.E. Parsons, rowing at 5, and the heaviest man in the crew, was obliged on doctor's orders to give up rowing. The replacement 5 '*was very slow with his hands and had a fearful bucket and naturally upset the whole boat.' (Captain's Private Log).* Fletcher pulled the boat together once more, and the House succeeding in making 4 bumps. Despite this, it was apparently decided that a trip to Henley was not worthwhile. Fletcher's contribution as coach over 2 years was marked by the gift of a silver tankard dating back to 1760

In memory of the never to be forgotten services which he rendered . . . by his wonderful coaching.

In 1904 the House crew for Eights suffered by not being able to find a satisfactory stroke. Eventually T.D. Roberts, a newly-arrived American from Yale, was put as stroke but was '*very slow into the water*'. The coaching of Sherwood and Fletcher saved the day, and the Eight made 3 bumps to move up to 3rd on the River. (They had risen 12 places in 3 years). '*If we had had a stroke capable of driving us we should, I feel certain, have gone Head of the River*' wrote Priestley. '*Owing to . . . our difficulty in finding a stroke, we decided not to go to Henley.*'

1905

When practice started for Eights Week, friction developed between Roberts and the coach, Sherwood, and Roberts was removed from the crew. However, when Fletcher came up to coach 10 days before racing started, Roberts was re-instated. Fletcher told T.G. Cochrane, the President of the Boat Club, that the House would do well not to go down 6 places. Indeed, on the first night they were caught by Univ. But for the remaining nights the crew held off repeated attacks by Balliol. '*Great credit is due to Roberts for the way he stroked and the unexpected qualities of pluck and endurance which he revealed*', wrote Cochrane.

Once again no House crew was entered for Henley, but 2 Christ Church men entered for the Diamonds under the College's name. One was Roberts, who had won the Junior Sculls at Oxford the previous year. The other was G.H. Woodard who had earlier been up at the House for only 1 year, and had been in the 1897 Henley crew. Nothing is known of his later rowing experience until 1905; it may be assumed that he developed some skill and success as a sculler. As it turned out, both Roberts and Woodard were beaten by the eventual Diamonds winner, F.S. Kelly, an Oxford Blue of 1903 now representing Leander, who recorded his third victory in 4 years in a record time of 8min. 10sec. which stood until 1938.

1906

It was decided that the Christ Church Eight would be stroked by H.R. Barker, with A.C. Gladstone, the stroke of the 1905 Eton Eight, which had won the Ladies', at 7, and Roberts at 6. Due to there being too many different styles of rowing in the boat, this crew did not settle well until Fletcher came up to coach. (Fletcher had earlier in the year coached the Oxford boat for the sixth and last time.) Starting in 4th place, the House bumped Univ. on the second night, thus regaining the 3rd place they had held 2 years before.

It was then decided to enter for Henley. Cochrane explained why:

> *With the idea of giving the younger members of the crew the advantage of further coaching, and also of seeing what good rowing was like, it was decided to enter for the Ladies' Plate at Henley.*

The making of arrangements affecting logistics, accommodation and catering fell to Cochrane, as President of the Boat Club.

> *A subscription list was opened and most generously subscribed to be nearly every member of the House and by the Dons, Canons, and old members. Leave was given for subscriptions, if desired, to be paid through Battels – a great convenience to many who find money scarce at the end of the Summer Term. It was decided to take the Barge to Henley, which I think should always be done, or at any rate some provision made for the accommodation of House men at Henley. In previous years the catering had always resulted in a heavy deficit, altho' high prices were charged for the tickets for luncheon and tea. W. Wyatt, the J.C.R. caterer, came to me and suggested that he should be allowed to do the catering, promising to provide the best luncheon in Henley at the lowest price. I went very carefully into the cost of everything with him, and decided on this occasion to get as large a number of people to make use of the Barge as possible, and therefore to charge as low a price for the tickets as possible compatible with not shewing a deficit on the catering account. The prices fixed upon were 4/- for luncheon and l/6 for tea, about half the prices charged anywhere else. The result, was most successful; the food excellent, the Barge crowded, the receipts roughly £90 and the expenses £80. Another year, I think a little more might be charged so as to help to pay for the cost of moving the Barge but for a first time I preferred to be certain of having a crowd and yet not incur any loss on the catering account, neither of which had been successfully done before.*
>
> *As my Schools were over I came into the boat vice Phillips at bow, whose rowing in Eights had not given satisfaction. We secured H.C. Bucknall (Merton) to coach us. We arrived at Henley on 18th June, having taken 90 Bell St., a house with a good garden reasonably near the river. The time at Henley was a very pleasant one, thanks to the general good-temper and liveliness of the crew. I was disappointed, however, with our progress, as we did not improve as we should have done. Halfway through practice we had to leave Hope out in favour of Fraser – Tytler as Hope was all to pieces and upset the boat badly. Nor did Barker improve as expected, but rather the reverse. But by the time the Regatta began we were a fair good crew.*

Because of the number of entries, the Regatta this year took place over 4 days. On the first day Woodard, who had again entered for the Diamonds, lost to H.T. Blackstaffe, the eventual winner. On the second day the House met Christ's, Cambridge, in the first heat of the Ladies', for which 8 crews had entered. The House crew was:

Bow	T.G. Cochrane
2	R.F. Hanbury
3	C.F. Gummer
4	J.R. Trench
5	J.F. Fraser – Tytler
6	T.D. Roberts
7	A.C. Gladstone
Str	H.R. Barker
Cox	A. St.J. Kekewich

> *Starting at 41 against 42, Christ Church soon drew to the front and at Fawley they were a quarter of a length to the good. At the mile they were ahead a length in front, and, despite a vigorous effort on the part of the Cambridge crew Christ Church won by half a length in 7min. 14 sec.*
>
> (*The Field*, 7 July, 1906).

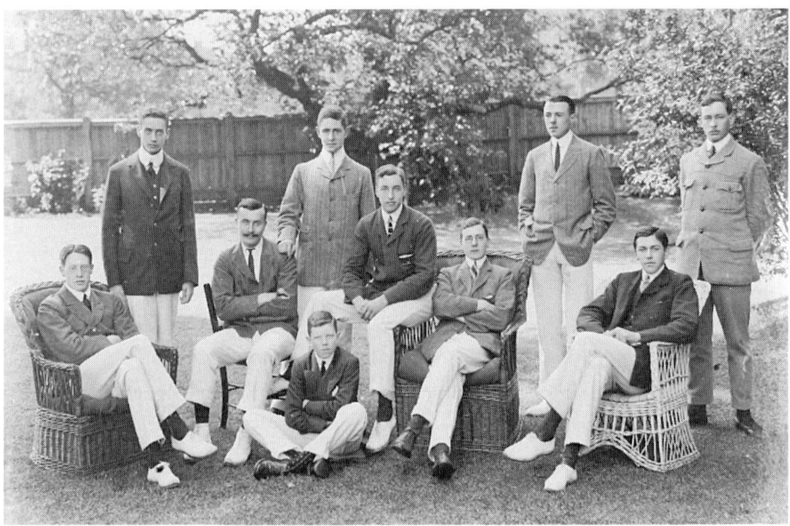

Henley Eight, 1906. HR. Barker is seated in the centre, and A.C. Gladstone on the extreme right.
Christ Church Archives

The next day they raced against Pembroke, Oxford. *The Field* reported thus:

> *A light wind was blowing up the course when this heat was rowed, Pembroke rowed 19 and 38, Christ Church 21 and 40, in the first half and whole minute. The last named drew right away from their opponents up Temple Island, and led by a quarter of a length clear at the quarter mile. Continuing to go much the faster, they reached the half mile two and a half lengths in front, rowing 34 to the 36 of Pembroke. The time of the leaders at Fawley Court Boathouse was 3min. 33 sec. Christ Church dropped their stroke to 32 at the three-quarter mile, while Pembroke went on at 34 strokes a minute. In the end Christ Church won an easy race. Time, 7min. 29½sec.*

The House had now qualified for the Final, in which, on the last day of the Regatta, they met First Trinity, Cambridge.

> *No. 7 in the First Trinity boat had caused some anxiety as he was not well, but, fortunately, was able to row. At the start First Trinity rowed 20 and 39 strokes, and Christ Church 21 and 40 to the half and full minute. For some way up Temple Island they were level, but at the upper end First had a few feet advantage, which they increased to nearly half a length by the time the quarter-mile post was reached. It was a good race to the half mile, where First still led by one-third of a length. But rowing 36 strokes a minutes,* [sic] *the time of First Trinity to Fawley Court Boathouse was 3min. 31sec. At the three-quarter mile post First had gained three quarters of a length, which they made into a bare length by the time they reached the mile, still rowing 36 a minute. Above the mile Christ Church were beaten, and dropped their stroke, First winning a good race by one and a quarter lengths in 7min. 23½sec.*
>
> (*The Field*).

Cochrane recorded the following impressions of the Regatta and its significance for House rowing:

> *Had we come on at Henley as much as I had hoped, we might quite well, in the absence of a good Eton crew that year, have won the Ladies'. As it was, we did not do badly, and I think quite satisfied our supporters. Bucknall did*

his best for us as coach, and brought us on a good deal before we left Oxford, but at Henley seemed somewhat out of his element and not able for some reason, possibly short sight (?), to pick out our weak spots at the greater distance from the towpath which crews row there. In any case our thanks are due to him for the trouble he took with us.

That we did well to go to Henley, I have no doubt, as going there advertises the House and encourages men who can row – and who always want to row at Henley once in their lives – to come up to it; so that it is desirable to go whenever possible and where there is a reasonable chance of success, especially when most members of the crew will be up for another year.

It had been the cause of much consternation at the Regatta that Leander had not entered a crew for the Grand, which they had won 12 times in the previous 15 years. The previous year Leander had beaten a Belgian crew, Sport Nautique de Gand, in the Final. The Ghent crew had struck a remarkable 44 in the first minute, despite their stroke having caught a crab at the fifth stroke of the race. Now, in 1906, the Belgians returned. Who could repel their onslaught? Not Magdalen, nor Third Trinity, beaten in heats. British hopes rested on Trinity Hall, who had beaten a strong Canadian crew, Argonaut, to get to the Final. To the embarrassment of the spectators, the Belgians took an early lead, and won by 3 lengths to become the first foreign club to win Henley's most prestigious prize.

While there was no resentment against Belgian crews for their success, they being well-liked as competitors, (they had entered for the Grand twice before, in 1900 and 1901, in both years reaching the third round, as well as in 1905, when they reached the Final), strong feelings had been aroused against Vesper Boat Club of Philadelphia. Vesper had competed in the Grand in 1905, and afterward there had been suspicions that not all their crew members were amateurs according to the Henley definition. This was despite the National Association of American Oarsmen having confirmed, before the Regatta, that

. . . we have carefully considered the amateur standing of each member of the crew as to whether he is qualified under your and our own Rules, and unhesitatingly indorse them . . .

In June 1906 the Committee of Management issued a statement regarding the controversy, and *The Field* reported on 30 June, that

> *The Committee of Management of Henley Regatta … have unanimously come to the following conclusion; that the cost of sending the Vesper crew to Henley was mainly defrayed by public subscription; that all members of the Vesper crew accepted money; and that sworn declarations of some members of the Vesper crew, made before a notary public were, in some particulars untrue.*
>
> *The Committee of Henley Regatta therefore unanimously agreed that no entry of the Vesper Boat Club of Philadelphia, or any entry comprising any member of that club's crew of 1905, be accepted in future.*

At the Committee of Management meeting Fletcher had given notice of his intention later to propose a resolution preventing any entry from the U.S.A. being accepted. In the event, in December a motion proposed by Fletcher was unanimously approved by the Stewards. It provided that

> *No entry shall be accepted of any Crew or Sculler out of the United Kingdom unless such Crew or Sculler belong to a Club which is affiliated to a Union of Federation having an Agreement with the Committee of Management of Henley Regatta…*

and required that any entry so made be authenticated by the Union or Federation. The motion also included the whole of the Henley definition of an amateur as it then stood.

1907

It had been evident for a year or two that Fletcher had been pondering the significance of the success of the Belgian crews. English rowing was committed to a style developed by Edmond Warre at Eton, and followed first by S.A. Donaldson and then by the great R.S. de Haviland, which came to be known as the "orthodox style" of rowing. The impact of the Eton style can be judged by the fact that between 1904 and 1913, 87 out of 180 Blues awarded by the universities went to Etonians.

> *Warre and his contemporaries had developed the principle of long body swing on fixed seats, and the slide had been introduced (1873, 8") and gradually*

lengthened to 16" to increase the length of the stroke. The importance of swing had continued to be proved by success . . .

Sir William Gladstone, *The Christ Church Style*, article in *Christ Church Boat Club Crew Competition and Racing Results, 1946-1993.* (This article is reproduced at the end of this section of this book).

The long body swing was facilitated by long oars with a long inboard length and thin blades. By contract, the Belgians' oars were shorter, both inboard and outboard, and the blades perhaps 1½ inches wider than those used by Leander. Though the Belgians by no means abandoned the long swing, their shorter inboard oar length, and proportionately longer outboard length, produced a long stroke, with the wider blades moving more water, and with a faster rate of stroking possible.

Fletcher had initiated experiments before Torpids in 1906, when he shortened the distance from the outriggers to the sill of the boat, and at the same time moved the buttons 2" towards the end of the handle. '*This*', wrote Cochrane,

'gave a long oar out board with a short leverage inboard, and enabled the crew to row with a long sweeping stroke without requiring to over-reach in the slightest degree. In fact they appeared to be short forward, tho' in reality their stroke, in the water, was the longest of any crew's.'

Small modification were made, and the Torpid rose from 7th to 3rd. As noted earlier, in 1906 the House made 1 bump in Eights Week, and reached the Final of the Ladies' Plate. For the 1907 Eight Fletcher had requested the adding of a set of '*new short oars*'. A.C. Gladstone (President of the Christ Church Boat Club from July 1906 to July 1907) commented in the *Captain's Log* that

. . . we came in for columns of unfavorable criticism in the press, the favourite hit being that we had "Belgianized" our rowing, the allusion being that they had taken the Grand out of the country in 1906.

The essence of Fletcher's technique which came to be known as "The Christ Church Style", is given by Sir William Gladstone:

> *Evolving the ideas of Warre and de Haviland, he appreciated that with the longest existing (16") sliding seat, the "quick catch" so vital to the English style might best be achieved by a broader blade and shorter oar, with a relatively longer inboard length, than by an excessively long body swing with a long oar and thin blade which had seemed the best combination for many years in spite of its tendency to "pinch" the boat and reduce the strength which could be applied at the beginning.*

In the Eights Week races the House bumped New College on the first night, and on the third night caught Magdalen, thus going Head of the River for the first time since 1849, a lapse of 58 years.

As might be expected, it was decided to go to Henley, and initially entries were made for the Grand and the Ladies', though entry for the latter was dropped. Since Fletcher was again a Henley Umpire, he felt unable to coach the crew; the coaching was undertaken by G.C. Bourne, twice a winning Oxford Blue in the 1880s. Woodard entered for the Diamonds for the third and final time, once again achieving no distinction.

There were 5 entries for the Grand, the other 4 being the Belgians, Leander, Thames and London. The Belgians beat a Leander crew including 7 Cambridge Blues (who had beaten London R.C. in the first heat), while the House took on Thames R.C. on the third day. The crew, with 3 changes from Eights Week, was:

Bow	T.G. Cochrane
2	C.R. Codrington
3	C.S. James
4	J.R. Trench
5	G.E. Hope
6	J.P. Purnell – Edwards
7	H.R. Barker
Str	A.C. Gladstone
Cox	A. St.J. M. Kekewich

The Times report (5 July) on the race reads:

> *Christ Church started at 43 strokes a minute and Thames at 41, the former slowly gaining, and being half a length ahead in a quarter of a mile. They had doubled this lead at the half mile, and at Fawley, reached in 3min. 43sec., they were a length and a quarter in front. They were only rowing 36 strokes a minute above there, but gained steadily, and they won by many lengths in 8min. 3sec.*

On the fourth and last day of the Regatta the Final of the Grand took place. *The Times* reported that

> *Although the Belgians again won the Grand Challenge Cup, which they last year took out of this country for the first time in its existence, they did not do so without a hard race with Christ Church. The result of the race might have been different had the stations been reversed, for the wind was blowing very strongly, partly downstream and partly off the bushes. Christ Church rowed an exceedingly plucky race, but had a stern chase for the whole distance. Both crews started at 44 strokes a minute, the Belgians at once leading, and being three-quarters of a length ahead at the quarter-mile. At Remenham Rectory they were rowing 38 strokes a minute, and Christ Church 40 just above it. The Belgians, however, were clear at the half-mile, and led by more at Fawley, reached in 3min. 32sec. They had increased this advantage to a length and a quarter at three-quarters of a mile, they reducing their stroke to 36 a minute above it, Christ Church still rowing 40 at the Grosvenor Club. At the mile the Belgians led by a length and a quarter, and increased the rate of stroke to 36 above there, Christ Church dropping to 39. Christ Church drew up a little, and the Belgians won by a bare length in 7min. 31sec.*

The Field added that

> *Christ Church, Oxford, were rowing in somewhat similar fashion to the Belgians, but failed to strike the water, with the blades together, in the dashing and effective manner of the Gand men, and were not nearly so steady in sliding forward.*

However, to have lost by only 1 length to a crew which had demonstrated its mastery of the river for 2 years in a row was no mean feat, and the House was in a good position to congratulate itself and wonder what good fortune the next year might bring.

Here is how A.C. Gladstone described the Henley experience in the *Captain's Private Log*:

> *Owing to the success of the Eight it was decided to go to Henley. Dr. Bourne kindly undertook the duties of coach, as W.A.L.F. did not feel at liberty to undertake as he was one of the umpires. We went to Henley 10 days before the Regatta. Trench came up to row at 4 in F-Tyler's place, Cochrane bow in Codrington's place and Codrington 2 instead of Paget. This strengthened the eight, but in spite of it we were probably not faster at Henley than we were in Eights. We entered for the Grand and Ladies', but soon abandoned the idea of the latter as any head of the river crew ought to be able to win the Ladies' easily and so perhaps it is hardly "sporting" to go for it. Also we really thought we had a fair chance for the Grand C.C., for which there were 5 entries, Leander, London, Thames, Club Nautique de Gand (Belgians) and Ch.Ch. The luck of the draw gave us Thames in the antefinal, whom we beat easily, while the Belgians beat Leander by 1/3 length in the other heat. Leander, composed of 7 Cambridge Blues, led till the Mile Post and were beaten on the post, an unprecedented thing for an English crew. They had the Bucks station and a big head wind gave them a distinct advantage for the first half of the course. The moral seems to be that the present Cambridge style, though it has justified itself on the tideway at Putney, is found wanting in a tight race on the Henley Course. The chief characteristics of it are a slow beginning and a tremendous thrust at the finish. The fact that Leander were only rowing 33 at the finish speaks for itself.*
>
> *This left Ch.Ch. in the final against the Belgians, who had Bucks, from which they in turn derived advantage for the first 3 minutes as there was a very stiff head wind blowing slightly off the Bucks shore and affording shelter to the Bucks boat. Ch.Ch. started at 42 and hardly ever dropped below 40, but were always behind the Belgians, having almost a length at the ½ mile and winning by a bare length. Full details in Secretary's book. According* [to] *the opinion of the coaches, the House eight could not have expected to do better under the circumstances, but it would have been interesting for them 1) to have met the Belgians on the same day with stations reversed or 2) to have met Leander.*

1908

Before the 1907 Regatta the Stewards had decided that, since the rowing Olympics – part of the London Olympics the following year – would take place soon after Henley, foreign entries would not be accepted for 1908. For House rowing 1908 was a bumper year. The first Torpid went Head of the

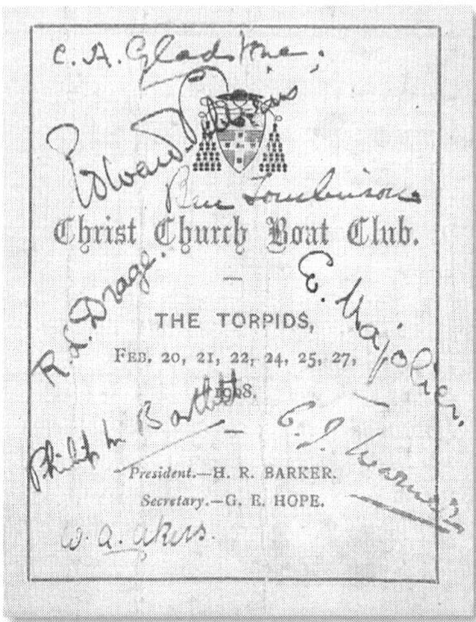
C. A. Gladstone

Christ Church Boat Club.

—

THE TORPIDS,

FEB. 20, 21, 22, 24, 25, 27, 1908.

President.—H. R. BARKER.
Secretary.—G. E. HOPE.

Counter clockwise from left: *Christ Church Torpids race card cover, with autographs, 1908.*

Christ Church Bump Supper Torpids Menu, 26 February, 1908.

Christ Church Eights Week Bump Supper Dinner Menu, 1908.

Parkhouse: J.F. West Album

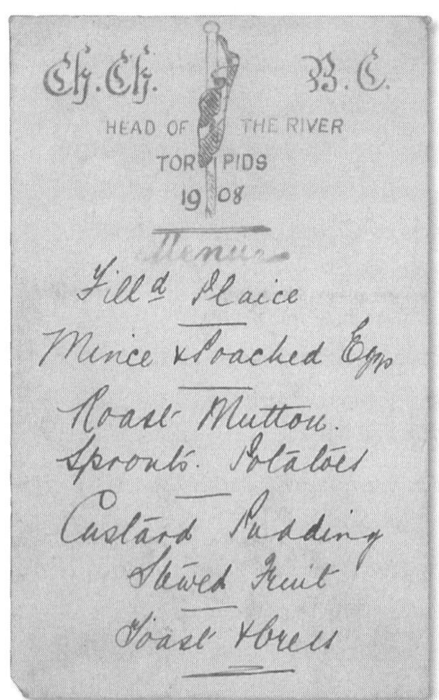
Ch. Ch. B. C.

HEAD OF THE RIVER

TORPIDS

1908

Menu

Fill^d Plaice

Mince & Poached Eggs

Roast Mutton.

Sprouts Potatoes

Custard Pudding

Stewed Fruit

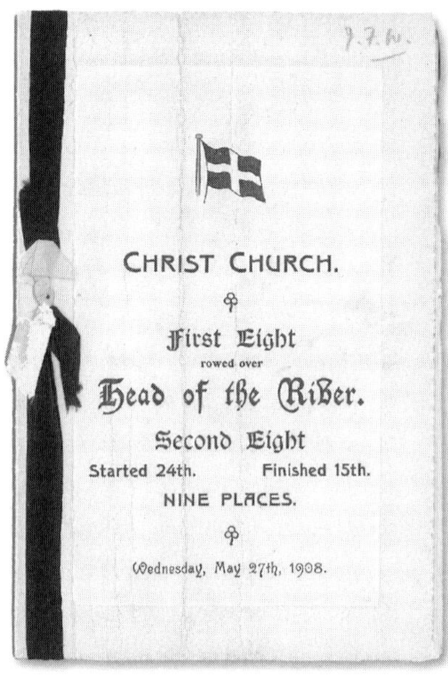
J.F.W.

CHRIST CHURCH.

First Eight

rowed over

Head of the River.

Second Eight

Started 24th. Finished 15th.

NINE PLACES.

Wednesday, May 27th, 1908.

River, the Eight retained its headship, A.C. Gladstone won the Varsity Sculls, and, partnered by his younger brother, C.A., the Varsity Pairs. The decision to enter for Henley was an easy one. It was decided to send 2 crews. The First Eight would enter for the Grand, and the Second Eight, (which had made 9 bumps), for the Thames. A.C. Gladstone and H.R. Barker also entered for the Goblets.

Because Leander and Cambridge University had been selected as Britain's 2 crews for the Olympic Eights, (each participating country was permitted to enter 2 crews), and because the Belgians (who would enter for the Olympics) were barred from competing at Henley, as noted above, the reduction in heavyweight competition for the Grand increased the number of entries for the event. As well as Christ Church, 5 Cambridge colleges, 2 Oxford colleges, Thames and London Rowing Clubs, and Eton, all entered. The House crews were as follows:

	GRAND CHALLENGE CUP	THAMES CHALLENGE CUP
Bow	A.B.G. Cherry-Garrard	J.F. West
2	W.A. Akers	M.H.B. Lethbridge
3	F.E. Villiers	P.M. Bartlett
4	A.C. Gladstone	G. Metaxa
5	G.E. Hope	B. Tomlinson
6	E. Majolier	J.P. Purnell-Edwards
7	H.R. Barker	G.R. Codrington
Str	C.A. Gladstone	K.T. Dowding
Cox	A. St.J. M. Kekewich	G.T. Hebert

Cherry-Garrard was later a member of Scott's Antarctic Expedition in 1910-13, about which he later (1922) wrote a book, *The Worst Journey in the World.*

The House's appearance on the first day in the third heat of the Thames, against Molesey Boat Club is described thus by Sir Theodore Cook in his *Henley Races* covering the period 1903 to 1914, and from which all the following commentaries on Henley 1908 are taken:

> *Both crews started at 20 and 39 in the first half and full minute. For half a minute they were level and then the House began to go quickly away, leading by three-quarters of a length at the quarter mile. From this point the time in the Molesey boat got erratic, and they dropped further behind,*

First Eight, Eights Week, 1908. "At the punt". Parkhouse: J.F. West Album

First Eight, Eights Week, 1908. "The first stroke". (Note: The blazers are now stored in the punt.) Parkhouse: J.F. West Album

The Thames Cup, 1908. Christ Church beat Molesey in a heat. Parkhouse: J.F. West Album

being at Fawley Court Boathouse a length and a quarter to the bad. The time of the leaders to this point was 3min. 34sec. Afterwards Christ Church, rowing the slow stroke of 32, maintained their advantage, winning easily by a length and three quarters in 7min. 29sec.

The following day the First Eight were drawn against Jesus, Cambridge.

This heat produced a magnificent race. Jesus started at 20 and 39 strokes in the half and full minute, the House rowing the fast rate of 22 and 43. For some strokes there was nothing in it; then Christ Church began to gain very slowly, having half a length's lead at the quarter-mile post. The same distance separated them at the half mile. The time to Fawley Court Boathouse was 3min. 22sec. Christ Church had gained no more at the three-quarter mile, but below the mile they spurted hard at 37, and gained a quarter of a length more by that point. Both crews spurted hard to the finish at a stroke of 36 to 37, Christ Church winning finely in the good time of 6min.59sec. by three-quarters of a length.

In the Thames, the House won a close race against Clare, Cambridge.

Christ Church led out at a fast stroke, Dowding starting at 21 and 41 to Clare's 18 and 36. The Oxford crew led by half a length at the quarter mile, but Clare pressed the leaders all the way to Fawley, where the Christ Church lead was no more than the forward canvas (time, 3min. 33sec.).

> *Clare were rolling rather badly, and Christ Church got very short before the mile post was passed, with Christ Church a quarter of a length in front. Both crews were tiring badly, but Christ Church lasted rather better than their rivals, who made a fruitless spurt at the lower end of the inclosure. Christ Church finally won a hard race by half a length. Time, 7min. 20sec.*

The Thames Cup, 1908. Christ Church beat Clare, Cambridge, in a heat. Parkhouse: J.F. West Album

On the third day, Christ Church met New College in the Grand.

> *Conditions were all in favour of fast time when this race was rowed, owing to a strongish breeze blowing up the course from the Berkshire bank. New seemed to be the quicker for the first few strokes, rowing 19 and 37 in the half and full minute to the 22 and 42 rowed by Christ Church. Along Temple Island the last named increased their pace, and, gradually forging ahead, led by three-quarters of a length at the quarter mile. Still going away, Christ Church were about a length in front at the half mile, passing Fawley Court Boathouse in 3min. 22sec., and still rowing 40 strokes a minute. At three-quarters of a mile Christ Church were one and a half lengths ahead, which was increased to two and a quarter lengths at the mile. The leaders had a "breather," and then spurted in to the finish doing the fast time of 7min. 1sec., and winning, of course, easily.*

In the tenth heat of the Thames, Kingston Rowing Club were the House's third opponents.

> *The crews rowed level up the Island, Kingston starting at 20 and Christ Church at 19 for the half minute, both rowing at the same rate for the minute. Christ Church had a few feet advantage at the top of the Island, and the length of their canvas at the quarter-mile post. At Remenham Kingston tried a spurt, but did not gain anything, Christ Church having rather over a quarter of a length at the half mile. The time of the leaders to Fawley was 3min. 30sec., both crews rowing 36 a minute. The Oxford college then drew away a little, leading by over half a length at the three-quarter-mile post. Kingston, spurting, regained a few feet after the mile, but could not do more, Christ Church winning a good race by half a length in 7min. 13sec.*

The Thames Cup, 1908. Christ Church beat Kingston in a heat. Parkhouse: J.F. West Album

When the final day of the Regatta started, Christ Church were in 3 Finals, those of the Grand and the Thames, and the Goblets, for besides Barker and Gladstone there was only 1 entry, J. Beresford and K. Vernon of Thames Rowing Club.

The Final of the Grand was the second event of the day. The House's opponents were Eton, who had defeated Pembroke, Cambridge, Caius, Cambridge, and Thames.

Christ Church, rowing the faster stroke of 22 to 42 to Eton's 21 and 40, had the best of the start, leading by a few feet up Temple Island. They added a foot or so before the quarter-mile post. Above this point they went away faster, rowing 37 to Eton's 36 a minute, and leading by half a length at the half-mile post. The time of the leaders to Fawley Court Boathouse was 3min. 26sec. Still gaining, the House led by three-quarters of a length at three-quarters of a mile. Eton tried to spurt, but the crew evidently felt the effects of their previous races, and could not gain anything. Christ Church led by between three-quarters and a length at the mile, Eton pluckily hanging on to what was certainly a faster eight. In the end Christ Church came in a length and a half in front, Eton slacking off just at the finish. Time, 7min. 10sec.

The Final of the Thames was against Wadham, who had beaten BNC. and St. Catherine's, Cambridge, on the way.

This race, which produced a tremendous struggle, was rowed in a dead calm. Christ Church second eight went away at 21 and 40 to Wadham's 18 and 36, and at once took the lead. At the quarter-mile post Christ Church led by a quarter of a length, but were hard pressed by Wadham, and had not improved their advantage at the half mile. Wadham were rowing well, and gained a trifle before passing Fawley, where Christ Church led by their canvas, in 3min. 30sec. A great struggle for the lead ensued, and at the mile mark the crews were dead level. At the lower end of Phyllis Court Wadham led for the first time. Opposite the inclosure Christ Church tried to quicken, but the effort died away, and Wadham, who stayed rather better, went away, and won by about a length. Time, 7min. 15sec., which has only twice been beaten in Thames Cup finals. It was Wadham's first win at Henley since 1849, when they won the Grand Challenge on a foul and the Ladies' Plate.

In the Goblets Barker and Gladstone led by only ¼ of a length at the half mile. But after Fawley

Christ Church began to leave their rivals, and led by two lengths at the mile. Christ Church steered a beautiful course, and, with the Thames pair rowed out and unable to spurt, Barker and Gladstone won easily by nearly four lengths.

Christ Church win the Grand, 1908. (I'he impression may be given, incorrectly, that the boat is being stroked from bow side). Sir William Gladstone

Barker (bow) and A. C. Gladstone in the Goblets, 1908. Sir William Gladstone

H.R. Barker, now Boat Club President, included these comments in his report on 1907-1908:

> *We decided to take both crews to Henley, the second being composed chiefly of first year men, and to enter the 1st Eight for the Grand, and the 2nd for the Thames. Majolier was included in the first eight on the strength of his excellent performance in Eights. Our practice was somewhat broken up by A.C. Gladstone and myself having to make frequent excursions to Putney and Henley to row in the Olympic crew which was at that time in process of formation.*
>
> *We had at one time thought of putting a four on as well at Henley, but as our few excursions did not show any great Merit we decided to abandon the idea and specialize in the eight oared events. The first eight won the Grand, beating Eton in the final, and the second was beaten by Wadham in the final of the Thames after a very fine race. A.C. Gladstone and myself entered for the Goblets, which we won beating J. Beresford and K. Vernon (Thames R.C.) in 8:26.*

The House had indeed had a wonderful year. Only 4 other Oxford colleges before had won the Grand. And more glory for individual members of the Boat Club was still to come, on the occasion of the rowing Olympics.

1908 Eight on the water at ChCh Barge. Parkhouse: J.F. West album

These took place at Henley between 28 and 31 July, 1908. The Olympic Regatta was organized, on behalf of the British Olympic Council, by the A.R.A. who set up a Committee of 10, the majority of whom were Henley Regatta Stewards. Fletcher was a Committee member, and together with F.I. Pitman, he acted as Umpire.

Six countries competed for the Eights, with the U.K. and Italy entering 2 crews each. For the Fours 6 countries entered, and for the Pairs 4 countries, while 11 scullers from 7 countries entered for the Sculls. United Kingdom entries won all the events. In the Final of the Eights Leander, with A.C. Gladstone at bow, defeated Royal Club Nautique de Gand, representing Belgium, by 2 lengths. (The club had been granted the "Royal" prefix in recognition of its wins in 1906 and 1907.) H.R. Barker rowed 2 in the Leander Four which lost the Final against a Magdalen crew, these 2 crews constituting the United Kingdom entry for the event. Barker went on to become a noted Oxford coach, being involved with preparations for the Boat Races of 1911, 1913, 1921, 1926-8, and 1932.

Leander's victory over the Belgians served to restore confidence in the paramountcy in Britain of orthodox rowing over the Belgian style. The Christ Church Style had severely irritated the upper echelon of Oxford rowing. Thus A.G. Kirby (a Magdalen man), OUBC President May 1907-May 1909, writing after the House went Head in 1907:

> *It is a great pity that these departures from the orthodox style were made, as Oxford rowing will be ruined if two styles appear.*

Following the 1908 Boat Race, in which A.C. Gladstone stroked Oxford, he returned to the attack:

> *There is no getting away from the fact that Gladstone at stroke never gave his crew a chance. In paddling he had learnt length, but when he rowed he went back to his old style, that damnable Christ Church style which has spoiled Oxford rowing for the moment.*

In fact, though some other colleges attempted, without success, to mimic the Christ Church Style, things soon returned to normal, and D. Mackinnon, the OUBC President following Kirby, noted, following Eights Week 1909, that:

The House retained their old measurements but were making a distinct effort to return to a long stroke . . . all other crews were coached on the orthodox style and it was satisfying to note that the House coaches were endeavouring to teach their crews to swing and row long.

Although it would seem that after 1908 Fletcher's role and influence as a Christ Church coach waned, he nevertheless, until his death, remained keenly interested in, and involved with, the life of the House.

Never in her long and varied history has Christ Church had a more loyal member or one more devoted to her best interests,

wrote a Student of Christ Church in an appreciation of Fletcher in the *Oxford Magazine* (28 February, 1919).

Leander Crew winning the Final of the 1908 Olympic Eight. Leander Club

Winning Leander crews framed in the 1908 Olympic winning-post. A.C. Gladstone on the right, one row from the top. H.R. Barker on the right, front row.
Peter Burnell

That Fletcher's innovations did not represent a revolution in rowing theory is explained by Sir William Gladstone.

> *Fletcher's Christ Church crews would, however, have looked ultra-orthodox to us today, and his alterations to the rig would have been regarded as marginal. There is a good photograph, slightly faded, of Christ Church rowing Head past the barges in 1908, showing the beginning of the stroke. Other photographs show how it was considered vital to start the shoulders back at the very beginning of the stroke, so that slide and body reached the end of the stroke simultaneously . . . and that there was a long lie-back at the finish, with the blades well covered, before the hands came smartly away.*
>
> *I believe the Christ Church Style to have been a new phenomenon in English rowing. Of course, there had been recognized variations in style*

> *since, say, the 1850s, and there were several occasions when a successful coach of one university had been persuaded to migrate to the other and had transferred his success with a recognizable change of approach. But there was no deliberate attempt to change the orthodox canons laid down by Dr. Warre and faithfully adhered to by his disciples and successors.*
>
> *The accusation that the Christ Church style was subverting the principles of English rowing was answered by the contention that Christ Church would have been equally successful with any rig, and A.C. Gladstone went some way towards proving the point by choosing the longest oars and thinnest blades in the University (from Merton) and winning the University Pairs with H.C.Bucknall in 1906.*

1909

The House faced Eights Week with some trepidation. Magdalen, behind them in second place, had a crew including 6 Blues (counting the cox) who had been in the winning Oxford boat in April, plus a former Captain of the Boats at Eton, Millington-Drake, who was to get his Blue 2 years later. (Barker and A.C. Gladstone were also in the 1909 Oxford boat for the second year running, Gladstone having earned 2 Blues before that.) The Christ Church Eight did not do well in practice.

> *As races came on we steadily seemed to get worse and our second (Eight) took half a length off us in a minute. All this came from slowness into the water and failure to hold it out.*
>
> (*Captain's Private Log*)

The remedy decided on was to make the slides run uphill ½ an inch; this with only three days to go before the first race.

On the first night Magdalen got within ⅓ of a length at the OUBC Boathouse, but were held off. But the Magdalen stroke had strained himself, and was unable to continue rowing for the rest of the series. This necessitated the reorganization of the Magdalen crew, the stroke of their second Eight being brought in. Nevertheless, Magdalen came after the House with a vengeance on the second night, and were level with the Christ Church stern at the Boathouse. '*This was the worst night in Eights, and made us very nervous about the remaining nights'.* The Magdalen threat was, however, held in check, and the House stayed Head of the River.

On the advice of Fletcher and C.K. Philips, an Old Blue and former Oxford coach, who had been coaching the Eight, it was determined not to defend the Grand at Henley, but nevertheless to send a crew. Only three men from the Eight would be available to row in 1910, and Barker and A.C. and C.A. Gladstone were invited to row for Leander in the Grand. So it was decided to form a crew from the Second Eight and enter it for the Thames Challenge Cup. At the same time, a Four was made up and entered for the Visitors' and the Wyfolds, and G.E. Hope, winner of the OUBC Sculls, and A.C. Gladstone, entered for the Diamonds. The crews were:

THAMES CHALLENGE CUP

Bow	R. Boumphrey
2	M.H. Raikes
3	O.B. Pratt
4	G.D. Pidgeon
5	A.S.R, Macklin
6	G.R. Codrington
7	N.M. Bruce
Str	N.A. Sprott
Cox	A.G.L. Owen

VISITORS', WYFOLDS

Bow	W.A. Akers
2	G.R. Codrington
3	G.E. Hope
Str	K.T. Dowding

On the first day of the Regatta Gladstone lost his heat of the Diamonds to J. de G. Edye of Auriol R.C. He was leading by ¾ of a length at the ¾ mile post, but was overtaken and lost the race by two lengths. Hope, racing the next day, had a lead of ¾ of a length against G.L.Thompson of Trinity Hall after ¼ mile. Thompson, however, led by the same distance at the ¾ mile mark, and went on to win. Edye and Thompson, in turn, lost later heats, and neither reached the Final.

Also on the first day the House met Trinity, Oxford, in the Thames. It was a close-fought race.

> *Trinity led out at 20 and 38 to Christ Church's 19 and 38, and, gaining slowly, had obtained an advantage of half a length at the quarter-mile post. Christ Church spurted, but could make no impression on the leaders, who*

passed Fawley just clear in 3min. 44sec. Christ Church never ceased to persevere,but, although they went up a little near the mile post, Trinity went away again, and won by a length in 7min. 48sec. The winners rowed in a new boat, which rode very lightly on the water. The rudder was placed underneath the boat, midway between the coxswain's seat and the stern end, and the boat appeared to answer to it well. (Cook)

The House Four had its first outing (on the second day) against London Rowing Club in the Wyfolds, and gained an easy win.

Christ Church rowed 19 and 35 strokes and London 21 and 40 in the first half and minute. The metropolitan crew were outpaced from the start, and were about three-quarters of a length behind at the upper end of Temple Island. The House added another quarter length by the time they had reached the quarter-mile post. The distance separating them was the same at the half mile, Christ Church having lost a little in steering. The leaders' time to Fawley was 3min. 48sec. Above this point Christ Church gained rapidly, leading London by two and a half lengths at the mile. London spurted hard there, but were clearly the losing boat, Christ Church rowing in three and a half lengths ahead in 8min. 6 sec.

(Cook)

Two races followed on the third day of the Regatta. In a further heat of the Wyfolds, the first race of the day, Christ Church took on Univ.

Christ Church got off nicely from the start, rowing 19 and 36 to the 19 and 38 rowed by University. The former went faster from the start, and led by nearly a length at the quarter mile. Above this point the House drew right away, leading by three lengths at the half mile, and reaching Fawley the same distance ahead in 3min. 51sec. They dropped to 32 a minute, University rowing 36, and held their advantage to the finish, winning easily in 8min. 10sec.

(Cook)

The last race of the day was a heat of the Visitors', which event had attracted 7 entries. In an earlier heat First Trinity, Cambridge, had beaten Balliol easily, the latter having steered into the piles before rowing a minute. First Trinity now met the House.

First Trinity started at 21 and 40 and Christ Church at 19 and 37 in the half and full minute respectively. They nearly collided at the end of half a minute, but both steered away, and Christ Church drew out, leading by a length at the quarter-mile post. Christ Church went away fast above, First steering badly, and they led by one and a half lengths at the half mile. The time of the leaders to Fawley was 3min. 47sec., and they were two lengths to the good. First then slowed down, and Christ Church rowed in easy winners in 8min. 11sec.

(Cook)

The House was now in 2 Finals on the last day. They first met Balliol in the Wyfolds.

Balliol rowed the faster stroke at the start – 21 and 41 to Christ Church's 19 and 36. There was less wind when this race was rowed. The crews steered well up the Island, and were level at the quarter-mile post, where the House came out into midstream, and Balliol went dangerously near the booms, but came out again. Christ Church led a trifle at the half mile and Fawley, which was reached in 3min. 44sec. Both crews were in midstream, and a clashing of oars was narrowly avoided. The race was a good one to watch; the crews being dead level at the three-quarter mile signal. Balliol spurted finely, and secured a lead of three-quarters of a length at the mile. Christ Church tried to quicken, but became erratic in their steering, and received Balliol's wash. Finding themselves outpaced, and with another race later in the day, Christ Church eased up opposite the enclosure, leaving Balliol to go on and win easily. Time 7min. 44sec.

(Cook)

The very last race of the Regatta was the Final of the Visitors', against St. John's, Oxford, who had in the heats beaten Trinity Hall and Univ. St. John's had earlier in the afternoon won the Ladies', beating First Trinity, and their Four was drawn from the same crew.

Christ Church went off with the lead, rowing 19 and 37; St. John's College rowed 20 and 39 strokes in the half and first minutes respectively. Just above the Island Christ Church steered towards the piles, and nearly fouled them, but they were leading by half a length which they increased to three quarters at the quarter-mile post. Both crews were steering indifferently, Christ Church always having the best of the race, however, and they were a length and a half in front at the half mile. St. John's were feeling the effects of their race in the eight, but spurted well to Fawley, reached by the leaders in 3min. 47sec. Above Fawley Christ Church settled down, and, rowing nicely and steering straighter, kept a length and a half from St. John's. The latter were steering badly at the mile, but stuck to their work well, being beaten in the end by one and a half lengths in 7min. 53sec.

(Cook)

Christ Church had every reason to be pleased with the visit to Henley; they had not had a win in the Visitors' since 1883. The 3 men who rowed in the Leander crew had not, however, fared very well. Cook noted:

Leander was not a good crew and failed to produce anything like the fine form shown by their eight for the Olympic Regatta of 1908.

With C.A. Gladstone at bow, A.C. at 3, and Barker at 7, they lost their first race to Jesus, Cambridge, by ⅓ of a length. Jesus went on to be beaten in the Final by the Belgians.

George Hope, successor to Barker as Boat Club President, made the following entry in the *Private Log:*

Were determined to go to Henley, but on Philips' and Fletcher's advice did not go for the Grand to defend it. In place we allowed Barker and Gladstone to accept an invitation to row in Leander. As none of the Eight, except bow- 3- stroke would be available next year, we made up a crew from the Second Eight.

These had been very disappointing. They were a very hardworking crew; 3-4-5-6-7 were all over 12 st. and all freshmen, as were 2 and str. In practice they came on well and did good times all over the course, but they had the same stroke and failing as the Torpid. They could not quicken, which prevented much success in races. The first night they got off badly and the cox made matters worse by not being straight and taking a bad course. In spite of this they got within ¼ length of Worcester. The second night Hebert, who coxed the second eight in '08, went cox. This night they got off well and rowed Worcester down, bumping them opposite the Barge. The third night they got within ¼ length of Lincoln at the boathouse, but ran into the bank in avoiding Wadham and Oriel, who had bumped just in front. Lincoln got round, but we broke 2 oars and only just escaped Worcester. Each of the three last nights they did the same thing, coming up steadily up to a foot of Lincoln but being unable to spurt and catch them. Whereas they should have bumped most of the boats in front, they only made one bump, as they rowed a course and not a race each night.

From this material we made up an Eight for Henley. Only bow and 3 of the first eight rowed and a very powerful looking crew was produced. As before they came on well for a time. The same man was stroke and set beautiful rhythm and soon made a fair crew. They rowed the same way and rate as at Oxford, but there was not sting about their rowing or drive from the stretcher. Mr. C.K. Philips very kindly took them, but even he could make nothing of them. Perhaps this was due to lack of experience, but they had now rowed in many races. A week before the Races we saw that some experienced man was needed, and so Codrington was put six.

Neither Akers nor myself, who were there with the four, could row in the Thames Cup since we rowed in a winning Grand crew. This improved them slightly but nothing could have made them more than very moderate. In their last course they rowed 32 the whole way except the first minute.

They entered for the Thames Cup, but drew Trinity, Oxford, who beat them by I length very easily in 7:48. Besides the eight, a four was made up. At first I hoped to have made it a training and teaching crew by putting a fresher at 2. Unfortunately we failed, and so made up a four to try to bring home some cup. It was finally made up. Akers bow, Codrington 2, Hope 3, K.J. Dowding stroke and steers. Owing to various causes we got very little practice. At Oxford we made one journey in a light four but no more owing to schools. When we got to Henley we were able only to go out 4 days out of the first week, as two of us had schools. The next week, to add to our troubles, Codrington had to row in the eight as well as the four, so we could only at best do one journey a day. Finally on Frid. 2nd July he got water in his wrist joint. Most pluckily he continued to row, but the four again suffered and only went out once in two days.

After all this it is not surprising that we rolled terribly, looked awful, and could not steer. We used to bounce and ricochet up the piles, and our steering added 300 yards on to our course. We also never had rowed: only 2 Fawles [Fawleys] and a 2 min. had we done.

We entered for both Visitors' and Wyfolds and were very lucky indeed in the Draw. We had fewer races than anyone and drew a bye on every possible occasion.

On 6th July, 1909, we beat London Rowing Club easily in the Wyfolds. On 7th July we beat University College, Oxford, easily in the Wyfolds, and First and Third Trinity, Cambridge, easily in the Visitors'.

Christ Church crews, 1909, with trophies won in 1907–09, as follows (from left to right): OUBC Sculls, Torpids Head of the River, Grand Challenge Cup, Eights Week Head of the River, OUBC Pairs, and Nickalls Challenge Cup. The Gladstone brothers (CA., left, and A. C., right) are seated either side of G. E. Hope (with moustache). HR. Barker is to the right of A. C. Gladstone. A.G.B Cherty-Garrard sits to the left of CA. Gladstone. Parkhouse: J.F. West album

We were thus in both Finals. On 9th July we first rowed Balliol College, Oxford, in the Wyfolds. Up to the Mile we were dead level. But then Balliol put in a spurt and got a lead of 1 ½ lengths, which we never reduced. They ultimately won by 3 lengths in 7: 18 which equals the Record.

In the Final of the Visitors' we had to row against St John's, Oxford. Up to the half mile we were level. There we spurted and got I length's lead which we added a few feet to, winning by a length and a half in 7:53.

Barker and Gladstone rowed bow and 7 for Leander [Hope is in error here. As noted, both Gladstone brothers were in the Leander crew with Barker]. *This crew had to be changed several times and ultimately was not very good. In the Grand they drew a bye in the first round and then met Jesus, Camb. There was a very strong bushes wind and they had the Berks. station. Nevertheless they were only beaten by l/3 length after a desperate race. On the same day Magdalen, who had also had the Berks. station, were beaten by the Belgians by a half length after a desperate race. In the final Jesus were beaten by the Belgians by 1 length.*

THE CHRIST CHURCH STYLE

by SIR WILLIAM GLADSTONE
former President, Christ Church Boat Club

The admirable 'Short History of the Christ Church Boat Club' by Richard Frost does not mention the Club's greatest triumph, the winning of the Grand Challenge Cup at Henley in 1908. True, this was an Olympic year, so competition was not as strong as ordinarily, but nevertheless this victory was the club's greatest in the short period of vintage years around it, and one which has never been repeated.

As the 'Short History' shows, Christ Church regained the headship of the River after a space of 58 years in 1907, and the Secretary wrote at length about their style of rowing: it was "most unfavorably criticized, on the ground that it was subverting the principles of English rowing by doing away with the swing".

The history of "style" in English amateur rowing starts in 1836. It works through Egan, Shadwell, Menzies and Warre on fixed seats; through Warre to de Havilland, Mclean and W.A.L. Fletcher ("the Flea") who developed the Christ Church style and started the first furore in the history of English rowing.

Egan as the founder of the English style of rowing deserves his place in the pantheon, but the great names are those of Warre and de Havilland. Warre coached the Eton eight from 1860 to 1884, won the Ladies' Plate eight times and reached the final of the Grand five times. Competition was not what it is today, but the school had to beat all the Oxford and Cambridge colleges to win the Ladies', and competed with the great tideway clubs (London and Thames) as well as Oxford, Cambridge and Leander in the Grand. De Havilland's Eton eights between 1893 and 1912 won the Ladies' twelve times and reached the final of the Grand once. My emphasis on Eton is deliberate: the school provided 3I2 of the 848 Oxford and Cambridge blues between 1863 and 1920.

Warre, de Havilland and their disciples evolved the methods from which modern racing oarsmanship has been developed. As with the English language itself, their language of oarsmanship was disseminated round the globe and evolved with a wealth of variations, each of which assumed itself to be in the orthodox tradition. Until about 1905 there is no history of any club deliberately developing an orthodox style. The amateur rowing fraternity was small and close knit, though extending to continental Europe and across the Atlantic, and each prophet, priest and king merely added his own contribution to the orthodox tradition of received wisdom.

Around 1905 occurred a sea-change. The number of clubs, both in Britain, Europe and America, had grown. Orthodoxy was developing areas of rigidity, where tradition and theory and interpretation of the Word of Warre overrode practice. The Belgians, wearing black beards and purple sock-suspenders and smoking cigars, won the Grand in 1906 and 1907. Something had to be done.

What was done is well known. It was no longer good enough to make up the Leander crew, which would probably win the Grand, from the winning Boat race crew (with perhaps 5 or 6 places), the remaining two or three going to the best oarsmen in the losing crew or an older hand. In 1908 the cream of several previous years were gathered together and actually trained throughout the summer. In order to make this possible for the genuine amateurs of those days, each oarsman was allowed a substitute of similar size and skill, who could take his place when necessary in practice. (A.C. Gladstone, the only Christ Church representative, had his brother C.A. Gladstone as his substitute.) Previously, and indeed until the 1950s, it had never been "done" for a Leander crew to be brought together for more than three weeks before Henley: any abandonment of this amateur spirit would have amounted to "pot-hunting". The 1908 Olympics were taken so seriously that the Leander crew did not compete for the Grand. The way was left clear for the best tideway, college and school crews; and Christ Church, Head of the River at Oxford, won – using the Christ Church Style.

The Style was introduced by W.A.L. Fletcher, a great coach of University crews in his own right. Evolving the ideas of Warre and de Havilland, he appreciated that with the longest existing (16") sliding seat, the "quick catch" so vital to the English style might best be achieved by a broader blade and a shorter oar, with a relatively longer inboard length, than by an excessively long body swing with a long oar and thin blade which had seemed the best combination for many years in spite of its tendency to "pinch" the boat and reduce the strength which could be applied at the beginning.

Warre and his contemporaries had developed the principle of long body swing on fixed seats, and the slide had been introduced (1873, 8") and gradually lengthened to 16" to increase the length of the stroke. The importance of swing had continued to be proved by success, and there is an impressive photograph of Leander winning the Grand in 1905, dropping their blades in at the extreme forward position. The caption to this photograph in Haig Thomas and Nicholson's 'The English Style of Rowing' (1958) says "one of the leading metropolitan coaches of today, when shown this photograph, remarked "What an extraordinary position to get into!" That crew beat the best American crew and the Belgians; but in 1906 and 1907 (and, indeed, in 1909) the Belgians won.

The Belgian blades were 7³⁄₁₆" wide, Leander's probably 5¾"or 6". The Belgian oars were shorter, both inboard and outboard. The Belgian swing was slightly shorter than that of the best English crews, but not much.

W.A.L. Fletcher had coached both Oxford and Cambridge winning crews around the turn of the century on entirely orthodox lines, using the traditional longer oars and thinner blades and the combination of swing and slide. He must surely have been influenced by the Belgians when he introduced wider blades and shorter oars to Christ Church in 1905 or 1906. His blades were not more than 6¾" (Head of the River 1908, reduced to 6½" for the longer Henley course in the Grand that year), but his oars were even shorter than those of the Beigians. This inevitably reduced the length of his crews' swing, and also gave the impression of a shorter stroke because of the reduced angle of the oars at the beginning.

Fletcher's Christ Church crews would, however, have looked ultra-orthodox to us today, and his alterations to the rig would have been regarded as marginal. There is a good photograph, slightly faded, of Christ Church rowing Head past the barges in 1908, showing the beginning of the stroke. Other photographs show how it was considered vital to start the shoulders back at the very beginning of the stroke, so that slide and body reached the end of the stroke simultaneously (not that the principle had been abandoned forty years later, and for all the author knows may still be preached today), and that there was a long lie-back at the finish, with the blades well covered, before the hands came smartly away.

I believe the Christ Church Style to have been a new phenomenon in English rowing. Of course, there had been recognized variations in style since, say, the 1850s, and there were several occasions when a successful coach of one university had been persuaded to migrate to the other and had transferred his success with a recognizable change of approach. But there was no deliberate attempt to change the orthodox canons laid down by Dr. Warre and faithfully adhered to by his disciples and successors. The notes by both de Havilland and Bourne in no way sought to contradict what Warre had written.

The accusation that the Christ Church style was subverting the principles of English rowing was answered by the contention that Christ Church would have been equally successful with any rig, and A.C. Gladstone went some way towards proving the point by choosing the longest oars and thinnest blades in the University (from Merton) and winning the University Pairs with H.C. Bucknall in 1906. In 1908 A.C. & C.A. Gladstone won the Pairs with 6" blades and A.C.G. with H.R. Barker (7 in the Christ Church Eight) won the Goblets with 6⅜" blades. The Fours, however, eluded Christ Church, who were beaten at least twice in the final by their arch-rivals Magdalen. It was from this era that the cry "God damn bloody Magdalen" or "GDBM", still in use at Christ Church in the 1940s, originated.

The House went Head of the River in Eights Week 1907 and remained Head in 1908 and 1909. It went Head in Torpids in 1908, and, as mentioned, won the Grand that year. I have no record of other successes, so it may indeed be that the vintage years were as much due to talented oarsmen and a brilliant coach as to any variations in style. As far as the rig was concerned, the shortness of the oars was evidently more important than the width and shape of the blades, but unfortunately the author of these notes has no complete oars in his possession, the blades having been cut off and preserved during the Second World War when it became difficult to keep the oars as a whole. We do know from the Secretary's account, quoted in the 'Short History', that the oars in 1907 were 11'10" overall, a major reduction from the standard Cambridge (and probably Oxford) I2'4", and a reduction even on the Belgian 12'½". The House had 3'7" inboard, as against the standard 3'8½" and the Belgian 3'6½". The inboard proportion is very close: House 30.496%, Standard 30.067%, Belgian 29.41%. The "Leverage" or thwartship distance was House 31", Standard 31", Belgian 32". So it seems that the salient factor which caused the furore was in fact the overall length of the oars, although a fuss was also made about the width of the blades. The Secretary in his account makes it clear that success with the shorter oars depended on "great lightness of the hands over the stretcher", an essential in any orthodox rowing but the more essential with a shorter stroke.

In 1919 Steve Fairbairn, an orthodox oarsman and hitherto an orthodox coach, started something far more radical, influential and permanent with the Jesus style. This was a return to first principles designed for unskilled oarsmen after the First World War, not a mere modification of orthodoxy, and thereafter British oarsmen have had to opt either for orthodoxy or for one new heresy or another. There was, however, no mere modification of orthodoxy of the same kind as the Christ Church style until the Lady Margaret style was developed after the Second World War. In many ways this was extraordinarily similar to the Christ Church style, insofar as it was practised by talented oarsmen, very well coached, for quite a short period, and disappeared from noteworthiness when those oarsmen had gone down; and insofar as it had one particular characteristic which anyone who saw it could latch on to (like the shorter stroke of Christ Church), this was the long finish and slow recovery of Lady Margaret. Since those days of the late 1940s, new styles and new equipment from all over the world have come apace, but it is probably still true even today that, the higher the standard of crews using different styles and different equipment, the more alike they look.

1910–1919

1910

THE HOUSE DID NOT HAVE A BIG PRESENCE AT HENLEY THIS YEAR. In Summer Eights they had lost the Headship to Magdalen, ending in 3rd place. It was decided to enter a Four in the Visitors'. C.A. Gladstone was invited to row bow in the Leander Eight entered for the Grand. A.C. Gladstone rowed bow in the Leander Four which lost its heat of the Stewards'. The Christ Church crew was:

Copyright.] THIRD DAY.
HENLEY
ROYAL REGATTA
(In accordance with the rules of the A.R.A.)
THE OFFICIAL
PROGRAMME
FOR
WEDNESDAY,
JULY 6th, 1910.
PRICE
6d.

Henley Royal Regatta programme cover, 1910.
Park:house: J.F. West Album

Bow	N.M. Bruce *(steers)*
2	J.F. West
3	O.B. Pratt
Str	W.A. Akers

The Four met Trinity Hall on the third day of the Regatta in a heat of the Visitors'. Trinity Hall had beaten the Old Westminsters the previous day in a heat of the Wyfolds.

Hall started at 37 a minute and Christ Church at one stroke more in the first minute. Although they were level for some strokes, Hall soon began to forge ahead, and had three-quarters of a length

> *advantage at the quarter mile. The Hall crew were steering straighter than on the previous day, and gained fast, being a half length of clear water ahead just above the half mile. They passed Fawley in 3min. 55sec., well clear of Christ Church, and reached the mile two lengths in front. From there they had the race well in hand, and steering over to the Berks side, won by two lengths in 8min. 18sec.*
>
> (Cook).

Trinity Hall went on to win the Final of the Visitors'.

In the Grand on the same day, Leander had met Magdalen. It was a remarkable race:

> *There was a strong wind off the Bucks bushes at mid-day, worth, at least, two lengths over the whole course, and suggesting an even greater difference at the start itself. Good judges gave 7.30 as a likely time for a fast crew under*

Henley 1910. ChCh lose to Trinity Hall in a heat of the Visitors'. Parkhouse: J.F. West album

the conditions, and the difficulty shown by Magdalen in keeping straight while Mr. Fletcher started them was a clear proof that the strong and gusty wind would be a real drawback. All precedents were thrown overboard, however, as soon as the word 'Go' sounded, for Fleming rushed away at 12, 22, and 42, while Bourne had to be satisfied with 10, 19, and 37. The result was that the College eight walked away as if their opponents were standing still, took a length in a minute, and were half a length clear in a quarter of a mile. With no hesitation Donkin [the Magdalen cox] *steered his men straight in front of Leander, and quite calmly appropriated all the shelter of the Bucks bushes, staying there until he reached Fawley, in 3min. 26sec., still half a length clear. Only after this point did Donkin look round at all to see whether there was any danger, and Fleming kept Magdalen ahead on a long and lively 36. Bourne was evidently determined not to stay in his somewhat invidious position until the very end, and spurted just before the mile. But Donkin only gave way slowly, and when at last he was driven out he went over at just the right place to secure the benefit of the towpath station, having thus succeeded in getting the best of two possible worlds in a way that can very rarely have been seen before at Henley. Leander, when they did get going, spurted very hard, but they only just managed to get past Magdalen's stern canvas, and Magdalen won by three-quarters of a length in 7min. 13sec., a very good time indeed, when it is considered that the weather was bad, and that the winners steered right out of their own course, into their opponents' water and back again.*

(Cook).

Magdalen's second race in the Grand was in the Final, where they met, and defeated, Jesus, Cambridge, by 2 lengths.

The Regatta as a whole was noteworthy for the number of close finishes. In 12 of the 23 races the winning margin was ½ a length or less, including 2 ft. in the Grand, 5 ft. in the Ladies', and 4 ft. and 6 ft. in the Thames.

In May of this year the Stewards amended the rules to prevent any crew or crew members entering both for the Thames and the Ladies' at the same Regatta. This decision followed a recommendation fro the Committee of Management after Fletcher raised the matter; he seconded the motion by which the Stewards endorsed the proposal.

1911

This year saw the House send a Four to Henley to compete in the Visitors' and the Wyfolds, and a Pair for the Goblets, one of whose members entered for the Diamonds. The crews were:

VISITORS'/WYFOLDS		GOBLETS		DIAMONDS
Bow	J.G.G. Leadbetter *(steers)*	*Bow*	N.M. Bruce	N.M. Bruce
2	A.F.B. Broadhurst	*Str*	C.A. Gladstone *(steers)*	
3	O.B. Pratt			
Str	G.L. Prestige			

W.A.L. Fletcher was out of the country during Henley, and his place as Umpire was taken by R.S. Bradshaw of London Rowing Club. One innovation this year was the sale of Regatta flags to the operators of the pleasure boats which lined the course. This potential idea had been proposed by Fletcher, in October 1910, to the Committee of Management as a way of increasing Regatta revenue, based on the favourable experience of Molesey and other Regattas. Cook reported in his comments on 1911 that:

> *The booms were lined with pleasure craft for a long way down the course, and a fair majority of the boats carried one of the flags which were sold for 2s. 6d. for the benefit of the Regatta funds. This scheme (introduced at Molesey Regatta for the first time in 1910) brought a substantial amount in contributions from the occupants of pleasure craft, whose presence on the course makes the expensive booming absolutely necessary.*

The sale of flags proved to be a good source of income for the Regatta in the years immediately following.

The Four did not perform well. In a Wyfolds heat, drawn against Pembroke, Cambridge, they did not steer well, and were beaten *'easily'*. Pembroke went on to win the event. In the Visitors', against First Trinity,

> *Nearing the top of the Island the House nearly took the piles, but managed to start out again. Bow in the Christ Church crew again pulled the boat around, and they crashed into the piles. From this point the race was a procession . . .*
>
> (Cook)

Bruce and Gladstone fared much better in their event, the Goblets. Drawn in a heat against First Trinity, they succeeded in gaining a lead of 1½ lengths at the mile, and held on, despite a fine spurt by their opponents, to win by ½ a length. In the Final they met Beresford and Cloutte of Thames, who had set a time record in dead-heating an earlier heat.

> *Cloutte went away at the fast stroke of 12, 22 and 41, which gave him the lead over Gladstone, who went away at 11, 20 and 38. Curiously enough, the Thames pair did not show that masterly steering which had so far distinguished them, and soon after the second signal Beresford seemed to have pulled Cloutte over so far that if Gladstone had not given way there would have been a foul that must have been in favour of Christ Church. Fortunately, however, nothing of the kind happened to spoil a magnificent race, and Beresford straightened his boat before Fawley (passed in 4min. dead), and never made a mistake again. Cloutte only had half a length advantage here, and a magnificent race ensued to the mile, where the veterans had increased their lead to one and a quarter lengths. From here Gladstone began a succession of spurts with the greatest courage and persistence, but he could not catch the leaders, who passed the post a length and a half to the good in 8min. 15sec., which equals Muttlebury's old record, but is not so good as that set up the previous day by Beresford and Cloutte themselves. It was a fine finish to a better Regatta than had been seen for many years, alike in weather and in the quality of the crews.*
>
> (Cook)

In the Diamonds Bruce beat Charleton of St. Catharine's, Cambridge '*easily*', the race, from the mile post onwards, being '*a procession*'. In the semi-final heat Bruce met E.W. Powell of the Vikings Club.

> *Powell got away at the start, sculling 20 and 35 strokes to Bruce's 17 and 32. The Old Cambridge Blue was very fast off the mark and obtained a lead which afterwards won him the race. Bruce sculled long and well, but although he was the faster sculler of the two some part of the distance after Fawley, he could never make up the ground lost in the first minute. Powell was two lengths in front at the quarter mile, and at 30 to Bruce's 28 kept the same*

distance past Remenham. At Fawley Bruce had knocked about half a length off Powell's lead when the latter passed that point in 4min. 3sec. The Oxford sculler was pushing Powell all he knew up to a mile and was only a length and a quarter down there. It was a splendid race in to the finish, Bruce coming up on Powell, but halfway up the Wall the leader had a fine spurt which carried him in the winner by one and a quarter lengths. Bruce stopped for a stroke opposite the grand stand and Powell slowed down also, nevertheless his time, 8min. 22sec., has only been beaten in Diamond finals by F. S. Kelly.
(Cook)

Powell went on to lose to W.D. Kinnetor, the holder of the Wingfield Sculls.

R.C. Bourne, President of the OUBC, was very flattering of Bruce and Gladstone.

Bruce in the Diamonds and Bruce and Gladstone in the Goblets were deserving of every praise and were a credit to Oxford Rowing.

It may be noted that the Grand, this year, was won by Magdalen, against Jesus, Cambridge. The Belgians had entered for this event, too, but stopped rowing, when ½ a length behind, opposite the Phyllis Court wall, in their heat against Ottawa R.C. Their 7 had severely strained his stomach muscles several days before the race, and they gave out in the race itself.

Incidentally, this was the first year in which the final day of the Regatta was a Saturday.

Of the matters considered by the Committee of Management between the close of the Regatta and the end of the year, 2 are as follows.

Harcourt Gold (the Leander coach) suggested an improvement to cancel out the advantage consistently held by crews rowing on the Bucks side of the course; due to the effects of the "Bushes wind" these crews had, statistically, a 60:40 advantage. Gold proposed starting 250 yards below the existing starting line (approximately where the 1908 Olympics races had started), with the finish line a corresponding 250 yards short of the existing finish line. The matter was considered by a sub-committee, which consulted all clubs which had competed over the previous 5 years. The result was that in 1912 the course was reduced in width by 10 feet, pushing it further towards the centre of the river and away from the Bucks side.

The second matter was the risk that an aeroplane might fly over the course during the Regatta. This was a mere two years after Blériot had flown the English Channel, so it was not as though the skies were yet full of aeroplanes. But during the course of the Regatta that year,

> *...unexpected excitement was provided by the arrival of an aeroplane which swooped down almost to the surface of the water and gave the occupiers of the boats an anxious moment until it passed out of sight.*
>
> (*The Times*)

It was for this reason, presumably, that in December the Committee agreed that an application should be made to the Home Office for the scheduling of the Regatta course as a place where aerial navigation was prohibited.

1912

This year the House decided to enter for the Visitors' and the Wyfolds, while Bruce competed once again in the Diamonds.

It was a big year for the Regatta, for, for the first time, a reigning King, and his Queen, attended on the Saturday. King George V and Queen Mary, who arrived by train, embarked on the royal barge, and were rowed under Henley Bridge to the Royal Enclosure, where they watched 2 races, the first of which, the Final of the Ladies' Plate, was won by Eton for the third year in a row. (In 1911 they had established a new record time for the event of 6min. 56sec.) The royal party was then rowed to the riverside home of the Hon. W.F.D. Smith (later Lord Hambledon) before returning to the course and boarding the launch "Maritana" to follow the Final of the Grand. At the end of the day Queen Mary presented the prizes to the winners from a special dais.

Following the success of this occasion, King George agreed to become Patron of the Regatta. H.T. Steward, Chairman of the Committee of Management, put on record his thanks to W.A.L. Fletcher for his assistance in handling the special arrangements which had been needed. Fletcher had additionally resumed his role as Umpire for this year's Regatta.

The House entered 2 crews (Christ Church I and II) for the Visitors', the second boat also being entered for the Wyfolds. Bruce again entered for the Diamonds. The crew members were:

	VISITORS' (Christ Church I)	VISITORS', WYFOLDS (Christ Church II)	DIAMONDS
Bow	J.G.G. Leadbetter	R.W. Lush *(steers)*	N.M. Bruce
2	A.F.D. Broadhurst	R.S. MacIver	
3	G.E. Hellyer	J.D. Chrichton	
Str	N.M. Bruce *(steers)*	A.C. Boult	

Boult was Adrian Cedric Boult, who went on to achieve great fame as Sir Adrian Boult, the orchestra conductor. He had come to Christ Church from Westminster. He maintained his membership of Leander throughout his lifetime.

On the first day Christ Church II were drawn against Lady Margaret, Cambridge, in a heat of the Wyfolds. Along the Island the House steered badly. They then hit the piles, Chrichton breaking his blade. Nevertheless, the House were leading at Fawley, until Chrichton caught a crab and Lady Margaret won by a great distance.

In the Diamonds, Bruce beat O. Mansell-Moullin by 6 lengths in his first heat, having been 1 length ahead at Fawley.

The next day saw Bruce take on G.E. Fairbairn of Jesus, twice a Cambridge Blue, in the Diamonds. Fairbairn, with P. Verdon, had been one of the 2 Leander Pairs representing Great Britain in the 1908 Olympics. He, too, had won his first heat.

> *Fairbairn put in 30 to Bruce's 29 in the first minute, and took the lead, the last named missing the water at the eighth stroke. At the first signal Fairbairn was half a length to the good. There was a hard tussle for the lead to the half mile, where Fairbairn still led by three-quarters of a length. At Fawley (time, 4min. 14sec.) Bruce came up very nearly level, and at the third signal only a quarter of a length separated them. Fairbairn then went ahead, and led by one and three quarter lengths at the mile signal. It was a hard fight in, but the old Cambridge Blue always held the upper hand, in spite of a very fine spurt by Bruce opposite the crews' inclosure, and he won by two and a half lengths in 8min. 43sec.*
>
> (Cook)

Fairbairn was to lose the Final of the Diamonds to E.W. Powell of Eton Vikings.

The third day saw both House Fours in action in the Visitors'. Christ Church II beat Trinity Hall by 1¼ lengths, and Christ Church I were easy winners against Pembroke, Oxford.

Since there were only 4 entries, the 2 House crew now met each other in the Final of the Visitors' on the last day.

> *Both rowed 18 and 35 strokes in the first half and minute, but No. 3 in the first crew came off his slide at the fourth stroke and the second boat led for a short distance. However, the first boat was much the better combination, and soon took the lead, having a half-length's advantage at the first signal. They were rowing steadier, and went away faster to the half mile, No. 2 steering badly there. No. 1 was one length and three-quarters ahead at Fawley, their time being 4min. dead. Above Fawley No. 1 drew right away, leading by three lengths at the mile, and won quite easily in 8 min. 19sec.*
>
> (Cook)

So another Henley victory had been secured. Meanwhile New College, the only Oxford or Cambridge college entered for the Grand, had met Sydney Rowing Club, New South Wales, in the fourth heat. Despite a strong effort on their part, New College were no match for the Australians, who won by 1 length and went on to beat Leander in the Final. For the purposes of this survey of House involvement at Henley Regatta, it should be noted that New College were coached this year by the House's H.R. Barker. In his commentary on the 1912 Stockholm Olympics Sir Theodore Cook, writing of New College's encounter (as 1 of 2 British Eights entered) with the Swedish first Eight, says –

> *. . . at the Boathouse* [R.C.] *Bourne, rowing a spirited 36, went right past the Swedes in splendid style, and won easily in 6min. 19sec., after as good a bit of rowing as New College had done that season, which did great credit both to themselves and to Mr. Barker, of Christ Church, their coach.*

New College defeated both Norway and Sweden in the Olympic Eights. They then met Leander, who won by 1 length.

1913

In Eights week the House, by bumping Univ., regained 3rd place on the River. This encouraged them to enter an Eight for the Ladies' and a Four for the Visitors'.

This year saw a record number of competitors enter for Henley, and there were 77 entries. (The Thames alone called for 17 heats and a Final). The Regatta, too, had continued over the years to attract more and more visitors; in 1902, for example, the Great Western Railway had run 28 trains to Henley, of which 12 were non-stop, and the visit of the King and Queen in 1912 had boosted public awareness of, and interest in, the event.

And yet signs of change could be observed. A *Times* leader of 2 July noted a

> *still diminished . . . demand for houseboats, and this year only nine are to be seen on the Regatta course, though there are others stationed in the backwater behind the bridge.*

What could explain such an occurrence as this? Why,

> *the ever-growing popularity of the motor-car bringing visitors to the town in the morning and taking them back at night . . .*

Another sign of the times was the threat of a demonstration by suffragettes. On 4 June, 1913, Emily Davison had thrown herself under the King's horse at the Derby. Henley Regatta, another major sporting event, one in which the upper classes and the "Establishment" took a great interest, and, to boot, with an event bearing the highly provocative title of "The Ladies' Challenge Plate", could be a prime target for another in the series of demonstrations being staged.

The Times leader referred to above called attention to this risk:

> *This year, unless the militant suffragists decide otherwise, the Regatta will rely for its success purely on its own peculiar charms. The militant suffragists, in fact, provide the only uncertain element in the situation. During the last few days it has been freely rumoured that a spectacular attempt will be made to interfere with the racing as was done at the Derby. The boathouses, protected by a ring of iron fences, are guarded at all hours and at night*

> *dazzling flares illuminate the various enclosures. . . . The precautions are so elaborate that there seems little chance of interference with the boats before racing starts, and it is with regard to the Regatta itself that particular anxiety exists. During the racing the boats must come within a few feet of the pleasure craft drawn up on the booms, and it is at this point that interruption is feared.*

In the event the Suffragettes' impact was minimal. *The Times* reported on Friday, 4 July, that

> *There is a persistent rumour in Henley that the militant suffragists intend to interfere with the Eton crew in one of their contests for Ladies' Plate, and there was some excitement yesterday afternoon when, just before the race between Eton and St. John's College, Oxford, four women paddled along the river in a punt decorated with the colours of the Women's Social and Political Union. On this occasion, at any rate, however, there was no cause for anxiety, for under the watchful eyes of the Thames Conservancy officials the punt was moored up under the trees and far away from the booms, and the race seemed to have little or no interest for the occupants of the craft.*

And the next day:

> *The rumoured threat on the part of the militant suffragists to interfere with the Eton crew has not materialized, for Eton were defeated yesterday in the semi-final of the Ladies' Plate, and the heat passed undisturbed. Near the starting point the course is not marked off by booms, and just after the race started a punt got on to the course. This, however, was believed to be an accident, and it was quickly removed with the help of the Thames Conservancy officials. The efforts of a number of the militant women to sell copies of their periodical from a gaily decorated punt were by no means facilitated by the persistence with which they were followed throughout the afternoon by another punt, bearing the name "Sufferingents", which apparently acted as a combined bodyguard and amateur police force.*

To return to the rowing at the Regatta, Christ Church, as stated, had entered for the Ladies' and the Visitors'. The crews were:

LADIES’		VISITORS’	
Bow	F.M. Fisher	*Bow*	J.G.G. Leadbetter
2	C.E. Driver	*2*	R.L.H. Nunn
3	G.H.S. Dixon	*3*	G.E. Hellyer
4	R.L.H. Nunn	*Str*	R.W. Lush *(steers)*
5	G.E. Hellyer		
6	O. Horsley		
7	J.G.G. Leadbetter		
Str	R.W. Lush		
Cox	M.A. Charlton		

The Eight met Radley in a heat of the Ladies' Plate in the first race on Thursday, the second day of the Regatta. Both crews got off to a fast start, but the House led by 1 length at the quarter mile. They maintained their lead, and won by 2 lengths.

In the last race of the same day the Four were drawn against Univ.

> *University had beaten Auriol in the Wyfolds earlier in the day after a good race. There was no wind, and they got away well, rowing 21 and 39, and Christ Church, at 19 and 37, were soon left. University had three-quarters of a length advantage at the top of Temple Island, and a length at the quarter. They steered rather badly at the corner, but straightened up again, and passed Fawley a quarter of a length clear of Christ Church in 3min. 56sec. The latter went up a little, and were but a length behind at the three-quarter mile. Tinné put in a spurt and drew away again to one and a quarter lengths at the mile signal and University won fairly comfortably by two lengths in 8min. 9sec.*
>
> (Cook)

Still with a chance in the Ladies', Christ Church met Trinity, Oxford, on the third day. Trinity had earlier beaten Beaumont College. The race between the Oxford colleges was a close one, despite the House being 1 length behind at the quarter mile. At the half mile they had reduced the deficit to ⅓ of a length.

> *Trinity were away the better, rowing 19 and 38 strokes. Christ Church, at the same rate in the half minute and one less in the full, were half a length behind*

> *at the upper end of Temple Island and the same at the quarter mile. Christ Church came up a bit to the half mile, and were but a third of a length behind there. Trinity reach Fawley in 3min. 28sec., and then spurted, and gained up to a bare half length at the three-quarter mile. Below the mile Christ Church, by an effort, came up again to within a quarter of a length. Along the wall Trinity spurted, and won a good race by half a length. Time, 7min.15 sec.*
>
> (Cook)

Trinity went on to lose the Final to First Trinity.

A.C. Gladstone rowed bow in the Leander Eight which won the Grand.

1914

The Regatta this year was an exceptionally busy affair, with (again) 77 entries, including 12 from abroad, and a total of 61 races. 4 foreign crews were entered for the Grand out of a total entry of 8, and all 4 English Eights were knocked out in their first heat on the first day they raced. So, for the first time the semi-finals were composed entirely of foreign crews, 1 from Germany, 1 from Canada and 2 from the U.S. In the Final Harvard beat the Union Boat Club of Boston by 1¼ lengths.

The House decided to go to Henley – this was the 10th year in succession of Christ Church entries – and set their sights on the Ladies'. The crew was as follows:

Bow N.L. Carrington
2 A.S. MacIver
3 R.L.H. Nunn
4 R.S. Partridge
5 E.P. Dale-Harris
6 O. Horsley
7 A. Dilberoglue
Str R.W. Lush
Cox K.W. Hogg

There were 12 entries. Christ Church's first race was against Univ., Head of the River in Summer Eights, on the first day.

The wind was blowing quite strongly against the crews in this race, the second after the luncheon interval. Both got away smartly, University at 20 and 37½, Christ Church 20 and 39. They were level for a minute, then Christ Church showed in front, leading by a quarter of a length at the first signal. Steadily gaining, Christ Church were half a length to the good at the half-mile mark, and they passed Fawley in 3min. 36sec. The wind was fairly strong at this stage, and Christ Church were very effective in their methods and went faster, having three-quarters of a length of clear water at the mile signal. University became ragged, especially on stroke side, and Christ Church rowed in rather easy winners by two and a half lengths. Time, 7min. 38sec.

(Cook)

On the second day they met Christ's Cambridge, who had drawn a bye in the first round of five heats. Christ Church was now the only Oxford college remaining in the Regatta. This race was tougher than that against Univ.

Christ's started at 20 and 38 strokes, Christ Church 19 and 37. The Oxford College led slightly at first, then the Cambridge crew came up, and a good race began for the lead, which was secured, after a hard race, by Christ's, who were a quarter of a length in front at the half mile, but were by no means safe. The time to Fawley was 3min. 38sec. Christ Church soon challenged Christ's again. and came up level in a splendid race at the three-quarter mile. Again they tried hard to get ahead by a fine spurt at the mile. At this point Oxford led by a quarter length, and after a fine finish won by three-quarters of a length. Time, 7min. 32sec.

(Cook)

This victory put the House in the semi-final, against Pembroke, Cambridge, who had defeated Shrewsbury School by 4 lengths in their heat.

Both crews rowed 38 strokes at the start. Pembroke gained fast after clearing the Island, and led by half a length at Fawley in 3min. 28sec. Pembroke rowed in first-class form and won comfortably by a length and a half. Time, 7min. 9sec.

(*The Times*, 4 July, 1914).

Pembroke went on to win the Final against First Trinity.

The close of the Regatta on 4 July marked the end of an era. One month later, to the day, Britain declared war on Germany and the Great War started. On 12 December the Stewards agreed that

> *. . . having regard to existing conditions, no steps be taken to fix a date or make any arrangements for the Regatta in 1915.*

This suspension remained in effect until the war ended.

1919

During the Great War Fetcher, who had won the DSO in South Africa during the Boer War, served as a battalion commander in France. During the night of 28-29 July, 1917, the 2/6th (Rifle) Battalion of "The King's" (Liverpool Regiment) returned from the front line to their base in the village of Armentières in France. They were subject to one of the first German attacks employing mustard gas, against which at that time there was no protection. Fletcher was badly gassed, and upon his recovery was very debilitated. On 23 July, 1918 he regretfully relinquished his command and returned to England. He had been twice mentioned in despatches, and had been made a Chevalier of the Legion of Honour by the French. The Armistice took effect on 11 November.

During the war the Henley Stewards had continued to hold their annual meetings. In December 1918 Fletcher, a member of the Committee of Leander since 1894, proposed a resolution that the club invite officials and members of all boat clubs affiliated to the A.R.A., and the Honorary Secretaries of Regattas, to a meeting to be held in January to consider steps to be taken in 1919 to revive amateur rowing. A further resolution proposed that Henley Royal Regatta not be held that year, but that the Regatta Stewards should organize an interim regatta to take place in July. Both resolutions were carried unanimously. On 23 January 1919, with Fletcher present, the Regatta Committee of Management met to consider an agenda for a forthcoming meeting of the Stewards to discuss organizing an interim Regatta that year, the proviso being made that the Regatta challenge cups would not be presented for competition, and that the event should be named "The Henley Peace Regatta". On 10 February Fletcher's membership of the Committee of Management was again renewed, and he was elected its

Chairman for 1919. Two days later he attended a meeting of the leading lights of rowing, organized by Leander, in line with the December resolution, and gained approval of his motion that no attempt be made – after such a long break – to organize first-class rowing for challenge trophies, but rather that races of a less serious character be arranged, and over a shortened Henley course.

Four days after his election as Chairman of the Committee of Management, Fletcher was dead, being overcome – at the time of the epidemic of Spanish influenza – by bronchio-pneumonia against which his damaged lungs had no defence. He was 6 months short of his 50th birthday.

The Peace Regatta did take place. Its events included the King's Cup for "Allied Eights" and the Leander Cup for "Allied Fours". These were restricted to crews whose members had *'served in the Navy, Army or Air Force of any country which fought for the Allied Cause'*. For example, 2 Australian Army crews, a Canadian Army crew, and an Oxford University Services crew competed for the King's Cup. Other events were open both to service crews and U.K. amateur clubs.

One of these events was "The Fawley Cup" for Senior Eights,

Christ Church crew on the water at Henley. The Fawley Cup, 1919. Christ Church Archives

Open to any crew of Amateur Oarsmen from the United Kingdom who are members of H.M. Navy, Army or Air Force, or who are members of an Amateur Club having its headquarters in the United Kingdom.

(Sir Theodore Cook's *Henley Records* had covered the years 1903 to 1914. The years between the 2 World Wars are covered by *Henley Records 1919 to 1938* (Hamish Hamilton 1939), by C.T. Steward, the son of H.T., from which this passage and others following are taken.)

The names of the crews entered, 12 in all, provide an interesting picture of the unique variety of backgrounds represented at the Peace Regatta. In addition to clubs which were traditional entrants, such as Thames, London, Marlow and Kingston Rowing Clubs, the second crews of Oxford and Cambridge Universities and crews from Christ Church and Eton College, there were represented crews drawn from the Royal Military College, Sandhurst, the Tank Corps, Rhine Army Officers, and Royal Engineers Officers. The House crew was:

		st. lb.
Bow	J.F.C. Richards	10. 13
2	A.T. Fripp	11. 5
3	M.M. Johnson	11. 11
4	R.P.R. Carpenter	11. 5
5	D.H. Amory	11. 12
6	R.S. Partridge	12. 7
7	E. Majoribanks	10. 12
Str	F.M. Fisher	10. 4
Cox	K.W. Hogg	9. 0

In its first heat it won easily against Rhine Army Officers. It then won by 2½ lengths against the Cambridge University No. 2 crew, which had earlier beaten the Royal Military College. In the semi-final the House beat Oxford University No. 2 crew (stroked by A.S. MacIver, also a Christ Church man), which had beaten both London Rowing Club and Eton, by 1½ lengths. In the Final, however, against Thames, the crews having been level up to the Mile Post, Thames spurted in the last few hundred yards and won by a length. *The Times* (7 July, 1919) commented:

The Thames R.C., well stroked by Mr. Beresford, a veteran of 52, won the Fawley Cup for Senior Eights, a success that should help in the revival of the sport among the clubs on the tideway. Christ Church gave Thames a great race and the result was in doubt until the last two minutes, each taking a lead alternately, but never by more than a few feet, and the third and fourth signals each showed the boats to be level. In the final spurt the greater experience of the Thames crew served them well. Christ Church appeared to be flurried, and they lost some of their dash with the result that Thames drew away and won by a length.

1920–1929

1920

THIS YEAR SAW A RETURN TO THE NORMAL SERIES OF ROWING RACES AT OXFORD, and the revival of Henley Royal Regatta in its traditional format. Both programmes had been suspended during the period 1915-1919. It is not known how Christ Church had been able to put together a crew in 1919 strong enough to reach the Final of the Fawley Cup, but 3 members of the crew were able to row the following year, and in Eights Week 1920 the House retained its place at 3rd on the River which it had held in 1913 and 1914. The decision was made to enter for the Ladies' Plate. *The Times* reported that '. . . *entries were the most numerous on record, seven crews for the Grand, 18 for the Ladies' Plate, and 18 for the Thames Cup.*' In all 400 oarsmen comprised the crews entered for all the events. The qualification rules for the Ladies' were changed to permit crews from the Royal Military College, Sandhurst, and the Royal Military Academy, Woolwich, to enter. The former did so. The House crew was:

		st. lb.
Bow	W.M. Binney	11. 5
2	R.P.R. Carpenter	11. 11
3	M.M. Johnson	12. 1
4	A.T. Fripp	11. 8
5	H.W. Paton	13. 10
6	R.S. Partridge	12. 12
7	E. Majoribanks	11. 1
Str	R.L.H. Nunn	11. 1
Cox	M.A. Lush	8. 3

Of these men, Carpenter, Partridge and Majoribanks had been in the 1919 crew.

The House met Bedford Modern School in a heat on the first day, led all the way, and won easily. On the second day they defeated Third Trinity, Cambridge, being clear at Remenham, having a 1½ length lead at Fawley, and winning by that distance. *The Times* commented that '*Christ Church . . . have improved very much since the Eights at Oxford . . . .*'

On the third day of the Regatta the House met Christ's, Cambridge, who had beaten Pembroke, Cambridge, the day before. The House gained an early lead, striking 39 to Christ's 37, increased it to ¾ of a length at the half mile, and won by 1¾ lengths.

> *Christ Church* (reported *The Times*), *have come on very rapidly at Henley, and today they again rowed well, slipping away from Christ's along the Island, and then gradually adding to their lead all the way up.*

In the Final on the last day Christ Church faced Merton, who had so far beaten Beaumont College, Lady Margaret, and Eton. The race was close:

> *Merton started at 40 and Christ Church at 37. The crews raced level up to the Island, when Christ Church began to go ahead and led by a quarter length at the second signal. Merton reduced this to a canvas at Fawley reached in 3.51.*
>
> *From here to the mile the post the positions remained practically unchanged but Christ Church, spurting well, drew ahead to win a good race by a length and a half in 7.30.*
>
> (Steward)

This was the House's fourth victory in the Ladies', the last occasion having been in 1889. In all Oxford colleges won 5 events, the Grand (Magdalen), the Ladies' (Christ Church), the Stewards' (Magdalen), the Visitors' (Merton), and the Goblets (Magdalen), a "sweep" approaching, though not matching, the success of Cambridge Colleges in winning all 8 events (5 of them by Trinity Hall) in 1887.

MacIver, partnered at bow by H.W.B. Cairns of Balliol, entered for the Goblets. They won their first heat, against Vikings R.C., easily, but lost their second race, a semi-final, to S.I. Fairbairn and B. Logan of Thames, who similarly won easily. This was the first time the House shared its name with another college to enter a composite crew. G.O. Nickalls (the son of Guy

Christ Church group photograph, 1920. The House won the Ladies' this year. Christ Church Archives

Nickalls) and R.S.C. Lucas won the Final for Magdalen, as noted. (G.O. Nickalls won 10 Henley events between 1920 and 1928).

The Diamonds were won – for the first of 4 times – by Jack Beresford, Jr., whose father, now 53 years old, stroked Thames R.C. in the Grand as he had in the Fawley Cup the previous year. Thames R.C. also won the Thames and the Wyfolds in 1920.

This year was notable for the controversy surrounding the attempted entry of J.B. Kelly of the Vesper Boat Club of the U.S.A. for the Diamonds. The Committee of Management had rejected the entry on 2 grounds:

1. In 1906 (as has been noted) the Committee had passed a resolution stipulating that no further entries from the Vesper Boat Club should be accepted in future, and
2. Kelly, who had been an apprentice bricklayer in his youth, was barred from entering because he was not qualified under Rule 1(e) of the General Rules of the Regatta, which made anyone *'who is or ever has been . . . by trade, or employment for wages a mechanic, artisan or labourer'*, ineligible.

The consequence of this decision was an outcry in the press on both sides of the Atlantic; in the U.S. the Stewards decision was portrayed as an attempt to prevent Kelly from winning the Diamonds. As it happened, Kelly defeated Beresford in the single sculls at the Antwerp Olympics, held in late August; partnering his cousin he also won the double sculls.

1921

This year, despite having 6 members of the 1920 Henley Eight, and the cox, available, the House lost 3 places in Summer Eights, moving from 3rd to 6th. The decision was made, however, to defend the Ladies' Plate at Henley, for which there were 15 entries. The crew was made up as follows:

		st. lb.
Bow	W.M. Binnery	11. 7
2	A.T. Fripp	11. 6
3	J.W.F. Treadwell	11. 4
4	R.P.R. Carpenter	11. 11
5	H.W. Paton	14. 4
6	R.L.H. Nunn	11. 9
7	E. Majoribanks	11. 5
Str	O.C.E. Ivelby	10. 4
Cox	M.A. Lush	8. 2

In the first heat of the event the House met Merton, who had bumped them in Eights Week, but whom they had beaten in the Ladies' Final in 1920. *The Times* reported that the heat

> *. . . furnished one of the only surprises of the day. Merton led over the first mile, but Christ Church made a good spurt along the enclosure and won a great race by a quarter of a length and so reversed the result of the racing in the Summer Eights at Oxford. After the race it transpired that D.T. Raikes, the Oxford President and Merton stroke, strained himself during the race, which may have accounted for Merton's failure to answer their rival's spurt.*
>
> (30 June, 1921).

The following day the House met First Trinity, Cambridge, who quickly doubled a 1 length lead, and won easily. The Final of the event on the last day, when the Prince of Wales was in attendance and presented the prizes, was won by Eton College. The remarkable J. Beresford, Snr. once again stroked Thames R.C. in the Grand, which was won by Magdalen for the second year in a row.

MacIver, partnered at stroke by M.M. Johnson, who had been a member of the House Eight at the Peace Regatta, entered for the Goblets. There were only 3 entries, and the Christ Church pair were drawn to race in the second race, the Final. Here they were beaten by Campbell and Playford of Jesus, Cambridge, who had won the first heat against Nickalls and Lucas.

For the 1921 Regatta the Stewards had amended the rules to

> *forbid substitutions except if the original competitor is prevented from rowing by circumstances which are outside his control, and not attributable to his having rowed in the Regatta.*

Caption: Ladies' Plate crew, 1921. Christ Church Archives

1922

The House rose 1 place in Eights Week and entered for the Ladies' and the Visitors' at Henley. The crews were:

LADIES' PLATE

		st. lb.
Bow	W.M. Binney	11. 6
2	J.W.F. Treadwell	11. 9
3	E.J. Pyke	11. 6
4	W.J. Rickards	11. 12
5	H.W. Paton	14. 7
6	G.E.G. Gadsden	11. 1
7	E. Majoribanks	11. 10
Str	A.V. Campbell	11. 3
Cox	Lord Settrington	8. 3

VISITORS' CHALLENGE CUP

		st.lb.
Bow	W.M. Binney *(steers)*	11. 6
2	J.W.F. Treadwell	11. 9
3	E. Majoribanks	11. 10
Str	A.V. Campbell	11. 3

Campbell was the first Christ Church Blue since 1910.

In the Ladies' the House met Eton in the sixth of 8 heats on the first day. They secured an early slight lead and won by ⅓ of a length. *The Times* noted that

> *. . the defeat of Eton by Christ Church caused some disappointment. Eton had one old choice in the boat, and lacked the stamina and experience of the fine eight which won the event last year. Christ Church led from the start and, although Eton hung on well and spurted strongly after the mile post, they were beaten by a third of a length.*

On the second day, however, the House was up against Magdalen, who did not enter for the Grand. Up to the ½ mile point the lead was exchanged between the 2 crews, but Magdalen led by a length at the mile post and won by 2 lengths. In the Final, they lost to BNC, who had beaten Bedford School, Emmanuel, Cambridge, and Oriel on the way.

1922 was the first year in which John Lowe (later Dean) came up to the House as a Rhodes Scholar from Canada. Judith Curthoys notes, in *The Cardinal's College*, that he rowed for Christ Church. This included stroking the First Torpid in 1924.

In the Visitors' the House succumbed in a heat to Third Trinity, Cambridge, who won easily. Third Trinity beat Lincoln in the Final.

1923

This year the House excelled in Summer Eights, rising 3 places to second on the River. On the strength of this they entered for the Grand, which attracted 8 other entries, including Christiana Roklub, Norway (which had competed the 2 previous years, having in 1921 set a new record of 7min. 7sec. in the Thames Cup and gone on to win the event that year), the Rowing Club of Paris, Leander, Thames (with Beresford, Jr. now replacing his father in the crew), and London R.C., Eton Vikings, BNC and Pembroke, Cambridge.

The Christ Church crew, which included 4 of the previous year's Henley Eight, consisted of:

		st. lb.
Bow	G.S. Thompson,	9. 11
2	C.E. Pitman	11. 0
3	O.C.E. Welby	9. 13
4	W.J. Rickards	12. 1
5	J.W.F. Treadwell	11. 12
6	M.R. Grant	11. 9
7	G.E.G. Gadsden	11. 7
Str	A.V. Campbell *(steers)*	11. 3
Cox	J. Craig, cox	8. 10

In their heat of the Grand they faced Thames, who quickly gained a 1 length lead and ended winning easily. *The Times* reported that

> *Thames led off* [the heats of the Grand on the second day of the Regatta] *by rowing down Christ Church (Oxford) quite easily. The winners were beautifully together in their easy style, and were able to slow down to a paddle after Fawley.*

Thames went on to win the event.

During the years since the 'New Course' was adopted, the advantage arising from the protection afforded to boats on the Bucks station when a "Bushes Wind" was blowing had resulted in 59% of wins being achieved on the Bucks side, this despite the course having been progressively narrowed by pushing it out from the Bucks side.

After the Great War ended, a survey was made to investigate the pros and cons of moving the start to the Berkshire side of Temple Island, which would do away with the Bucks advantage. Burnell tells what happened:

> *The Berkshire channel was then very much a winding back-water, shallow in places, and it was clearly not possible to achieve the full Henley distance. Nevertheless the Stewards decided as an experiment to try out a straight course on the Berkshire side of the river, although this meant starting above the Island and accepting a shorter course.*
>
> *In 1923 this Experimental Course produced 53.2% wins for Bucks and 46.8% for Berks. This was much better than the 59%–41% advantage which Bucks had shown before, but unusually calm weather meant that the Bushes Wind effect had not been in evidence in 1923. Nevertheless, according to Tom Steward, the feeling generally was that there must be advantages in moving the course to the Berkshire side of the river. The decision was made; Lord Hambleden agreed to give up land on the Berkshire bank, Mr W. D. Mackenzie likewise agreed to a trimming of the Temple Island bank; 10,000 cubic yards of material were excavated, 800 feet of new campshedding erected, and the new Straight Course, 80 feet wide and back to the original one mile and 570 yards length, was ready for the 1924 Regatta.*

The result in the change in the course was satisfactory. Not only was there, for the first time, a straight course, with the booms at a width of 80 feet, but, to use a statistic covering all races from 1939-1984, there was no advantage in either station, the percentage for the station with the highest ratio of wins (neither station consistently prevailing) never exceeding 51.

The Duke of Connaught attended Henley this year.

1924

This was, as noted, the first year of the Straight Course at the traditional length. It was also a great year for the House in Summer Eights. The Headship of the River was regained for the first time since 1909, and was to be retained in the greatest period of Eights Week pre-eminence enjoyed by Christ Church in the twentieth century. Following this success, it was only proper that an entry be made for the Grand. 5 members of the 1923 Henley Eight, (including Gadsden, who had won his Blue in the 1924 Boat Race), plus the cox, were in the crew:

		st.lb.
Bow	H.A.G. Howard	9. 8
2	C.E. Pitman	11. 3
3	P.W. Murray-Threipland	12. 8
4	W.J. Rickards	12. 5
5	G.C.S Curtis	12. 3
6	M.R. Grant	11. 10
7	G.E.G. Gadsden	11. 7
Str	A.V. Campbell	11. 3
Cox	J. Craig	8. 7

In the first heat of the event, held on the second day, the House were drawn against Leander. Steward provides a brief description of the race:

> *Leander starting 39 to Christ Church's 37 took the lead but were only a canvas in front at the first signal. Christ Church came up and were slightly in front at the half-mile and held the lead at Fawley in 3.55. The crews were level at the third signal but Christ Church led by half a length at the mile, then Leander came up and ultimately won a good race by one length in 8.5.*

The Times hailed this tussle as '*one of the best races of the day*'. Leander went on to win the event.

Gadsden and Pitman (stroke; steers) represented the House in the Goblets. Steward and *The Times* have conflicting reports regarding their first (Heat 4) opponents. The latter (Friday, 4 July) reported that Christ Church rowed over, their opponents, Delfteche Studenten Roeivereeniging, having withdrawn. The former, (considered by this author to be more reliable), held that the House men's opponents were G.K. Hampshire and W. Phillips of Magdalen, whom they beat easily. Gadsden and Pitman's next opponents, in the Final, were Eley and Macnabb of Third Trinity who, taking an immediate lead, won easily.

Hampshire and Phillips had had an unusual and unexpected win in their first heat (Heat 2 – Burnell mistakenly calls it the Final) against Nickalls and Lucas. As Steward explains:

> *The result of this race was entirely unexpected for Nickalls and Lucas were considered the probable winners of the Goblets. It was not generally known, however, that as well as being famous oarsmen they were no mean amateur carpenters and always carried a set of tools. Whilst waiting at the Start, Stroke, thinking that the boat was unnecessarily heavy, cut away some of the bigger timbers and on the first stroke of the race Bow pushed his stretcher through the skin and she started to leak.*
>
> *However, they soon took the lead and before going far, Hampshire and Phillips hit the booms and Nickalls and Lucas waited for them.*
>
> *On restarting Nickalls and Lucas again took the lead and were a long way ahead at Fawley, reached in 5.30. Here it became obvious that something was wrong for the boat was floating lower and lower in the water. In spite of the handicap they kept well ahead and it became more of a race against the leak than against their opponents. At the Mile Post it was clear that the leak was gaining on them fast and at the bottom of the Enclosure the cut-water disappeared and then the boat sank amidst execrations that were visible but inaudible at the Winning Post.*
>
> *All this time Hampshire and Phillips were entirely unconscious of what had happened to their opponents whom they had not seen since about half way up the Island. When they came up with them they were not a little surprised to find them swimming and so stopped rowing. Ultimately they paddled in to complete the Course in 12.0 and immediately offered to row the race again. The Committee, however, could not allow this, pointing out that as they had passed the Winning Post the race was over and that a boat must abide by its accidents.*

Gadsden also rowed bow in the Leander Four, stroked by A.V. Campbell, in the Stewards'. This crew won its heat, but lost its Final to a Four from Third Trinity.

This year the qualification rule for the Ladies' was amended to permit entry by Trinity College, Dublin. In December the Henley Stewards, in view of the rising number of entries, decided to restrict clubs to 1 crew for any eight – or four-oared event. Rule VI of the General Rules now read:

No Club shall enter more than one crew for any eight-oared, or four-oared, race; nor shall any individual be entered twice for the same race, except as a substitute in both cases. No one who has rowed in a race shall row in another crew for the same race.

1925

This was the second successive year of the House's Headship of the River. The Oxford Blue Boat (which became waterlogged in the race and had to stop) had contained no fewer than 5 Christ Church men, and C.E. Pitman had in May been elected President of the OUBC, the first time that the House had held this honour since W.A.L. Fletcher's presidency in 1892.

It was again only fitting that another attempt be made at winning the Grand, and the following crew was entered:

		st.lb.
Bow	C.E. Pitman	11. 3
2	M.R. Grant	11. 11
3	P.W. Murray-Threipland	12. 6
4	A.V. Campbell	11. 9
5	W. Rathbone	13. 1
6	T.W. Shaw	12. 4
7	G.E.G. Gadsden	11. 9
Str	E.C.T. Edwards	11. 13
Cox	A.W. Parker	8. 8

Of these men, Pitman, Grant, Campbell, Gadsden, and Edwards were Blues, and Rathbone had been Oxford's spare man.

The other entrants were Leander (the holders) Thames, London Rowing Club, and Maidenhead Rowing Club (who had won the Thames Cup the previous year), along with Jesus, Cambridge, (1924 finalists), a Granta crew consisting of Cambridge Blues from 1921 to 1925, and a Dutch crew, Amsterdamsche Studenten Roeivereening.

The House were first drawn against the Dutch entry. It was an exciting race, according to *The Times* report of Friday, 3 July:

> *The Dutch crew caught a "crab" at the fourth stroke, but it had little effect on the result of the race. Christ Church led throughout and reached Fawley in 3min. 23sec., a length up. The Dutch crew made a wonderful spurt, but were beaten by a quarter of a length in 7min. 7sec.*

The other winners in the first round were Thames, Leander, and London Rowing Club. It fell to the House to next meet Thames in the semi-finals. Steward gave his customary matter-of-fact account:

Christ Church (Bucks station) beat Amsterdamsche Studentenverein Roeivereening in a heat of the Grand, 1925. Hodgkin Collection, Christ Church Archive

> *Rowing slightly the slower stroke Christ Church went away and led by half a length at the first signal and three-quarters at Fawley, reached in 3.20. Thames reduced this to a third of a length at the third signal and were level at the mile. Continuing to gain they got home by three-quarters of a length in 6.58.*

The Times, however, brought out the drama of the encounter:

> *The pace of the other heat* [of the Grand rowed on the third day, Friday] *was terrific. True to expectations, Christ Church, starting off at 40, had a lead of three quarters of a length at the First Signal, and all but a length at the Second. Between there and Fawley they showed signs that the pace was too fast, and at Fawley, which they reached in 3min. 19sec. they only led by half a length. They could not, however, hold the pace any longer, and Thames went level at the Mile Post, and, spurting to 36, eventually won by three-quarters of a length. But for the fact that they were all unfit, Christ Church should have won. They were a fine, fast crew, and their rowing was very gallant. Gadsden, in particular, though far from fit, rowed one of the best races that he has ever rowed, but the "Schools" had taken their toll.*

The nature of the indispositions experienced by the House men, if such were responsible for the unfitness, is not known.

In the Final Thames met Leander; Leander won by ¾ of a length.

The House crew returned to Oxford with its honour fully intact. Both the Cambridge crews entered for the Grand had lost their heats; the Oxford flag had been nobly kept aloft by the Christ Church men; no other college had entered for the event, and no Oxford college won any Henley event this year.

Nono Rathbone's 1925 Head of the River medal. Bill Rathbone

1926

The Christ Church dominance of Oxford rowing continued. The Eight was Head of the River for the third year in a row, and there were not 5, but 6 men in the Blue Boat, namely Rathbone, Murray-Threipland, Shaw, E.C.T. Edwards and his younger brother H.R.A., and Pitman. (H.R.A. Edwards did not row in the Christ Church Eight, having been rusticated). Unfortunately, in the Boat Race Cambridge's winning streak, which had started in 1924 and was to run unbroken until 1937, continued.

Given the power of the House Eight, it could have been expected that they would again enter for the Grand, but no doubt due to the difficulty of keeping the crew together after the end of term, it was decided to enter a Four for the Stewards' and the Visitors'. The same crew, as follows was entered for both events:

		st.lb.
Bow	E.C.T. Edwards	120
2	T.W. Shaw	121
3	W. Rathbone	130
Str	P.W. Murray-Threipland	128

It will be noted that all 4 men were Blues.

On the first day of the Regatta, Wednesday, the House met Merton in the Visitors', and got off to an excellent start.

> *... Christ Church with their four Blues rowing for them, steered a beautiful course, while Merton wandered badly over the course. Christ Church soon had the race in hand and eventually won easily. They will have a much harder race to-day, when they will meet the holders, Third Trinity. In their race with Merton, Christ Church reached Fawley in 3min. 51sec. and won easily in 8min. dead.*

Nono Rathbone's 1926 Visitors' Cup medal. Bill Rathbone

(*The Times,* 1 July, 1926).

The following day they were drawn against Third Trinity in the Stewards'. Third Trinity's stroke, Hamilton-Russell, had also stroked the winning Cambridge boat earlier in the year.

> *Third Trinity travelled slightly the faster to Fawley, reached in 3.40, where they were half a length ahead. From there Christ Church began to gain and led by a quarter of a length at the mile and, continuing to gain, won by a length and a half in 7.38.*
>
> (Steward).

On Friday the House had 2 races, a heat of the Visitors' rowed at noon, and an encounter at 6:15 p.m. with Thames in the Stewards'. The Visitors' race, one of 2 semi-finals, was against the same Third Trinity crew beaten the previous day.

> *The semi-final heats of the Visitors' Cup resulted in an Oxford final. This, considering all things, is a very satisfactory result for them, but four Blues in a boat ought to be too good for this race. In the first heat Christ Church repeated their success over Third Trinity. They started off in a most unpromising fashion, after keeping level at 36 against their opponents' 40, by taking the booms at the top of the Island. This lost them more than a length, and they did not really get into their stride again till Fawley, where they were still three-quarters of a length down in 3min. 43sec. By the Mile they had reduced this to a canvas, and rowing with great length and smoothness, went ahead to win by three-quarters of a length in 7min. 44sec. They are a really stylish four, and it was a good achievement to row down Hamilton-Russell in this manner.*
>
> (*The Times,* 3 July, 1926).

In the Stewards' however,

> *. . . Christ Church, in spite of their neatness, could not repeat their success in the Visitors'. Thames led them off the mark, and, though Christ Church pressed them all the way, they rowed as a tired crew and could not quite get on terms. Thames won by a length and a quarter in 7min. 42sec.*

In the Final of the Visitors', the House's opponents were Corpus, Oxford, who had, in their only previous race in the event, defeated BNC by 2 lengths. The encounter was not impressive, in the opinion of *The Times:*

> *The Visitors' Cup provided a poor race by contrast. Both crews rowed a very slow stroke, Christ Church, on Berkshire, 35, to the 36 of Corpus. The latter went a long way ahead and, passing Fawley, in 3min. 53sec., won in a paddle in 8min. 15sec, The losers, like many other crews, steered badly, but the winners steered very well.*

However, since *The Times* got the winner and the loser the wrong way round, the validity of its opinion may be doubted.

This was the first Christ Church win at Henley since 1920, and its first in the Visitors' since 1912.

Rathbone teamed up with J.D.W. Thompson of Univ. to enter for the Goblets; they lost their heat to Leander, but won the OUBC Pairs that year.

Gadsden had again rowed bow for Leander in the Stewards. The crew won its heat, but lost the Final to Thames R.C. But Gadsden had also rowed bow in the Leander crew which beat Lady Margaret, Cambridge, to win the Grand.

At this point an aside is in order, firstly to note H.R.A. ("Jumbo") Edwards' collapse in the 1926 Boat Race, worth referring to in light of his later resounding successes as an oarsman and his amply demonstrated powers of endurance, and, secondly, to explain why, after 1926, he disappeared from the Oxford rowing scene for 4 years.

Richard Burnell puts the matter of the 1926 Boat Race bluntly:

> *Cambridge had the best material in 1926, but Oxford managed to hold them as far as Chiswick Eyot when H.R.A. Edwards, their No. 6, blacked out altogether for several strokes. There had been questions about Oxford's fitness during training, and Edwards was diagnosed as being over weight.*

In his autobiography *(The Way of a Man with a Blade.* Routledge & Kegan Paul, 1963*)* Jumbo Edwards good-naturedly acknowledged his lack of preparedness:

Christ Church Henley Eight, 1926. Christ Church Archives

On going up to Oxford I hoped to follow in my brother Sphinx's footsteps and get a blue, but above all, for pleasurable rowing, to get into the Christ Church Head of the River crew. We won the Fours and I won the Silver Sculls my first term, and it was inevitable that I should be selected for the 1926 'varsity crew. I was the only freshman in the crew. I was young for my years, shy and reserved but nevertheless rather conceited. Having been deservedly squashed once or twice by other members of the crew, and with the feeling that being an Oxford crew we couldn't possibly win, I became most unhappy, and that resulted in my not giving of my best, and holding something back throughout boat race training. With the lack of any additional exercise which I always needed I put on too much weight, and was far from fit at the end of training. This was observed by several critics and in particular by Guy Nickalls who wrote in the press about my 'baby blubber'. I collapsed in the race and only one critic had the humanity to say that it was honourable to row yourself to a standstill. That was Steve Fairbairn.

However, there may have been an alternative, or at least a complementary, explanation. Jumbo adds – and in this he is supported by Hylton Cleaver in his *A History of Rowing* (Herbert Jenkins, 1957), – that

> *Afterwards the X-ray photographs showed that I had a dilated heart.*

Hylton Cleaver's comment is:

> *H.R.A. Edwards collapsed in the race of 1926 suffering from dilation of the right side of his heart, which had apparently come up against his breast-bone, causing a black-out.*

Jumbo Edwards had come up to Christ Church from Westminster as a freshman in 1925. His academic career was interrupted due to his failure to pass Mods. In 1927 his rustication continued. He spent the years 1928 and 1929 as a schoolmaster. Having with the aid of a "crammer" succeeded in passing Mods., he returned to Oxford, the completion of his degree being a necessary path to gaining a commission in the Royal Air Force. He rejoined the Oxford Boat Race crew in 1930. He had represented Westminster in the Ladies' for 3 years (1923-25), and was to go on to enter for Henley events 18 more times between 1927 and 1933, in 11 of these as a member of London Rowing Club crews.

1927

This year E.C.T. Edwards, Rathbone and Shaw all rowed in the Oxford boat, which again was defeated. In May Shaw became President of the OUBC. The House was Head of the River for the fourth straight year.

For Henley the Second Eight was entered for the Ladies', and a Four, containing 3 Blues, for the Stewards' and the Visitors'. Shaw and Edwards entered for the Goblets (Gadsden again rowed bow for Leander in the Grand, and for Eton Vikings in the Goblets). The House crews were:

LADIES'

		st.lb.
Bow	D.G. Bird	11. 6
2	A.L. Binney	11. 2
3	T. Newman	11. 3
4	R.G. Pettiward	12. 7
5	The Marquis of Graham	14. 11
6	W.M. Acton-Adams	10. 6
7	A.J.D. Winnifrith	10. 13
Str	J.M.O Barstow	11. 1
Cox	A.W. Parker	9. 4

STEWARDS' AND VISITORS'

		st. lb.
Bow	J.L. Merrill	11. 10
2	P.W. Murray-Threipland	12. 2
3	T.W. Shaw	12. 3
Str	E.C.T. Edwards, *(steers)*	12. 6

GOBLETS

Bow T.W. Shaw
Str E.C.T. Edwards

No fewer than 21 crews entered for the Ladies' and the House's heat was Heat 12 of the event. Here the crew met Christ's, Cambridge, who eliminated them. *The Times* commented:

> *The Oxford head of the river college was only represented by their second eight, and, although they led at the start, the Cambridge crew soon drew level, and won by many lengths.*

In the Visitors' Christ Church met Lady Margaret in the first heat on the first day of the Regatta.

> *The holders, Christ Church, with three of last year's winning crew again rowing, removed one of their strongest opponents in the Visitors' Cup when they beat Lady Margaret, Cambridge. Christ Church rowed a slower stroke throughout, but steered a much better course than the Cambridge crew, and they were nearly clear at Fawley. They won eventually by one length, Edwards stroking and steering the crew finely in a heavy rain-storm. First Trinity beat Pembroke, and so qualified to meet Christ Church in the semi-heat.*
>
> (*The Times*, Thursday, 30 June).

According to *The Times'* comment on that semi-final encounter, rowed on the third day, Friday,

> *. . . in a great race, Christ Church the holders, jumped into a lead of half a length, and kept it till Fawley, where First Trinity spurted and got up level at the Mile Post. In a terrific race from there to the finish Christ Church drew away once more, thanks to their better steering, and two lengths from the finish had half a length's lead when they hit the booms. Christ Church rowed the slower stroke throughout. The First Trinity crew rowed with great courage and deserved their victory.*

Christ's, Cambridge, beat First Trinity in the Final.

Meanwhile, on the previous day the Four, in a field of 4 was eliminated from the Stewards' by Leander. *The Times'* comment was:

> *Leander went away steadily at a faster stroke and soon obtained a comfortable lead. They were able to take things easy over the last half of the course and won by one and a quarter lengths.*

E. C. T. Edwards strokes Christ Church from bow side, Henley, 1927. David Edwards

Leander had also been the House's opponent in the Goblets. They were 2½ lengths ahead at Fawley, and held off a spurt by Shaw and Edwards along the Enclosure to win by ½ a length. Also competing in the Goblets, as mentioned, was Gadsden, who, partnered by A.G. Wansbrough, entered for Eton Vikings. They, too, were beaten in their heat by the same Leander pair. Gadsden and Wansbrough (a 1925 Cambridge Blue) also rowed at bow and 2 in the Leander crew – which lost its heat – in the Grand. H.R.A. Edwards rowed in the London R.C. crew which was defeated in the Final of the Grand, and – without success – in the club's Four in the Stewards'.

1927 was the last year of William Rathbone's appearances for Oxford and Christ Church. "Nono", as he was nicknamed, for he was the ninth William Rathbone, was a 2-time Blue, had won the University Fours, the University Pairs, and the Visitors' at Henley, and had been a member of the Head of the River crew 3 years running. He went on to give good service as coach to his old college, and in 1936 came to the rescue of Oxford as they prepared for the Boat Race. The circumstances of this occurrence are explained by George Drinkwater in his *The Boat Race* (Blackie & Son, Limited 1939).

> *For the 1936 race, preparations at Oxford never went happily at all. R. Hope was elected president in May 1935 but resigned in the Autumn term, B. S. Sciortino taking his place. The coaches arranged originally were K.M. Payne, Haig-Thomas, Brigadier Gibbon and Jerram Escombe. The last named was, however, far from well and withdrew early in practice. It had originally been intended to put Winser at stroke, but he was so decisively beaten by Hope in the trial eights that the latter was installed with good results. As training progressed his rhythm fell off. J.T.W. Davis was tried, and then Winser, when the crew were training at Henley under Haig-Thomas. This led to disagreement between Haig-Thomas and Brigadier Gibbon, and finally W. Rathbone, the old Christ Church Blue, was brought in to coach. Under him a rather distracted crew found peace and improved very fast, and were able to put up a very good race for half the course, for they proved themselves better watermen than Cambridge in rough water.*

However, after Hammersmith Bridge, water and wind conditions improved, and Cambridge won by 5 lengths.

The next year, 1937, Rathbone was 1 of 3 Oxford Boat Race coaches, taking charge of the final week of preparations. After a false start Oxford, rowing a slower stroke, held on to Cambridge, and the boats shot Hammersmith Bridge dead level. Two slight fouls ensued, with Oxford giving way, but they were clear at Barnes Bridge, and won by 3 lengths. The 13-year run of Cambridge successes was at an end.

"Nono" Rathbone became a Steward of Henley Royal Regatta in 1959. His son was, in turn, to be a member of a House Head of the River crew.

The House had made 4 appearances at Henley during the years in which the Headship of the River at Oxford was held. The level of success – one win in the Visitors' – was not impressive, but needs to be balanced against the overwhelming Cambridge dominance of the period, not just in the Boat Race, but at Henley, too. For example, in the 4 years 1924-27, Cambridge colleges won the Ladies' and the Thames twice each. Only R. Lee, of Worcester, winner of the Diamonds in 1927, and the Christ Church 1926 Vistitors' crew, won any events for Oxford at the Regatta during this time.

1928-1929

The next few years were lean, indeed, for the House in terms of success in Eights Week. In 1928 they went 4th, in 1929 6th, in 1930 back to 4th, and in 1931 to 5th. Small wonder, then, there were no entries at Henley in the last 2 years of the 1920s. However, H.R.A. Edwards entered for 3 events in 1928, and for the same number the following year.

In 1928 he rowed 3 in the London R.C. Grand crew, which beat Union Boat Club of Boston, U.S.A., before being beaten by a Thames crew which went on to win the event. On the strength of this success, the Thames Eight was selected to represent Great Britain in the 1928 Amsterdam Olympics, where the crew won silver medals, losing by ½ a length to the United States.

In 1928 Edwards also rowed 3 (steers) in the Wyfolds for Courtenay Lodge, without success, and competed in the Diamonds as an Old Westminster B.C. entry, winning his first heat but being beaten in his second by R.T. Lee, that year's losing finalist.

In 1929 Edwards was 5 in the London crew in the Grand, beating Argonaut R.C. of Canada in a re-row, following an exciting dead heat in the initial race; in the Final Leander beat London. Because of the 2 races against Argonaut, which took place at 12:20 p.m. and 6:00 p.m., Edwards scratched from the Diamonds; his heat was scheduled for the same afternoon. He again rowed (at 3), however, in the Stewards', this time for London. There were only 3 entries, and London drew a place in the Final, where they lost to First Trinity, who had beaten Third Trinity in the heat.

The row over the entry of J.B. Kelly in the Diamonds, and the introduction of the New Course, apart, the 1920s were not marked by any serious modifications to the Regatta rules or the way it was conducted. In 1924 clubs were restricted, as has been noted, to entering 1 crew only in any eight- or four-oared event. (Burnell quotes the 1924 decision (p.25), but then adds, (p.26), that in 1928 clubs were barred from making double entries in the Ladies' and the Thames; the reason why the restriction needed to be re-emphasized in 1928 is not clear). In 1928 a limit was set on the number of entries per event, 32 for the Thames' and 16 for all other events. This necessitated the introduction of Eliminating Races. The limitation on numbers for events was, however, withdrawn, for all events except the Diamonds, in 1933. The number of entries for all events had risen from 75 in 1920 to 91 in 1927.

1930–1939

THE 1930S WERE, AS WILL BE SEEN, NOT GREAT YEARS FOR HOUSE CREWS IN SUMMER EIGHTS. Nevertheless, the tradition of entering crews for Henley was maintained, and the early years of the decade brought great glory to the Christ Church due to the successes of House oarsmen.

1930 and 1931

No House crew was entered for Henley in 1930, when the Eight was in fourth place on the River, but H.R.A. Edwards, who had returned to Christ Church and won his second Blue in the 1930 Boat Race, entered for the Diamonds under the name of Christ Church. Although he did not survive his heat – being beaten by the eventual winner – he shared in 2 important wins in other events. Firstly he rowed 5 in the London R.C. "A" crew in the Grand, where Leander were beaten in the Final. Secondly, he again rowed 3 (and steers also) in London's "A" Four in the Stewards'. Having beaten Jesus, Cambridge, and Third Trinity in heats, London beat Leander by 1½ lengths in the Final. On the strength of the win in the Grand, the London crew was selected to represent Great Britain in Eights at the first-ever British Empire Games, held in Hamilton, Ontario. A ½ length win over New Zealand brought Edwards his third win of the year.

In 1931 the House lost 1 place in Summer Eights, but a crew was nevertheless entered for the Goblets, H.R.A. Edwards teaming up with Lewis Clive. Clive had been Captain of the Boats at Eton, had rowed for Oxford, at 6 to Edwards' 5, in the 1930 Boat Race, had rowed again in the 1931 crew, and had rowed in the House Eight both these years, including at stroke in 1931. Edwards and Clive were both big men, well-matched at just over 13 stone each. Edwards rowed bow and steers, and Clive stroke. Clive also entered for the Diamonds in 1931.

Edwards, as had been the case for the 2 previous years, was also picked for the London crews for the Grand and the Stewards'.

The London "A" crew, with Edwards at 5 for the third successive year, beat, first Harvard and then Berliner Ruder Club, in heats of the Grand, to face Thames in the Final. London's ½ length lead at Fawley was gradually whittled away by Thames, but London won by ⅓ of a length.

In the Stewards, with Edwards again 3 and steers of the London "A" crew, there were only 3 entries. BNC were beaten easily in the heat, and in the Final London achieved a 3 length win over Societa Canottieri Vittorino Da Feltre Di Piacenza.

In the Goblets, Edwards and Clive first beat the Offer brothers, T. and J.S., of Kingston R.C. *The Times* reported:

> *In the Goblets Edwards put the finishing touches to a splendid day's rowing. In the first minute he and Clive collided with the Offers in neutral water. They were a little quicker away after the clash, and led at the first signal by half a length. Then the brothers took a similar lead at the signal. Clive spurted nearly level at Fawley. At the next signal the position was practically unchanged, and then the Offers took the booms. Edwards and Clive gained about two lengths by this, and though they spurted the Offers could not make much impression on them. The verdict was 2½ lengths. Had the Offers not taken the booms there would have been a wonderful race, but I think the extra strength of Clive and Edwards would just have won, though the Offers showed by far the better combination.*

Edwards and Clive then met Sambell and Luxton, 2 Australian Blues of Pembroke, Cambridge, in the Final, where they achieved a win by 4 lengths.

In the Diamonds Clive first beat West of London R.C., but then lost to Bradley (also of Pembroke, Cambridge,) who in turn lost the Final.

It will be noted that Edwards had won 3 Henley Finals, first the Grand, next the Stewards', and lastly, the finishing touch, of the Goblets. To win 3 events in 1 year was a feat not accomplished since 1903, but Edwards' successes – never since equalled – were all achieved on 1 day, and indeed

Christ Church (Edwards and Clive) win the Final of the Goblets, 1931. David Edwards

(Below) Edwards (left) and Clive with a Goblets trophy, 1931. David Edwards

in the space of 5½ hours, the race for the Grand Final having been at 12:15 p.m., that for the Stewards at 3:30, and that for the Goblets at 5:45. Edwards later joked that he was so tired rowing in the Goblets Final that he let Lewis Clive do all the work while he contented himself with steering the boat!

Edwards had indeed put to rest, with a vengeance, those doubts about his stamina raised following the 1926 Boat Race. That he was the dominant oarsman of the Regatta, *The Times* left its readers in no doubt.

> *For the second year in succession H.R.A. Edwards was the outstanding figure of the regatta. He is a powerful man and his style is now the model for coaches of boat schools and he is a perfect waterman.*

The Duke and Duchess of York (later King George VI and Queen Elizabeth) attended the last day of the Regatta, the Duchess presenting the prizes.

In 1931 E.C.T. Edwards won the annual King's Cup air race around Britain. In 2008 his trophy as winner became the trophy for the Prince of Wales Challenge Cup event for quadruple sculls at Henley, this event, added to the Henley calendar in 2001, having been inaugurated, with its royal patronage, in 2007.

1932

The House's performance in Eights Week was again mediocre, and the Eight dropped another place to finish in 6th place. It was, however, decided to enter for the Thames, and Clive again entered for the Diamonds, but it was Edwards and Clive, in the Goblets, who once more added lustre to the College's rowing reputation. The Thames crew was as follows:

		st.lb.
Bow	A.J. Rickards	10. 13
2	S.B. Wingfield-Digby	11. 3
3	R. St. J. Yates	11. 1
4	J.M. Couchman	11. 13
5	L.O. Prichard	11. 10
6	P.R.S. Bankes	13. 4
7	W.D.C. Erskine-Crum	12. 6
Str	S.M.F. Woodhouse	11. 6
Cox	W.M.A. Potts	9. 8

Erskine-Crum had won his Blue in 1931 and 1932, and was to row for Oxford again in 1933. In its first heat the crew had a narrow win over Downing, Cambridge, on the second day of the Regatta, but lost in what was an easy victory for Imperial College, London, who went on to defeat both Thames and Trinity, Dublin, before losing the Final to London R.C.

In the Diamonds Clive was knocked out in the very first heat. Edwards once again rowed in his usual positions for London in the Grand and the Stewards'. In the Grand London won their first heat comfortably, but then were overcome by the Leander crew, who beat Thames in the Final. In the

Stewards' 3 crews were entered. London lost to Berliner Ruder Club in the heat, and Thames "A" won the event. In the Goblets Edwards and Clive first met Sambell and Luxton, whom they had defeated in the Final the previous year. Once again the House men prevailed, leading all the way. The following day they again met the Offer brothers, C.T. Steward described the encounter as follows:

> *Both pairs went off at 34. Edwards and Clive touched the booms at the top of the Island and the Offers drew away to lead by a length at the Barrier. This lead they held to Fawley. After that Edwards and Clive began to draw up, and rowing the faster stroke just got on terms at the Post to make a dead heat. Times, 2.33, 4.16, 9.2.*
>
> *The race was re-rowed on the following day at 6.40 p.m. Edwards and Clive rowed 38 against 34 and led from the start, were a length up at the Barrier and a length and a half at Fawley. At the mile, the Offers being two lengths behind, stopped. Times, 2.33, 4.20, 9.37.*

Edwards and Clive had now earned a place in the Final, where they met Migotti and Lascelles of Gordouli B.C. They took the lead after the Island, and won by 3 lengths.

Edwards and Clive win the Goblets Final, 1932. Henley Royal Regatta

1932 was an Olympics year, the rowing Games being scheduled to take place in Los Angeles. As was customary, the British crews were selected with very heavy emphasis on those who had been successful at Henley.

Edwards and Clive lead near the end of the Olympic Pairs Final, 1932. Getty Images

Jumbo Edwards (3) in G.B. Four, 1932 Olympics. Getty Images

For the Eights, the Leander crew which had won the Grand was chosen. This crew was also the winning Cambridge Boat Race crew of 1932. For the Coxless Fours the Stewards'-winning Thames crew was chosen, and for the Coxless Pairs, Edwards and Clive. L.F. Southwood (who had beaten Clive in the Diamonds) was selected for the Single Sculls. He was not a Diamonds winner or finalist, but the Diamonds had last been won by a native Briton in 1927. No British crews were entered for the Coxed Pairs or Coxed Fours.

In the Olympic Regatta Britain secured 2 wins. The Eight, and Southwood both came in fourth. Edwards and Clive beat New Zealand by 1 length in the Coxless Pairs, and

Olympic Four, 1932. Jumbo Edwards one from right.
David Edwards

Jumbo Edwards (left) and Lewis Clive, 1932 Olympics. Jumbo is holding the official Olympics team hat.
David Edwards

the Thames crew won the Coxless Fours. The Thames crew was not, however, exactly the same as the Stewards' crew. T.H. Tyler, who had rowed 2, became sick in Los Angeles a few days before the Fours race, and Edwards was recruited as a substitute, joining the crew at 3, while 3 moved to bow and bow to 2.

It should be noted that Edwards' 2 Olympic wins were both secured on the same day. It is believed that this achievement by an individual has never been matched, before or since, in Olympic rowing. In just 2 days' racing in 1932, therefore, he succeeded in winning 3 Finals at Henley, and 2 in the Olympics.

The Thames Four, incidentally, was stroked by J.C. Badcock, who, as well as winning the Stewards' 4 times, the Grand twice, and the Wyfolds once, for Thames between 1925 and 1932, had also won a silver medal at the Amsterdam Olympics in 1928. Badcock was not a Christ Church man, but the name Badcock will appear again later in this survey of House rowing.

The success of Edwards and Clive in winning Olympic Gold for the House must rightly be ranked, along with the 1908 Grand win, as the most prestigious success for the Christ Church Boat Club in the first half of the 20th century, while Edwards stands as the greatest oarsman of this era, as Fletcher had been of the 19th century. Lewis Clive was killed in action in 1938 during the Spanish Civil War.

1933

Christ Church fell 2 places in Summer Eights to 8th. A crew was entered for the Visitors', and E.L. Dams teamed up with J.O.V. Edwards of Keble to enter for the Goblets. J.O.V. was the younger brother of E.C.T. and H.R.A.; he went to Keble because he was originally destined for a career in the Church. J.O.V. Edwards and Dams won the OUBC Pairs 2 years running. H.R.A. Edwards and Clive also entered for the Goblets in 1933. The crews were:

VISITORS'

		st. lb.
Bow	S.M.F. Woodhouse, *(steers)*	11. 8
2	L.O. Prichard	12. 5
3	P.R.S. Bankes	13. 11
Str	J.M. Couchman	12. 7

GOBLETS

CHRIST CHURCH & KEBLE			**CHRIST CHURCH**
		st.lb.	
Bow	E.L. Dams, (steers)	10. 1	H.R.A. Edwards, (steers)
Str	J.O.V. Edwards	11. 3	L. Clive

In a heat of the Visitors' the Four beat the Jesus, Cambridge, "A" crew easily.

> *Christ Church rowed 35 in the first minute, Jesus hitting the booms after 10 strokes. Christ Church gained two lengths before Jesus got going again. At Fawley, reached in 3min. 50sec., Christ Church were over two lengths ahead. Jesus continued to steer badly and the Oxford crew drew right away to win easily in 7min. 51sec.*
>
> (*The Times,* Thursday, 6 July)

They then met Trinity, Oxford, and were beaten.

> *Christ Church rowed 10, 19½, and 37 to 9, 17, and 33 by Trinity in the first quarter, half and full minute. Christ Church led at once but both crews found steering difficult in the head wind. Christ Church led by half a length at the Barrier, but near Fawley they hit the booms and Trinity went ahead and reached Fawley in 4min. 16sec. At the Mile Post Trinity led by two lengths, but Christ Church gained slightly along the Enclosure, Trinity winning by 1¼ lengths in 8min. 44sec.*
>
> (*The Times*)

In the Final Trinity lost to Christ's, Cambridge.

J.M. Couchman also rowed 2 for Leander in the Stewards'. Leander won their first heat, but lost the second to London, the losing finalists.

In the Goblets Dams and Edwards lost in the second heat to Powell and Gilmour of Eton Vikings. Eton Vikings rowed 36 and the Oxford men 35 in the first minute. Then Vikings led up to the Island and were a

> *… quarter of a length ahead at the First Signal. They were clear at Fawley in 4min. 3sec. The Oxford pair steered very badly and lost a good deal,*

> *Edwards being rather tired after his race in the morning. The Vikings won by 1½ lengths in 8min. 31sec.*
>
> (*The Times*)

Eton Vikings went on to win the event.

Edwards and Clive beat Brown and Ward of Thames R.C. by ½ a length, before being beaten in turn by E.F. and T.S. Bigland of Royal Chester R.C., who thus entered the Final, where the winners were, as indicated, Powell and Gilmour.

Jumbo Edwards explains in his autobiography, referring to his frame of mind after the Los Angeles Olympics, when he had already commenced his distinguished career in the Royal Air Force, that

> *I now decided to give up rowing, I had perfected my rowing to the highest degree of which I was capable, and the rowing world had no more prizes to offer, and I ceased to take any further interest in the sport. Flying had now become my major interest. Lewis Clive begged me to row in a pair in 1933, and weakly I agreed, but a further handicap was that I was about to become affianced. The rowing suffered, and of course we were beaten. After that I cut myself off from the river for 16 years.*

1934

This year saw the House regain 1 place in Summer Eights. A Four was entered for the Visitors', and a heavyweight Pair, who had rowed in the Four the previous year, for the Goblets.

VISITORS'

		st. lb.
Bow	A.J. Richards *(steers)*	11. 1
2	D.A.E.C. Philips	11. 13
3	B.O.P. Eugster	13. 7
Str	D.P. Paton	11. 12

GOBLETS

		st. lb.
Bow	J.M. Couchman *(steers)*	12. 10
Str	P.R.S. Bankes	13. 12

Neither crew distinguished itself. In the Visitors' the Four met, Univ., '*who won very easily in 8 min.*' (*The Times,* 6 July, 1934). The Pair met the Bigland brothers (of Royal Chester) in the very first heat of the event on the first day. The Biglands had, as indicated, lost the Final in 1933, and were to do the same thing this year. The heat race was an embarrassment for the House crew.

> *The crews raced together up the Island, after which the Oxford pair showed ahead, and were half a length up at the First Signal. They were the same distance in front at Fawley in 4 min. 6sec., but at the Mile Post Royal Chester led by a few feet. On the Enclosure the crews were level, but the Oxford pair fouled the booms and capsized, leaving Chester to finish alone.*
> (*The Times,* 6 July).

Christ Church's honour was, however, partially restored by Couchman, who rowed 2 for Leander, winners of the Grand in a new record time of 6min. 44sec., which stood until 1952. (Couchman had won his Blue in 1933, and did so again in 1934 and 1935, though, regrettably, never rowing in a winning Boat Race crew. P.R.S. Bankes also rowed for Oxford these 3 years.)

In December 1934 the Qualification for the Ladies' Plate was updated to make it clear that the "Universities" referred to in 1856 version were Oxford and Cambridge. The revision also banned 2 or more Boat Clubs from a single college, or from different colleges, combining to create a composite entry.

Leander (Couchman, Christ Church 2) win the Grand, 1934. Henley Royal Regatta

1935

This was a more successful year in Eights Week for the House, who rose to 5th place on the River, the best position since 1931. The decision to enter for the Ladies for the first time since 1927 was, therefore, quite reasonable. The crew were:

		st.lb.
Bow	W.G. Gordon	11. 0
2	R.D. Barlas	9.13
3	E.J. Bickersteth	11. 8
4	D.P. Paton	12. 7
5	B.O.P. Eugster	14. 2
6	P.R.S. Bankes	14. 1
7	H.J.R. Barker	11. 2
Str	J.S. Lewes	12. 5
Cox	P.L. Carter	8. 13

Barker was the son of H.R, Barker who, as earlier noted, had featured prominently in the success of Christ Church crews in the early 1900s.

The first heat in which the House was engaged was against Bedford Modern School.

> *An Oxford victory was gained by Christ Church, who very easily defeated Bedford Modern School. The latter led for the first 10 strokes, but once the House had settled down the issue was never in doubt, and over the second part of the course the Oxford crew were actually striking nine strokes a minutes less than the schoolboys, and still retaining their lead without difficulty....*
>
> *Bedford struck 11, 21, and 41 to 11, 20, and 38 by Christ Church in the first quarter, half, and full minute. Bedford led for 10 strokes, and then Christ Church went ahead. The House were nearly a length up at Remenham Barrier in 2min. 11sec., and then dropped to a strong paddle at 28, being a length up at Fawley in 3min. 40sec. Although striking about nine strokes to the minute less than Bedford, Christ Church easily held their own. Won by 2½ lengths in 7min. 37sec.*
>
> (*The Times*, Thursday, 4 July, 1935).

The next day the opponents were Trinity, Oxford. Another comfortable win was secured.

> *Trinity rowed 16, 20, and 38 to 10½, 20½, and 39 by Christ Church in the first quarter, half, and full minute. Trinity soon got a lead of a few feet but Christ Church were on them before a minute, and at the First Signal Christ Church led by half a length. They had this lead at Remenham Barrier (2min. 9sec.) but at Fawley, reached in 3min. 19sec., Christ Church were nearly a length ahead. Although striking 29 to 33 by Trinity, Christ Church continued to increase their lead and they drew right away along the Enclosure. Won by three lengths in 7min. 34sec.*
>
> (*The Times*)

Meanwhile, Radley had defeated Monckton Combe School and Selwyn, Cambridge. Now came the race between Radley and the House.

> *Radley, at 43 against 39, had gained half a length at the first signal but Christ Church brought them back to a quarter of a length at the Barrier. Past Fawley and nearly to the mile, the boys held their lead, but Christ Church were coming up again and took the lead at the bottom of the Enclosure, and got home by a quarter of a length. Times, 2.7, 3.33, 7.22.*
>
> (Steward)

These 3 wins secured a place in the semi-final against Eton, who had disposed of Keble, Queens', Cambridge, and Bedford School. It happened that R.D. Burnell, rowing 6 for Eton, had strained his back, and it was agreed to postpone the race until 7:00 p.m. (on the third day).

> *When the Ladies' Plate race between Eton and Christ Church, which had been put off till the evening to give Burnell's strained back a chance to recover, was finally rowed, Burnell was still obviously troubled by his back. Eton, however, started off very cleanly at 11, 21½, and 40½ to the 11, 20 and 38 of Christ Church. Eton were a canvas ahead at the First Signal and, at the Barrier, reached in 2min. 6sec., had gained more. At the Half-Mile Eton were half a length ahead, rowing 36 to the 31 of their heavy rivals. At the next two signals Eton had a length's lead and were rowing*

> *with far more life and dash. It was not until the Enclosure that Christ Church spurted and then it was too late. Burnell was in great discomfort, and in the last half-minute Christ Church gained half a length. They were quite outgeneraled by Napier, the Eton stroke, who got the crew home with half a length to spare just as they looked like cracking.*
>
> (*The Times*, Saturday, 6 July).

Richard Burnell, the son of C.D. Burnell, a 4-time winning Oxford Blue (1895-98) and 7-time Henley winner, was to win a Blue himself in 1939, having been Captain of the Boats at Eton. He had the distinction of winning the Double Sculls in the 1948 Olympics; (his father had won a gold medal in 1908). Burnell won the Grand in 1946 and 1949, and the Double Sculls in 1951. He was President of Leander, rowing correspondent of *The Times* and *The Sunday Times,* the author of the history of the first 150 years of the Regatta, already referred to, and, like his father, a Henley Steward. His son. P.C.D., was to win his Blue in 1962.

This year Couchman was again in the Leander Grand crew, this time at 6. Leander lost the Final to Pembroke, Cambridge.

1936

The House hung on to its position of 5th in Summer Eights. J.S. Lewes of Christ Church, an Australian who had stroked the House Ladies' crew in 1935, and who in 1936 rowed in the Boat Race, was elected President of the OUBC in May.

There were 109 entries for Henley, the highest number to date. The House entered for the Wyfolds and the Goblets. The Wyfolds crew was as follows:

		st. lb.
Bow	E.J. Bickersteth	11. 13
2	R.D. Barlas	10. 7
3	P.J.S. Windham-Wright *(steers)*	12. 13
Str	J.F. Davis	12. 6

In the fourth heat they met Reading R.C.

> *Both crews rowed 39 in the first minute, but Reading jumped away at once and were clear at the top of the Island. Reading were three lengths up at Remenham Barrier in 2min. 18sec., and even more so at Fawley in 3min. 57sec. Reading dropped to a hard paddle at 28. Won easily in 8min. 29sec.*
>
> (*The Times*, Friday, 3 July, 1936).

Reading went on to lose the Final to London Rowing Club.

W.G. Gordon, bow of the 1935 Ladies' crew, and J.S. Lewes won their first heat of the Goblets against the composite crew of J.M. Couchman (Christ Church) and E.E.D. Tomlin (Univ.) Gordon and Lewes lost their second heat, however, to a Vesta R.C. crew who lost in the Final.

Couchman also once again was in the Leander crew in the Grand, rowing once more at 6. Leander got to the Final for the second year running, but were again beaten, this time by Zurich Rowing Club.

1937

This was the year in which, as noted earlier, Oxford broke Cambridge's Boat Race run of 13 consecutive wins. Great credit for this is given by Richard Burnell in his *One Hundred and Fifty Years of the Oxford and Cambridge Boat Race* (1979), to Lewes:

> *Lewes believed that men should be picked for their racing ability rather than for their style. He insisted that his crew should race, during practice, as often as possible. For the first time he kept an Isis crew training alongside the University crew throughout practice, and when Isis won, which they quite often did, changes were made. This may seem to be a glimpse of the obvious in 1979, but it was not so in 1939. In the end, dissatisfied with his own form, Lewes stood down, against the advice of his coaches. But without doubt it was his leadership which at last turned the tables on Cambridge.*

The House, who had ignominiously dropped to 11th place in Eights Week, nevertheless decided to enter for the Thames, for which there were 30 entries. The crew was as follows:

		st. lb.
Bow	M.J. Starforth	12. 0
2	G.J. Boyd	10. 6
3	G.M. Blundell	11. 4
4	J.F. Davis	12. 0
5	A.S.H. Kemp	12. 6
6	P.J.S. Windham-Wright	13. 4
7	D.J. Orde	10. 13
Str	P.R.A. Birley	10. 10
Cox	W.R. Younger	8. 8

They met Lensbury R.C. in Heat 11 in what proved to be an exciting race.

> *Lensbury rowed 39 and Christ Church 40 in the first minute, and the tideway crew went away steadily to lead by a third of a length at the First Signal. They led by the same distance at Remenham Barrier in 2min. 10sec., but Christ Church spurted and the crews were level at Fawley in 3min. 42sec., with both crews rowing 34. The lead changed repeatedly over the second half of the course. Won* [by Lensbury] *by two feet in 7min. 53sec.*
>
> (*The Times,* Thursday, 1 July).

Lensbury won their next race, but then succumbed to London, who went on to lose the Final to Tabor Academy from the U.S.A.

Couchman's last appearance as a competitor at Henley took place this year, when he rowed 2 in the Leander Four in the Stewards'. Leander's success in beating Thames in the Final gave him his second Henley win.

This year a plan was adopted, to be implemented in 1938, to ease the pressure on schools who entered for the Ladies'.

> *There was a strong feeling that it was not fair to make Schools row two races on one day if their second race was against a College.*
>
> *Eventually a scheme was devised by which Schools and Colleges were kept apart though the preliminary and first rounds, these two rounds being rowed on the first day.*
>
> (*Henley Records* (Steward)).

Leander (Couchman 2) win the Stewards', 1937. Henley Royal Regatta

At a Special General Meeting of the Stewards held in June, the definition of an amateur was amended such that all references to manual labour, mechanics, artisans and labourers were removed. The change was triggered by an embarrassing occurrence the previous year when an Australian crew, on its way to the Olympic Games, was denied entry to Henley Regatta on the grounds that its crew, of policemen, were manual workers and, therefore, by Henley standards, not amateurs. Later in the year the ban on professional coaches was removed.

1938

The House gained 4 places in Eights, moving up to 7th place, and entered for the Ladies'. The crew was:

		st. lb.
Bow	D.J. Orde	11. 0
2	H.P.L. Attlee	11. 5
3	A.S.H. Kemp	12. 6
4	P.J.S. Windham-Wright	13. 9
5	M.J. Starforth	12. 12
6	T. Stainton	13. 2
7	G.M. Blundell	11. 8
Str	J.S. Story	11. 1
Cox	P.R.F. Burton	9. 2

The Times (30 June) commented on the House's heat with Corpus Christi, Cambridge:

> *Corpus rowed 37 and Christ Church 39 in the first minute. Corpus led at once and were three-quarters of a length ahead at the First Signal and clear at the Barrier, in 2min. 5sec. Rowing very strongly, Corpus were nearly two lengths ahead at Fawley, in 3min. 29sec. They dropped to a strong paddle over the second half of the course, but easily kept the lead..*
>
> *Won by 1½ lengths in 7min. 28sec.*

Corpus were a strong crew. As *The Times* also noted:

> . . . [They] *confirmed their good form in the Mays and at Marlow by disposing of Christ Church without difficulty.*

They went on to beat First Trinity, but lost the Final to Radley, who then enjoyed their first-ever win in the event.

Christ Church on the water, Henley 1938. Christ Church Archives

1939

The House, now once again 5th on the River, entered the following crew for the Ladies':

		st. lb.
Bow	D.J. Orde	11. 1
2	R.H.F. Scott	11. 1
3	V.F. Ellis	12. 9
4	A.S.H. Kemp	12. 4
5	M.J. Starforth	13. 12
6	T. Stainton	13. 1
7	G.M. Blundell	12. 0
Str	J.S. Story	11. 3
Cox	P.R.F. Burton	9.12

In a field of 28 for the event, which included crews from 12 Cambridge colleges as opposed to only 5 from Oxford, the House was drawn against Trinity College, Dublin. As with the race against Lensbury 2 years earlier, the encounter had an exciting finish.

> *Dublin rowed 10, 20 and 40 to 10½, 20 and 38 by Christ Church in the first quarter, half and full minute, and the Irish crew led at once, being a canvas up at the first signal and half a length at the Barrier, in 2min. 20sec. Trinity College gradually increased their lead and were nearly a length up at Fawley in 4min. 11sec. They retained this lead until reaching the Enclosure where Christ Church spurted splendidly, but they could not quite get level.*
>
> *Won by a canvas in 8min. 21sec.*
>
> (*The Times,* Thursday, 6 July, 1939)

The Times added:

> *Oxford colleges made a bad showing and not one of them succeeded in winning a heat. Christ Church, who got to within a canvas of Trinity College, Dublin, did best, for they were a length behind at the bottom of the Enclosure.*

Trinity, Dublin then fell to Pembroke, Cambridge, in their next heat. The event was won by Clare, Cambridge.

This being the centenary year of the Regatta, a special race was added to the programme, the Centenary Double Sculling Race. In 1946 a Challenge Cup and medals were added, and the event, the Double Sculls Challenge Cup, open to all amateurs, has continued ever since.

As has been seen, the House did not fare well in its appearances at Henley between 1933 and 1939, the last year of the Regatta before the outbreak of World War II. However, 2 points are worth emphasizing. The first is that the House, in entering, was abiding by a College tradition to send a crew to Henley, if possible, withou restricting such appearance to years in which it was in a dominant position on the Isis. Thus, in the 20 years between the wars when the traditional Henley Regatta events took place, Christ Church was an entrant no fewer than 18 years.

Secondly, during the 1930s Cambridge dominated the Boat Race, and did the same at Henley. The Ladies' was won by Cambridge Colleges 8 years out of 10 and by an Oxford College crew not once. In the Visitors' Cambridge again won 8 years, with only B.N.C. and Oriel winning once each. Edwards' and Clive's 2 wins in the Goblets were the only Oxford successes in this event during the decade. So in terms of rowing ability at the College level, Oxford was dwarfed by Cambridge, and it would have been amazing, indeed, given the House's moderate performance in Eights Week, had it succeeded in winning any of the events entered for, Edwards' and Clive's successes excepted

1940–1949

1945-1946

1946 SAW THE RE-LAUNCHING OF HENLEY ROYAL REGATTA AFTER A GAP OF 7 YEARS. The fact that a House crew was then entered was remarkable given the perilous state of Christ Church (and Oxford) rowing at the end of the Second World War. During the war rowing at the university had continued on a curtailed and sporadic basis, with Christ Church, Pembroke and BNC joining forces, for example, in 1941 and 1942 to create a composite crew, and with Dean Lowe himself undertaking coaching duties in 1941. Four unofficial Boat Races took place, though plans for one had to be abandoned, while for another (1942) Oxford could not raise a crew. In 1940 and 1945 such "Boat Races" took place at Henley, in 1943 at Sandford, and in 1944 at Ely.

The experiences of the Christ Church Boat Club in getting going again after the war have, fortunately, been recorded by R.J. Gould, President of the Christ Church Boat Club from after Eights Week, 1948, until Hilary Term, 1949, and a member of the First and Henley Eights in 1947 and the Henley Four in 1948. Dick Gould was kind enough to write about the immediate post-war years in an article, *Christ Church Boat Club 1945-1948* which appeared in this author's survey of *Crew Composition and Racing Results 1946-1993*. Dick's report is reproduced at the end of this section of this book.

In Trinity Term 1945 the Boat Club had only one member, J.R.L. (Jimmy) Carstairs, twice a war-time Blue. (Full Blues for rowing were not awarded between 1939 and 1945). The return of many ex-servicemen resulted in the number of recruits to the Boat Club growing, and 2 Christ Church crews could be put together for Torpids in 1946. The First Torpid made 6 bumps. This, and Carstairs' membership of the winning Oxford crew in 1946 – the first "official" post-war Boat Race, sparked further interest. Carstairs was President of the Christ Church Boat Club. In Trinity Term, 1946, the First Eight – starting 5th in its finishing position in Eights Week, 1939 – lost 2 places, but, despite this modest showing, out of respect for the Club's Henley tradition a crew was entered for the Ladies'. The crew was the First Eight save for a substitute at 2 and a substitute cox, the latter going on to twice cox the Blue Boat. The crew was:

		st. lb.
Bow	A. Chenevix-Trench	9. 6
2	R.H. McClure	10. 11
3	J.D. Gott	10. 7
4	C.H. Pemberton	11. 0
5	D.C.L. Gibbs	11. 10
6	J.R.L. Carstairs	12. 3
7	C.I. Mellor	11. 0
Str	P.D. Stuart	10. 0
Cox	A. Palgrave-Brown	8. 13

Henley Regatta was attended by the Princesses Elizabeth and Margaret Rose. Princess Elizabeth presented the Prizes, and the Princess Elizabeth Cup, for schools, was inaugurated.

The House was drawn against Bryanston School in a heat of the Ladies', for which there were 21 entries. Up to the mile post Christ Church held a lead of a canvas or less, but Bryanston drew ahead and won by ¾ of a length. Bryanston went on to win another heat before being beaten in the semi-final by Trinity College, Dublin, who lost the Final.

Entering for Henley Regatta may have produced an undistinguished result, but it helped to re-establish the high standard which marked the Christ Church Club's long history, and set the pace for a revival of House rowing; crews were to go to Henley for each of the following 4 years. A minor success was, indeed, achieved that summer by a Christ Church Coxed Pair, all 3 of whose members, C.I. Mellor, A. Chenevix-Trench, and A. Palgrave-Brown, were Old Salopians; they carried off the Open Pairs at Shrewsbury Regatta. Tony Chenevix-Trench (later Head Master of Eton), bow, had returned to the House after suffering severe deprivation as a 5-year prisoner of war of the Japanese; Cim Mellor (who succeeded Carstairs as President of the Boat Club) has commented on the possibility that in this crew bow might well have weighed less than cox.

1947

The year got off to a good start with the First Torpid making 3 bumps and ending in 2nd place. This was followed by the First Eight making 3 bumps and rising to 4th place in Division 1, the Second Eight making 6 bumps, and Mellor and E.W. Gladstone reaching the Final of the OUBC Pairs.

A return visit to Henley was, not surprisingly, decided on, and the First Eight, with 1 substitution (at 4) was entered for the Ladies', as follows:

		st.lb.
Bow	C.I. Mellor	11. 6
2	J.C. Soulsby	10. 6
3	R.J. Gould	11. 2
4	J.H.E. Whitfield	12. 2
5	R.A. Noel	12. 13
6	D. Barraclough	14. 6
7	D.C.L. Gibbs	11. 8
Str	E.W. Gladstone	11. 1
Cox	A. Palgrave-Brown	8. 13

The House was drawn against St. Edward's School in Heat 4 of the event. The result was no more impressive than that of the previous year. St. Edward's took a small early lead, which they extended to a length at Fawley, and won by 1¼ lengths. They then fell to Magdalene, Cambridge in their next heat. (See R.J. Gould's comments on what was, for the House, *'little short of a fiasco'*.)

D.C.L. Gibbs and E.W. Gladstone were both Presidents of the Boat Club during this year. E.W. and his younger brothers Peter and Francis (J.F.) were the sons of the Christ Church oarsman of the early 1900s, C.A. Gladstone, and the nephews of C.A.'s brother A.C. from the same era. Each of these five family members, in their turn, were Presidents of the Christ Church Boat Club.

1948

Following the House win in the Long Distance Race in Michaelmas Term, 1947, the First Torpid went Head of the River. R.A. Noel (now President of the Christ Church Boat Club) rowed 5 in the Blue Boat, which lost to Cambridge.

Unfortunately, in Eights Week the First Eight was bumped by BNC., so dropping one place to 5th.

It was decided to enter a Four in the Visitors' at Henley, as follows:

		st. lb.
Bow	E.W. Gladstone *(steers)*	11. 1
2	D.H. Tahta	11. 11
3	R.J. Gould	11. 12
Str	J.R.L. Carstairs	12. 1

Gould was, by now, as noted President of the Boat Club.

The Four met Jesus, Cambridge, in its heat of the Visitors'. Jesus had a 2-length lead at the ¾ mile, and won easily. This gloomy result was, however, quite outshone by the high spirits of the Christ Church crew. E.W. Gladstone (known to his friends as Willie, and later to become Sir William) drew a number of humourous cartoons, with commentaries by Dick Gould, recording aspects of the crew's living arrangements at Henley and of the maxims of their distinguished coach, Ian Fairbairn, son of the great Steve Fairbairn.

1949

The First Eight rowed over in 5th place. It was decided to enter for the Visitors' and the Wyfolds, with the same crew rowing in both events:

Gerald Percy had stroked the Isis boat early in the year. Gladstone was now again President of the Boat Club until Michaelmas Term.

In the Wyfolds the House was beaten easily in a heat by SEH, having hit the booms near the top of the Island, and being 3½ lengths behind at the ¾ mile. SEH won 2 further heats before themselves hitting the booms after being just ahead at the mile mark, so losing to Royal Chester, who in turn lost the Final to Lensbury, the latter's first ever Henley event win.

Leander (J.R.L. Carstairs, Christ Church, 3) win the Grand, 1949. Henley Royal Regatta

In the Visitors' the Four was drawn against Pembroke, Cambridge who, 2½ lengths ahead at the ½ mile, won easily.

T.R. Ticher (for 2 years cox of the First Eight, and Secretary of the Boat Club in 1950) coxed Royal Chester in the Thames.

J.R.L. Carstairs rowed 3 in the Leander Grand crew, which in its second heat beat Trinity, Oxford, in a time which equalled the 1934 course record, (6min. 44 sec,.), and then won the Final against Thames R.C. Carstairs also rowed bow in the Leander Four which lost its heat of the Stewards' to Trinity, Oxford, who won the Final.

Starting in 1946, a number of new events were added to the Henley programme. While they merit mention, and are summarized below, none of those for which the House was eligible to compete attracted an entry from the Christ Church Boat Club in the remaining period covered in this book.

In 1946 the Princess Elizabeth Cup was introduced (as has been noted) over a shortened course, to accommodate school crews not up to the standard needed for the Ladies' Plate. Starting the following year the event took place over the full Henley course. In 1963 the Prince Philip Challenge Cup for coxed Fours was initiated, the entry qualification for which being the same as for the Grand.

In 1968 a new event for coxed Fours, restricted to crews from the U.K. and Ireland, with no composite entries being allowed, came into being, known in its first years as the "Henley Prize", and from the following year as the Britannia Challenge Cup following the donation of a trophy by Nottingham Britannia Rowing Club. In 1981 came the Queen Mother Challenge Cup, for quadruple sculls, the qualification being the same as for the Grand.

In 1981 3 invitation races for women, over a shortened course, were introduced. They were discontinued after the next year. It was felt that open events for women would only be possible if some existing event or events were curtailed or withdrawn, given the tightness of scheduling the existing programme into 4 days.

CHRIST CHURCH BOAT CLUB 1945-8

by R.J. GOULD
former President, Christ Church Boat Club

I entered the House as a freshman in October 1946 after five years' service in the Army. Because of this service I was able to take a shortened degree course of seven terms, and went down in December 1948. I was married in December 1946, at the end of my first term, and became a father in January 1948. I begin this story in the year before I arrived on the rowing scene.

My own previous rowing career had been at Winchester. Most of this had been in fours with fixed seats, but in my last two years an eight was successfully trained using the facilities of Southampton University and a boat loaned by them. In 1941 an informal regatta attended by 11 public schools rowed three or four abreast between the anti-seaplane poles erected down the shortened course at Henley above Temple Island. I stroked and captained Winchester whilst Willie Gladstone coxed Eton. The regatta was rowed in two heats: an open draw in the morning and races between firsts, seconds, thirds and fourths in the afternoon. Eton won overall.

When I was elected President of the Ch. Ch. B.C. in 1948 I suggested that we should put together a Newsletter and send it to all old members whose addresses we could find. This was agreed, partly in the hopes of stirring up some financial support, partly to arouse interest in possible coaching, and mostly for general goodwill. I wrote this myself and although I have not kept a copy of the printed version, I do still have the manuscript.

1948 NEWSLETTER

"At a general meeting of the Ch.Ch.B.C. held in June 1948 it was voted that a report should be prepared for the benefit of old members to review the rebirth of the Club after the Second World War; and also to outline in more detail the events of 1947 -8 with a view to publishing in future a short annual report. For several reasons this is an apt moment to pause and take stock, for it would seem tlat the Boat Club is entering a new phase, the third since the war. The first was one of endeavour, the second one of achievement, whilst the future is once again left in the hands of but few men of experience, although this time they have a very healthy following of enthusiastic new blood.

In Hilary Term 1945 the combined Ch.Ch.-BNC Togger fared disastrously, and an entry in the President's Book reads thus: "One was forced to *beg* people to row. In consequence, when the bulk of the Togger went down in April, the combined Boat Clubs comprised but three members, two of whom were in BNC." Thus in Triniry Term it was decided not to enter a boat for the Summer VIIIs. Surely this was the lowest ebb to which a Club could sink without extinction! One might however add that the only survivor was a wartime Blue, so that the Ch.Ch.B.C. was simultaneously 100% Blues!

Michaelmas Term 1945 was given to training, mostly in tubs, a welcome number of voluntary recruits, many of them returned ex-Servicemen. Torpids 1946 returned to the 1939 order on the river, and the House boat started 11th. They went up every night, each time within three minutes of the start, bumping Corpus, Univ., Exeter, Balliol, Pembroke and Trinity. The second Togger went up one place. This was followed by Oxford winning the first resumed Varsity Boat Race with a House man at 5; and by Isis coming second on the same day in the Putney Head of the River Race with House men at each end (bow and cox). These successes, combined with an excellent Bump Supper, revived interest and keenness within and without the Boat Club, providing the Club with its greatest asset.

Trinity Term 1946 was perhaps disappointing, for the lst VIII dropped from 5th to 7th and the 2nd VIII went down every night. But the first crew was little altered from the 1st Togger, and averaged only 11st 21b; and the rowing proved that, although we were only 7th, the 8th boat, which had recorded 6 bumps, was definitely not as fast. As for the 2nd VIII, the achievement was that one could be raised at all.

After VIIIs three House Old Salopians entered for, and won, the Open Coxed Pairs at Shrewsbury Regatta.

An VIII was entered for Henley "lest an undesirable precedent be established." This was much enjoyed, and the first race went well up to the mile, at which

The House led, but "youth, innocence and weight", in the form of Bryanston School, told eventually and the schoolboys won by ¾ length.

This might be regarded as the end of the first phase of endeavour, not without its own successes.

Michaelmas Term 1946 brought up a number of freshmen with rowing experience, even if it was rusted by years away at the war. The coxless IV had little chance of success since a very light IV in training before the beginning of term was split up to include two of these freshmen, so there was no time to find balance and wind up muscle. It was beaten by Magdalen I who were beaten in the final by Oriel I. Our sole representative in the University Sculls was beaten in the first round. The House eschewed the Clinker IVs, rowed in place of Godstow Regatta, in favour of tubbing and preliminary VIIIs training for Torpids. Two House oarsmen and a cox were awarded Trial Caps.

The 1st Togger of Hilary Term 1941 was by general acclaim the fastest boat on the river. This was achieved by concentrating on a well-held-out finish and boat control. It had very bad luck. It started 5th. On the first three nights it bumped Magdalen, St Edmund Hall and St. John's in 30 strokes, before the Stone and opposite Timms respectively. Then the river froze, during which time two members of the crew went sick, one with 'flu and the other with mumps. Starting 2nd on Thursday (after three days' postponement) with two substitutes it was missed by St. John's by ⅓ length one night and by 4ft the next. On the last night St. John's were bumped by Trinity and we finished 2nd behind New College, who had improved a lot during racing. The 2nd Togger went up once and down four times.

The House was unrepresented in the 1947 Boat Race crew, but again provided bow and cox in what was a much less successful Isis crew.

Starting 7th in Summer VIIIs the House was full of hope to reach the first three on the river. This might well have been achieved either if we had rowed as well every night as we did on the last; or if New College, in front, had dealt more promptly with Oriel. As it was, bumps were recorded on the first, second and last nights, and the House finished 4th. The 2nd VIII went up every night, never having to row more than 2½ minutes. A 3rd VIII was raised which went down twice and up once.

A spectacular success was achieved in the University Pairs. The House pair beat the Magdalen pair, later runners-up in the Goblets and a potential Olympic pair, in the first round by 2 secs. In the final they lost by 5 secs to a strong Trinity pair.

Henley 1947 was little short of a fiasco in which failure to the House was only made less conspicuous by the failure of Oxford rowing generally. Only one change had to be made in the crew from the Summer VIII, albeit an important one, but due partly to mistakes in coaching, partly to over-confidence, partly to having the crew divided into widely separated billets, and no doubt also due to many other things, an undoubtedly fast and promising crew in practice fell, in the first race, an easy and dispirited victim to St. Edward's School.

Thus a very successful year ended in disappointrnent which was relieved, however, by the fact that most of the lst VIII had at least one more year's rowing before them.

The coxless IV of Michaelmas 1947 had to be reformed twice owing to injuries. It thus did quite well to win two heats and to lose to Magdalen in the semi-finals after hitting the bank at the start.

This term the Godstow Races were revived as the Long Distance Race from Sandford Lock to the Black Bridge on the Radley water, to be rowed as a Thames Head of the River race. The House decided to enter for this race two crews to be the same, if possible, as the 1st and 2nd Torpids for the following term. University Trials robbed us of one man, otherwise no plans were upset. The 1st VIII settled down to long stretches of hard paddling, worrying little about rate of striking, which came up naturally. The 2nd VIII did the same, but less of it. The result on the day was a good, hard row with no panic and no misadventures, and the satisfaction of winning by nearly 20 secs from Balliol in 16m 47sec. The 2nd Crew might have come in before many 1st crews, but the cox took the wrong turning round the island, hitting the bank and losing many lengths. In spite of this they finished 20 of 23, and 4th of the 2nd boats. A good send-off for Torpids.

"Torpids were a triumph", reads the President's book, "in that 1. we went Head of the River (for the first time since 1925), 2. our 2nd Torpid made four bumps, and 3. we raised a 3rd Torpid for the first time since the War. This last was also involved in a bump, with the result that the Ch.Ch.B.C. had the Great Distinction of Enclosing the River." The 1st Torpid was conspicuous for boat control and sustained performance, both due to the mileage covered the previous term. Fast times were recorded in practice, 57 secs for Green Bank and 7.11 for the full course. It was past its best in the races, and when for four nights it rowed over behind New College it became worried, although it never missed them by more than a canvas, and once all but overlapped. But on the fifth night it caught New College about 90 yards from the finish in front of a huge crowd attracted by the close racing of the previous nights. Much credit must go to the Waterman who altered the rigging overnight to prevent over-reaching and to ensure a hard finish. On the last night we rowed over comfortably. A good Bump Supper was held. This point was the zenith, to date, of the post War period.

Once again the House was represented at 5 in the Boat Race, but not in Isis, which suffered badly this year by neglect from above and disinterestedness amongst those approached to row in it.

Hopes naturally ran high for Summer VIIIs, with two Blues and two Trial Caps (including the cox) to add to the Head of the River Torpid crew. Great promise was indeed shown in the early days of practice, but for a number of reasons we reached Eights Week stale and dispirited. Nonetheless it came as a shock that we finished outside our distance with New College on the first night, and more so when on the next night BNC came within a length of us in the Gut. Saturday we rowed over uneventfully. On Monday, however, in spite of a very lively morning outing, BNC, owing partly to optimistic gunning and tremendous support from the bank, caught us opposite our own boathouse amongst pagan expressions of delight. Though not bumped again, our spirit was shattered, about which more later.

The second VIII was more successful than had seemed likely. Though not a good crew they bumped Oriel II, Herts and Cat's. A 3rd and 4th VIII were raised, the former dropping one place and the latter just failing to get on the river in a qualifying race, about 80 boats having entered for the 73 available places.

A new President and Secretary were elected after Eights, and to them fell the responsibility for raising a crew for Henley. Though no one who was needed was prevented by Schools or other valid excuse from rowing, it was with one or two exceptions impossible to persuade the senior members of the Club to row in a Ladies' Plate crew. After much deliberation it was decided to make an VIII out of the available material and to enter it, if up to standard, for the Ladies' Plate; otherwise to enter a IV for the Visitors' Cup. Proposals to have a trial run at Marlow were decisively out-voted. Reluctantly the VIII had to be abandoned, and in the last week of Term a IV started practice. It made surprisingly good progress, but on going to Henley one member got a poisoned hand and a substitute was put in with eight days to go. There was never a chance, but thanks to vigorous and most entertaining coaching, the practice and Regatta were enjoyed tremendously. Though we lost to Jesus (Cambridge) by 4 lengths in the first round, we performed quite well to Fawley, and certainly much was gained from the Regatta in many ways.

This ends the second of the post War periods. At the beginning of the Michaelmas Term 1948 there was no old active member of the Boat Club with so much as a Leander Cap nor any prospect of one. One freshman had rowed for Eton two years before, and one or two for Westminster. Over half the members had never rowed before. Since Michaelmas Term to Henley comprises the rowing year, an account of the great endeavour to maintain the House's position on the river by building right from the foundations must be left over for the next report. Suffice it to say that the endeavour and the response at the outset were worthy of the tasks ahead.

A word must be said about coaching. First, there is the well-known shortage of coaches generally. This has led us to rely more and more on our Waterman, to provide the constant background of our coaching which, in the opinion of the writer, had been a very good thing. A less good result has been that the Colleges, notably New College and Magdalen, are on the same lines, though with their own variations, and it seems to be inevitable that changing methods should be evolved to suit changing circumstances.

The Ch.Ch. B.C. has in three years grown from one member to over forty members, and has re-established the reputation to be classed as one of the rowing Colleges. In the face of many difficulties it enters a new phase cheerfully resolved to maintain, and in course of time perhaps to improve upon, this satisfactory achievement".

The MS ends here. I returned for one more Term and rowed in the University Fours. On this occasion I changed with Willie Gladstone to stroke the boat, but we did not do well. Because I then went down with my shortened degree, Willie was elected President in my place.

(The reference to Enclosing the River gave rise to much enquiry and debate. It was not at all clear what the term might mean. The solution, independently arrived at by both Willie Gladstone and Dick Gould, was that the phrase would apply when one's crews occupied both head and bottom positions on the river. The reference to the 3rd Torpid being "involved in a bump" meant, it turned out, that it was bumped and therefore went bottom. It was apparently the joking idea of Jimmy Carstairs, R.J. Gould informed me, to use initial capitals for the key words, (Great Distinction etc.), copying the style of 'Winnie-The-Pooh'. G.C.P.)

1950–1959

1950

WITH 2 BROTHERS, JIMMY AND MATTHEW CARSTAIRS, in the crew, Peter Gladstone (brother of E.W.), a 1950 Blue, at 6, and with T.R. Ticher (described by Dundas in the Christ Church Report as *'the elegant and bijou cox of the first Eight'*) holding the rudder lines, the Eight bumped BNC. on the first day of Eights Week to go 4th on the River, but hit the bank at the start on the fifth day and were caught by Merton, to finish in 5th place where they had started.

With D.A. Faulkner and J.D. Remers substituting for J.R.L. Carstairs and Gerald Percy, and with Peter Gladstone moving to stroke, the House entered for the Thames at Henley. The crew was as follows:

		st. lb.
Bow	M.W. Carstairs	11. 0
2	D.A. Faulkner	10. 11
3	J.D. Remers	11. 0
4	A.P. Graham-Dixon	11. 0
5	C.D. McDougal	13. 6
6	J.T. Regan	13. 7
7	H.L. Craig	10. 12
Str	P. Gladstone	12. 11
Cox	T.R. Ticher	8. 6

In their heat they met Magdalene, Cambridge and lost by 1 length. Magdalene were in turn beaten by Thames R.C., who lost to the Kent School, U.S.A., by 2½ lengths in the Final.

Jimmy Carstairs had been invited to row, at 3, for Leander in the Grand. Leander beat Dartmouth Rowing Club, U.S.A., in their first heat but lost by ½ a length to Studenten Roeivereeniging Njord of The Netherlands in their second. The Dutch crew lost the Final to Harvard University. Jimmy also rowed bow in the Leander Four in the Stewards. This crew won 2 heats, but lost the Final to Hellerup Roklub of Denmark.

In 1949 double entries had been banned in the Thames and the Princess Elizabeth Cup, and in 1950 this restriction was extended to the Ladies'.

1951-1954

The First Eight did not fare well in 1951, losing 2 places in Eights Week and finishing 7th. The following year, with Peter Gladstone President of the Boat Club for his second Eights Week – he had won his second Blue in the winning 1952 Oxford crew – the Eight held on to its position. With all but one member of the crew being available, it was decided to enter for the Ladies' at Henley, the crew being as follows, with Peter Gladstone moving from stroke to 4, and R.A. Plumptre coming in at stroke:

Bow	H.L. Craig
2	A.S. Kwiatkowski
3	C.K. Foster
4	P. Gladstone
5	G.C. Parkhouse
6	R.J.E. Liddiard
7	C.R.C. Owtram
Str	R.A. Plumptre
Cox	A.W.N. Bertie

With 19 entries for the event, the crew was 1 of 6 obliged to compete in an Eliminating heat, and was beaten by Selwyn, Cambridge.

In 1953 the Eight made a bump on the first day of Eights Week, but were later caught by Univ., and so stayed in 7th place. The following year, (in which the number of days' racing was reduced from 6 to 4), Univ. were bumped and the House finished in 6th place. In neither 1953 nor 1954 was a crew entered for Henley.

In 1951 the ban on past winners competing in the Grand and the Stewards' was removed. In 1954 the ban on double entries in the Thames and the Stewards' was removed; the qualification for the Thames was, therefore, the same as for the Grand. Double entries were still prohibited in other events for Eights.

1955

Torpids produced encouraging evidence of a revival of the House's rowing successes. In 6 days of racing the 3 Torpids crews between them made 14 bumps, including 5 by the First Torpid. Indeed, on the last 4 days of Torpids each House crew bumped every day. A '*noisy and rather riotous*' Bump Supper (according to Dundas) – the first since before World War II – degenerated into '*an improper amount of damage*' being done, including the burning of the Choir School's goal posts.

A further bright spot was the selection of Gavin Sorrell, a freshman in the very first term (Hilary Term) in which he matriculated, to stroke the Oxford boat in the 1955 Boat Race. Such selection of a freshman was believed to be unique in Boat Race history.

Nevertheless, the Eight was bumped by Queen's on the last day of Eights Week. Confidence was, however, high enough for a visit to Henley to be considered worthwhile, and, with one change being made, the following crew was entered for the Ladies':

		st.lb.
Bow	J.M. Grierson	11. 4
2	C.L. Ionides	11. 8
3	H.N. Cannon	11. 1
4	J.H.M. Edwards	11. 13
5	P.F. Barnard	14. 4
6	T.W. Meade	12. 8
7	G. Sorrell	12. 0
Str	J.N.F. Turner	11. 2
Cox	D.G. Crowley	8. 12

The first heat, on the first day, was against Pembroke, Cambridge. The House led by ½ a length at the Barrier, and ¾ of a length at Fawley, and went on to win by 2 lengths. The next day's heat was against First and Third Trinity, the holders, who had beaten Christ's, Cambridge the previous day. Unfortunately, First and Third had the misfortune to have a member of their crew become unfit, such that they were obliged to withdraw. As *The Times* reported on Friday, 1 July:

> *In the Ladies' Plate the greatest sympathy was felt for First and Third Trinity. On the way down to the start their bow, A.M.D. Lee, hurt his back and collapsed. Under the Henley rules, the committee could not permit the substitution of a spare man, and so First and Third Trinity lost an excellent chance of winning the Ladies'. Incidentally this is a rule which has practically nothing to recommend it. No one would ever use a substitute save as a last resort, and the rule, as it stands, encourages the rowing of men who are not fit to row.*

This unfortunate occurrence enabled the House to move on to the semi-final, against Queens', Cambridge, who had beaten Balliol and Eton. Queens' led throughout, being 2 lengths ahead at Fawley and 4 lengths at the Mile, and winning easily. In the Final Queens' beat Lady Margaret by 1½ lengths.

Reaching the semi-final of the Ladies' represented the House's best result at Henley since winning the Goblets in 1932. The success betokened greater things to come, and this indeed turned out to be the case.

1956

The House gained 3 places in Eights Week, rising to 4th on the River. J.H.M. Edwards, who had rowed in the Eight the previous year, and was spare man for the 1956 Oxford crew, was joined by his brother David (D.C.R. Edwards). They were the sons of the legendary Jumbo Edwards. David was to be President of the Boat Club from Eights Week 1958 to Torpids 1959.

With Sorrell coming in at stroke for C.J. Bell, the Henley Eight, again entered for the Ladies', was as follows:

		st. lb.
Bow	J.M. Grierson	11. 7
2	F.H.F. Schofield	11. 1
3	S.G. Sandford	11. 3
4	H.C. Wraith	12. 9
5	P.F. Barnard	14. 2
6	D.C.R. Edwards	12. 4
7	J.H.M. Edwards	12. 1
Str	G. Sorrell	12. 3
Cox	D.G. Crowley	9. 2

Four of the crew also made up a Four entered for the Visitors', namely:

Bow	J.H.M. Edwards *(steers)*
2	D.C.R. Edwards
3	P.F. Barnard
Str	G. Sorrell

On the first day the Four beat Jesus, Oxford, by 4 lengths in the Visitors', and the Eight beat B.N.C. easily in the Ladies', being 3 lengths up at the Mile. The next day they met Clare, Cambridge, in the Ladies', while the Four were drawn against Merton

The race against Clare produced an unusual result. As *The Times* (Friday, 6 July) reported:

> *. . . there had been great excitement in the Ladies' Plate, when Clare, after being led by three-quarters of a length at Remenham Club, came up to force a dead heat with Christ Church, the second in two days' racing at Henley.*
>
> (The previous day the Royal Air Force and London R.C. had dead-heated in the Wyfolds.)

A re-row was necessary; this took place 4 hours later. This was

> *. . . another close race. They were level at the Barrier. Then Christ Church led by a few feet a Fawley and by a canvas at the Mile. Both finished at 37,*

and Clare led by a canvas at the 1½ mile and won a fine race by ½ length.
(*Henley Royal Regatta 1939-1968; Volume I, 1939-1958.*
Compiled by H.B. Playford).

Two and a half hours later the Four was on the water to face Merton, who had not previously raced. Merton went steadily ahead, and led by 2½ lengths at Fawley. Their final margin of victory was the same.

Outside Eights Week and Henley, the year 1956 brought success to Christ Church men. Bell and D.C.R. Edwards lost the Final of the Rowe Double Sculls (won in record time), while J.H.M. Edwards reached the final of the Silver Challenge Sculls. The Edwards brothers won the Coxless Pairs in the National Championships held at Nottingham. (The trophy was a half-size copy of the Grand Challenge Cup). Sorrell, partnered by R. Barrett, Pembroke, won the OUBC Pairs, beating Barnard and M.S. Murray-Threipland. The latter had rowed in the Eight in 1955, had been President of the Boat Club for Michaelmas Term 1954 and Hilary Term 1955, and who was the son of P.W., the Oxford Blue and Christ Church oarsman of the 1920s. In the OUBC Fours the House won both the First and Second Divisions – the first college ever to do so. A member of the Second Four (along with Sorrell, C.J .Bell, and T.W. Meade) was W. Rathbone, the son of Nono, the great House and Oxford oarsman and coach.

1957

For the first time since the end of the War, the House won 2 seats in the Blue Boat. Sorrell, now President of the OUBC rowed at bow, and Barnard at 5. D.C.R. Edwards stroked Isis in the Putney Head of the River race, where Goldie were beaten into second place.

In Eights Week the First Eight bumped Balliol on the third day, to go 3rd on the River, its highest position since the end of the War. Sorrell, partnered by T.A.G. Raikes of Trinity, won the Double Sculls, beating Bell, partnered by R.W. Snow of Magdalen, in the Final. Sorrell also won the Silver Sculls.

It was decided to go to Henley in force. The Eight (with D.O. Lloyd-Jacob replacing Meade) entered for the Ladies', while 2 Fours were entered, a First Four in the Visitors', and a Second Four in the Wyfolds.

The crews were as follows:

LADIES'

		st. lb.
Bow	D.O. Lloyd-Jacob	12. 4
2	J.T. Lewis	12. 8
3	W. Rathbone	13. 4
4	G. Sorrell	11. 9
5	P.F. Barnard	14. 1
6	F.D.M. Badcock	12. 11
7	J.H.M. Edwards	11. 10
Str	D.C.R. Edwards	12. 7
Cox	P.H.D. Wetton	9. 7

VISITORS'

		st. lb.
Bow	J.H.M. Edwards	11.10
2	G. Sorrell	11.9
3	P.F. Barnard	14.1
Str	D.C.R. Edwards	12.7

WYFOLDS

Bow	S.T. Olivier
2	J.T. Lewis
3	W. Rathbone *(steers)*
Str	F.D.M. Badcock

The Wyfolds Four failed to win their Eliminating race, but the other crews had significant successes. On the morning of the first day the Eight met Eton. *The Times* (3 July, 1957) gave this guarded advance assessment of the possible outcome:

> *No doubt the race of greatest popular interest this morning will be that between Christ Church and Eton. In a year when the general standard of school rowing does not seem to be quite as high as recently, Eton have returned to the Ladies' Plate and there are those who think that they may do well. But it is important for a school crew to make a good start, and, if the following wind holds, Christ Church could be dangerous.*

In the event, the House gained a victory in what was, to *The Times* correspondent in his next day's report, an unexpected result:

Then came the surprise of the morning, when Christ Church rowed Eton down at the Mile. Eton led by nearly three quarters of a length at the Barrier, but Christ Church put in a great effort, and gradually closed up. At the Mile the crews were level, but in the row-in Eton dropped instead of raising their rating, and Christ Church drew away to win by one and a half lengths in 6min, 55 sec.

Christ Church (Bucks Station) near the finish of the Final of the Ladies', 1957.
This photograph, the gift of Bill Rathbone, hangs in the Christ Church Buttery.

In the early evening of the same day the Visitors' crew took on First and Third Trinity. The crews were level at the ¼ mile, but the House then gradually went ahead, building up to a lead of 1½ lengths at the finish. *The Times* noted that

. . . this Christ Church win meant that P.F. Barnard, who faltered and apparently blacked out in the Boat Race this year, had won two close races during the day, in exceptionally gruelling conditions – proof, if any were needed, that his Boat Race misfortune was not due to any lack of racing spirit.

The following morning the Eight took on Magdalene, Cambridge who had won their first heat against SEH. This was an extremely tough race, described thus in *Henley Royal Regatta 1939-1968*:

> *Magdalene led by a canvas at the top of the Island and held that to the Barrier. Christ Church drew up level at the ½ mile, but Magdalene led again, by a canvas at Fawley and by ¼ length at the ¾ mile. Christ Church led by a canvas at the Mile and by ½ length at the 1½ mile and then gained fast.*

The Times confirmed that the race was, indeed, hard:

> *. . . Christ Church had a hard and exciting race to beat Magdalene after being half a length down at Remenham and level at the Mile.*
>
> (Friday, 5 July.)

The Four's race was in the evening, when they took on Clare, Cambridge, for whom it was their first race in the event this year. The House led by ½ a length at Fawley, and by 1 length at the ¾ mile, but at the Mile this lead was halved. Nevertheless, the crew persisted and won by 1¼ lengths to be, with Queen's, the only Oxford crew in the final 4.

The Christ Church opponent in the Ladies' semi-final on the third day was Emmanuel, Cambridge. Once again the race was hard fought:

> *They were level at the ¼ mile. Emmanuel were just ahead at the Barrier. They were level at Fawley, but Emmanuel led by ¼ length at the ¾ mile. They were level again at the Mile. Christ Church led by a canvas at the 1-⅛ mile and kept ahead to win the race.*
>
> (*Henley Royal Regatta 1939-1968*)

The Four again needed to race before the day was over.

> *By the evening Christ Church, who had already raced five times in three days produced another thrilling finish in the Visitors' Cup to hold off Magdalene, Cambridge by a quarter of a length after leading by three-quarters of a length at Fawley and losing the lead at the bottom of the Enclosures.* (*The Times,* 6 July, 1957)

The House had thus earned the right to race in 2 Finals on the last day of the Regatta, both against Pembroke, Cambridge, in the Ladies' and the Visitors'. The stern four of the Pembroke Eight made up their Four.

In the Final of the Ladies'

> *Pembroke gained fast from the start and led by a length at the ¼ mile and by 1¼ lengths at the Barrier. They held this lead until past the Mile. Then Christ Church made repeated spurts but could only close the gap a little.*
>
> (*Henley Royal Regatta 1939–1968*)

In the Final of the Visitors' the House led at the start, but Pembroke were ahead by ½ a length at the Barrier and ¾ of a length at Fawley. The House made up a little of the distance but Pembroke's lead was the same at the Mile, after which they pulled ahead to win by 2 lengths. *The Times* (Monday, 8 July) gave this graceful acknowledgement of the Christ Church crew's determination:

> *As was almost inevitable, Pembroke College, Cambridge, were too strong for Christ Church, and achieved the coveted Ladies' Plate and Visitors' Cup double at their expense. In the Ladies' Plate Christ Church rowed most*

Christ Church (Berks station) in the Final of the Visitors', 1957. Henley Royal Regatta

> *gallantly, but Pembroke, greatly improved since Marlow, were clear at the Barrier, and were never again overlapped. If possible Christ Church raced even more desperately in the Visitors', reducing Pembroke's lead from a length to half-a length after Fawley. But Pembroke, rowing smoothly and powerfully, were never in serious danger.*

Here it is perhaps permissible to mention Cambridge's complete domination of the Ladies' in the 1950s. Between 1951 and 1959 8 Cambridge colleges secured 9 wins in the event. In the Visitors' Cambridge won 6 times to Oxford's 3.

The year ended with the House once again winning both Divisions of the OUBC Fours; the First Four '*romped home*' according to the *Cherwell* report. Both these crews, as was the case with so many House crews – not to mention the 1973-1978 Blue Boats – were coached by George Harris.

1958

This was the year in which the House achieved its greatest success on the Isis in 31 years. In Eights Week the First Eight bumped Merton on the first day, and Queen's on the second, to finish Head of the River for the first time since 1927. The crew included 2 first-time Blues, D.C.R. Edwards at stroke, and F.D.M. Badcock at 5. (Sorrell had also made his third Boat Race appearance at bow, but was not a member of the Eight). Five of the crew, and the cox, had been in the Henley Eight the previous year. The crew was:

		st.lb.
Bow	M. Aikin-Sneath	12. 7
2	L.L. Farrar	12. 8
3	W. Rathbone	12. 13
4	S.G. Sandford	11. 11
5	F.D.M. Badcock	13. 0
6	D.C.R. Edwards	12. 8
7	D.O. Lloyd-Jacob	12. 6
Str	J.R.H. Lander	11. 10
Cox	P.H.D. Wetton	9. 7

The scene on the Isis for the final race of Eights Week was admirably caught by the correspondent of the *Oxford Mail:*

> *Relaxed, determined and justly confident, a powerful Christ Church crew had little difficulty in rowing over in the Head of the River position when the Oxford University Summer Eights drew to a successful conclusion on Saturday.*
>
> *Christ Church were off to a fine start and they maintained their distance over the whole course. Once out of the Gut they were never in danger and were able to watch the following crew, Queen's fighting grimly to stave off the persistent challenge of Merton.*
>
> *The showers early in the afternoon had no effect on the crowds which, if anything, were larger than ever for the lower divisions.*
>
> *By the time the Division I race was due many thousands lined the towpath, four and five deep in places, while barges and boathouses were filled almost to overflowing.*
>
> *It made a colourful and exciting climax to the four days' racing, with one of the largest crowds in front of the Oxford University Boat Club and opposite the Christ Church boathouse.*
>
> *The House were given a great cheer as they moved off to the start and they certainly justified the confidence in them as they went through most impressively to their 24th Head of the River title since the races started in 1815, but their first success since 1927.*
>
> *TWO BLUES*
>
> *Two Blues were included in their crew, which was: M. Aiken-Smith* [sic] *(bow), L. L. Farrar, W. Rathbone, S. G. Sandford, F. D. M. Badcock, D.C.R. Edwards, D. O. Lloyd-Jacobs* [sic] *J. R. H. Lander (stroke), P. H. D. Wetton (cox).*
>
> *As they rowed back to their delighted boathouse, their success was acknowledged from both sides of the towpath and from every barge and boathouse.*
>
> *Pistol shots acknowledged them as they took in their boat and everyone waited expectantly for the traditional "ducking of the cox" ceremony. Wetton, who had steered Christ Church for two years, made a glorious struggle for survival, but in the end weight of numbers sent him plunging into the water.*

The crew's success was a source of special pride to the families of 4 of its members, for the fathers of each came to Oxford on the same day to watch their sons row. David Edwards (President of the Boat Club) was Jumbo's son, Bill Rathbone the son of Nono, and F.D.M. Badcock the son of J.C. Badcock;

Four fathers and four sons, Eights Week, 1958. From the left, HN.H. Lander, JR.H Lander, Jumbo Edwards, David Edwards, F.D.M Badcock, JC. Badcock, Bill Rathbone, Nono Rathbone. Oxford Mail

the exploits of these senior men from the 1920s and early 1930s have been highlighted in commentaries on the various Henley Regatta years in which they were involved. In addition H.N.H. Lander, the father of J.R.H., had rowed in the First Trinity Ladies' "A" crew in 1930, and had stroked the college's "A" crew in 1931 as well as the "A" Four in the Visitors' that year.

Bill Rathbone's 1958 Head of the River medal. Bill Rathbone

Not surprisingly, the decision to enter the Eights crew (unchanged) for the Ladies' at Henley was easily taken.

The first heat was against St. John's, Oxford, which the House won by 1 length. The second was against Lady Margaret, Cambridge. LMBC led by a canvas at the Barrier and by a little more at Fawley, but the House drew level, led by a ½ length at the Mile, and won by the same distance. *The Times* pointed out, the day before the race (3 July), that

> *Christ Church are handicapped by examinations, which seem to have limited their progress.*

However, its report of the race struck a more positive note:

> . . . *Christ Church rowed well up to their form, and though they were led by half a length, they rowed boldly past Lady Margaret at Remenham and won by half a length.*

Christ Church was now the only Oxford college left in the event, the other 3 survivors being Pembroke, Jesus, and Emmanuel, all of Cambridge. The House next faced Pembroke.

Once again the race was neck and neck. The House led by ¼ of a length at the end of the Island and ⅓ of a length at Fawley. The lead was increased to ½ a length at the Mile, and this was maintained to the finish line. In the other semi-final Jesus comfortably beat Emmanuel. The Final was a cliff-hanger.

> *Christ Church started at 40, and did not drop below 34 and rowed 36 after the Mile. Jesus started at 38½, continued at 35 and rowed 36 from the Mile, finishing at 38. Christ Church led by ½ length at the ¼ mile, by ¾ length at the ½ mile, and by ½ length at the ¾ mile. They still had 6 feet at the Mile, but Jesus passed them and led by 6 feet at the 1⅛ mile.*
>
> (*Henley Royal Regatta 1939–1968*)

Jesus crossed the line ¼ of a length ahead. Their time of 6 min. 51 sec. was the fastest of the 15 races constituting the Ladies' event.

The Times (Monday, 7 July) honoured the Christ Church crew with the finest accolade possible:

> *To Jesus one can pay no higher compliment than to say that Christ Church's performance in the Ladies' Plate was the greatest triumph for Oxford rowing since 1949.*

Its report on the race continued:

> *Christ Church raced from the start to lead by half a length at the first signal, and by nearly three-quarters of a length at the barrier, reached in 1 min. 58 sec., two seconds outside the record. Then inch by inch, Jesus began to pull them back. At Fawley, Christ Church still led by a quarter of a length, at the three-quarter-mile post by a canvas, and at the mile post by three feet. In a storming finish Jesus came home with a quarter of a length to spare. Christ Church would wish no excuses, but one hopes that D.C.R. Edwards can add the Oxford examiners to the list of those he defeated last week.*

Christ Church (Berks station) near the finish of the Final of the Ladies', 1958.
This photograph, the gift of Bill Rathbone, hangs in the Christ Church Buttery.

Another former Christ Church oarsman also made an appearance at this year's Henley. J.H.M. Edwards, now following his father in a career with the Royal Air Force, stroked a Four representing RAF Medmenham in the Wyfolds; the crew succumbed to London R.C. in its first heat.

During the year the First Eight won the Grand Challenge Cup at Reading Amateur Regatta, and the Edwards brothers, representing Wales, were fourth in the Pairs at the Empire Games, and third, at bow and stroke, in the Coxless Fours. Lloyd-Jacob and Aikin-Sneath won the OUBC Junior Pairs. The First Four won the OUBC Fours (First Division) for the third year running and the Second Four lost its Final by only 4 seconds.

1959

After the excitement of the previous year, 1959 proved to be something of an anti-climax, thought D.C.R. Edwards was 6, and J.R.H Lander stroke, of the Blue Boat which defeated Cambridge by 6 lengths, Oxford's first victory for 5 years, and its biggest win since 1912.

In Eights Week the First Eight held on to the Headship for 3 days, but were caught by SEH on the final day.

The Eight was entered for the Ladies' Plate at Henley, and a Four for the Visitors'. Lander was chosen to stroke Isis in the Grand. The crews were:

LADIES'

		st. lb.
Bow	J.C.W. Mitchell	12. 5
2	S.T. Olivier	10. 10
3	S.G. Sandford	11. 9
4	N.G. Mills	13. 0
5	F.D.M. Badcock	12. 9
6	M. Aikin-Sneath	12. 12
7	D.O. Lloyd-Jacob	12. 11
Str	D.C.R. Edwards	12. 9
Cox	R.A. Chanter	9. 4

VISITORS'

		st. lb.
Bow	J.C.W. Mitchell	12. 5
2	M. Aikin-Sneath	12. 12
3	S.G. Sandford	11. 9
Str	D.C.R. Edwards *(steers)*	12. 9

The Edwards brothers entered for the Goblets.

In the Ladies' the House's opponents on the first day were First and Third Trinity.

> *Christ Church led almost to the mile, though never by more than half a length. A fine spurt put 1st and 3rd Trinity on terms, and they came away up the enclosures to win by half a length.*
>
> (*The Times*, Thursday, 2 July, 1959.)

In the Visitors' the crew first comfortably beat Trinity Hall, leading by 1½ lengths at Fawley and winning by 3½ lengths. They next met New College, whom they beat even more comfortably by 4 lengths. In the semi-final their opponents were Pembroke, Cambridge. Pembroke drew ahead, led by 2 lengths at Fawley, and won by 3½ lengths. Pembroke finished by winning the Final against Lady Margaret.

J.H.M. and D.C.R. Edwards won their first race in the Goblets, beating a pair from Stratford-upon-Avon Boat Club narrowly by ½ a length. They next met Beresford and Porter of London R.C. who, leading by ⅔ of a length at the ¼ mile, increased this lead to 3 lengths at the ¾ mile, and won easily. They themselves were beaten in the Final.

In the Grand Isis met Harvard on the second day, Harvard having beaten London on the first. Isis led up to the ¾ mile point, and then Harvard drew ahead and won by ½ a length. They then beat Thames in the Final. D.C.R. Edwards joined the Isis crew for Senior Eights at the Serpentine Regatta, from which they went on to win their event at the All Kansai Regatta in Japan. David Edwards' reflections on his experiences in Christ Church crews at Henley in the 1950s appear at the end of this section.

Christ Church's several successes in getting to Henley Finals in the 1950s needs, to do the crews justice, to be viewed against the overwhelming dominance of Cambridge rowing in the decade. Cambridge won 7 Boat Races to Oxford's 3, and, as mentioned, Cambridge colleges completely dominated the Ladies' and the Visitors' during the decade.

THE HOUSE AT HENLEY IN THE FIFTIES

A Recollection by DAVID EDWARDS

I went up to Christ Church in 1955; my brother John had gone up in 1953 so I had already had the opportunity to get to know several oarsmen. Christ Church had had some lean years in the early fifties but were very definitely on the way up and so I was lucky to be in at the start of some successful years.

In those days, the House (like other colleges and clubs) would take a house at Henley and spend two weeks practising there before the regatta week. This gave the opportunity to work up after eights week, exams, and end of term parties. Christ Church had been staying at the Vicarage in Wargrave – a large Victorian building with a large garden and lots of rooms – so the eight plus spare men and the coach could easily stay with the vicar there as well and his family without noticeably clashing. Christ Church would send a lorry with beds, mattresses and bedding; and recover them after the regatta was over.

In 1956, my first year rowing at Henley, Peter Barnard, the president, had decided that the cost and disruption of eating the evening meal at Henley or in a pub at Wargrave was not conducive to success. He therefore invited the popular girl friend of one of the then current Blue Boat to do the cooking for us at the Vicarage. She had said 'Yes', perhaps jokingly, that she couldn't actually cook and certainly wouldn't be able to cook solid and substantial meals for 10 hungry men three times a day. Crisis!

Peter knew our family from Blue Boat coaching, and rang my mother (christened Michael for some reason and known universally in the rowing world as Mike) to ask if she knew of anyone who would be able to cook for us. She said 'I'll do it', and her offer was gratefully accepted. We were in time to get Christ Church to send over with the beds a load of saucepans and cooking utensils from the kitchens. These were the sort that nowadays would be displayed in an 'olde worlde' kitchen reconstruction in a National Trust grand house; huge copper pans, enomously heavy and not easy to pick up at all unless you were a weight lifter. And so began an era of excellent home cooked fare for the Henley period.

In those days Wargrave High Street had two general grocery stores, a butcher, a fishmonger, and greengrocer, so it was easy to get all the needed provisions delivered to the Vicarage. The main problem experienced by Mike was that when she turned on the electric cooker to get things warm for cooking breakfast, the vicar would creep in and turn it off to save electricity which was included in the 'all in' price charged for our stay.

We would have two or maybe three outings a day. This was usually two in the eight but normally also a coxless four from the eight was entered for the Visitors. The eight would be entered for the Ladies Plate. The spare men would run, scull, or row in a pair, and usually enter for the 'spare mens pairs' which was a semi-official race just before the regatta itself.

A great deal of posturing and one-upmanship was practised. One might pick up another crew as they paddled or rowed past and try to match their speed or cover; and would often try starts or short pieces of rowing by agreement. One of our tricks when a crew agreed to row a start and said: 'Shall we go ten strokes?' was to say: Oh let's do quarter of a minute at least'. There was also much spying on the opposition to know what times they were doing to the Barrier, Fawley, or over the whole course. Equally, we would take steps to try and escape from scrutiny ourselves when doing a full course trial.

When Jumbo was coaching and we had done a timed piece of rowing he would then drop a cigarette packet into the water, time its progress the length of a boom, get out his slide rule and calculate the speed of the current and then work out our speed (or that of the opposition) in feet per second and record it carefully on a Senior Service cigarette packet. The make was significant; Senior Service had a British sailor's head on the packet which was otherwise mainly white so leaving plenty of room for writing detailed comparisons of speeds. Years later, clearing up his records after his death, I came across various little piles of cigarette packets unfolded and kept within the pages of note books or rowing recordings and notes of various crews.

Another method of getting one up, when the draw had been made and one knew ones future opponents, was to invite them to dinner. This would be carefully structured to establish one's superiority in every way. We would dress in Henley evening rig of Christ Church blazer, black bow tie (or Leander if members) and white flannels. The table would be laid with silver candlesticks and such silverware as we had won during the year. I can remember the OUBC IVs Cup and Pazolt Cup (which were both a Christ Church preserve for most of my time at the House), together with the Reading and Marlow Regatta eights Challenge Cups on the table one year. The invited crew (who probably had to fight in the scrum of a pub somewhere in the Henley area) would be given an excellent dinner on plates with the Christ Church crest. The whole thing was planned to give them a sense of inferiority.

After another year at the Vicarage, there was a change of vicar; The Reverend Llewellyn Jones who was a rowing man himself, and used to coach Radley. We expected that he, too, would be happy to have a crew for Henley, but to our dismay and at rather short notice he said no. I was then President, and left with a frantic search for a new place. We liked and knew Wargrave and fortunately managed to find Orchard House was vacant, in the High Street, with the Jackson family. This was a surprisingly spacious house with a good size garden and a very amiable family. We stayed at Orchard House for several years, until the Jacksons sold and moved to Crazies Hill just above Wargrave.

Christ Church moved with them! Long friendships were established through our stays at Wargrave; the author married a Wargrave girl and has had somewhere to stay for Henley ever since!

One of the perennial problems of living in a neighbouring village was that of car parking at Henley. As I recall the ration of competitors' car park tickets was one for the crew and one for the coach. We were able to solve the problern because the daughter of our house took a temporary job every year in the Regatta Secretary's office. We were usually able to cadge a couple of extra parking tickets from her.

Another feature of Henley in those days was the funfair, which operated throughout Henley week on part of Lion Meadow which has now become car parks and additional enclosures. It was a traditional funfair with bumper cars, helter skelter, roundabouts and shooting galleries. It was always popular once one was no longer competing and provided opportunities for old rivalries to be renewed on the bumper cars or elsewhere. This perhaps came to a head when a fracas between Eton and Radley boys resulted in a fractured Etonian jaw: It is said that the headmaster of Radley demanded: 'Find the boy responsible – and give him his boxing colours!' Sadly, the funfair along with other relaxations and slightly wild but essentially harmless fun has fallen victim to seriously bad behaviour and has been curtailed or banned.

At that period Henley was a four day regatta, finishing on Saturday, so the Saturday evening was an opportunity for celebration, win or lose, with Sunday to get over the hang-over. There were parties everywhere, but the best was that given by Felix Badcock at Hedsor Wharf, near Cookham. Felix had rowed for Thames Rowing Club in the 30s, very successfully, and had been in the gold medal winning coxless IV at the Los Angeles Olympics in 1932 in which Jumbo Edwards had been substituted at short notice. His younger son, David (or Bonzo as he was always known) came up in 1956 and rowed in the House and OUBC crews. Felix's Henley Saturday party was very relaxed; crews he had coached, Thames Rowing Club almost in its entirety, the House crews and lots of others. Plenty of beer and other refreshments and much talk of rowing, races won and lost, old friends and juicy scandal. In 1961, I was rowing in an OUBC crew, thinly disguised as Leander, and we raced the Soviet National crew, thinly disguised as 'Soviet Navy' in the final of the Grand. Later that evening we managed to spirit away No, 5, Yuri Semenov (we called him Yuri because it seemed Russian and we could not pronounce his real name), from his minders and took him to Fledsor. He deeply impressed everyone by his (typically Russian) ability to demolish enormous quantities of strong liquor, and we took him back roaring drunk at five in the moming to the house near Twyford where the Russian crew were living. The chief Commissar, who had obviously been rehearsing his excuses for his trial for allowing a defection, was extremely relieved to have his charge back safe, if inebriated!

One year we decided to row the boat down to Henley, partly because it was cheaper than sending it on a lorry, but mainly to get back into trim after the break from Eights week. I seem to remember that we did it in one day, with a welcome break for lunch at the pub at Clifton Hampden which was by the riverside, and about halfway. The weather was wonderful and I remember getting a fine tan. The main problem on a trip like that was to avoid getting into a lock with a Salter's Steamer. They were then still steam driven, and would let out a loud whistle when half a mile from a lock to tell the tired lock-keeper to keep the gate open so that they were not delayed too much. Fitting an eight and a Salter's boat into a lock, particularly a deep one, always resulted in much shouting and fending off so the secret was to get far enough ahead that you could get the lock gate closed and the paddles opened before the dread whistle was heard.

They say that rowing builds character; but it also seems to breed characters, or as some might say, eccentrics. There was no shortage of colourful characters to be found at Henley during the late 50s. Jack Beresford was a senior figure in the rowing world then, but his father, 'Old Berry' would also be encountered either sculling or on the towpath. He had rowed in the Goblets in 1908 with a partner with whom he was barely on speaking terms and each was always trying to pull the other round. In the semi-final, it is said that they continued rowing as far as Henley Bridge continuing this personal duel! We would rather mischievously ask him the secret of his longevity. "It's the deep breathing exercises" he would say, "like this." He would then wheeze through a set of exercises until he seemed on the point of collapse.

One of the joys of the rowing world has always been its informality. The most senior and distinguished figures have always been content to be known by Christian name or nickname even by the most junior. Sir Herbert Thompson had had a distinguished career in the Indian Civil Service, but in his retirement devoted his time to coaching any crew who approached him. Known to all as "Tommy", his presence anywhere was signified by his coaching bicycle, of the "sit up and beg" variety, painted in vivid stripes. He explained that it helped him to find his bike in a crowd; and that if it was ever borrowed, someone was sure to recognise it and know where it should be returned.

Henley Sunday was available for hangovers to subside, and for relaxed conversations with old friends and acquaintances. One of the regulars at Leander Club in those days was Roger Bates. He was American, of elderly but indeterminate age, and said to be still working at a doctoral thesis at the Sorbonne whence he would bicycle each summer to Henley. I never discovered his rowing background, but he would converse at length on the merits of the various crews in the premier events. Unfortunately his accent was so broad and convoluted that only a small proportion could be understood, and as the regatta continued and the alcohol built up, it decreased to zero. But we knew that next year he would be back.

Part of the build up to the regatta itself was the Draw, on the previous Sunday in the Town Hall. Being the days before seeding it was always intriguing to know who one would be facing and the venue was always packed. Gully Nickalls, the Chairman of Stewards, would pick the names out of one of the Challenge cups with great ceremony and the draw for the Grand might go something like this: 'Yale versus Cornell' (a revenge match); 'Krasnoe Znamia versus CSFAF France '(both national crews – let them fight it out together in the heats); 'London Rowing Club versus Thames Rowing Club' (traditional enemies): 'Leander Club, a bye'. The hall collapsed in laughter, and the Commissars could never believe that the draw had not been rigged.

Those used to the sight and/or the experience of six or more crews racing abreast might consider that the secret of winning at Henley consists of going over the course in the minimum time. To an extent that is true, but leaves out the very important element of crew morale and confidence once the race is underway; and also the lower degree of strength and fitness typical of even senior crews in the fifties compared with today. So what is different about side by side racing? Put very simply, it is the sense of superiority generated by gaining and holding a lead; and the fact that once a crew has a significant lead, it generates a sense of hopelessness in its opponent which is difficult to overcome.

Let us consider how to set about gaining that edge over the opposition to enable one to win with the least effort. We would get boated in good time, to allow for going well down past the start to turn and have a couple of starts coming back upstream. Then on to the stake boat; but make sure you do so after your opponents, though not so late that the umpire has started bawling you out! You look round at the finish – it seems to be steeply uphill!

The flag drops, and you are off. Felix Badcock, who won many races at Henley, always said that the easiest way to win was 'to be out of sight by the top of the Island, and out of earshot by the Barrier'. If that is the way your start goes, then it is true. If not, the work of stroke and cox really begin. A good cox can give advice on how the opposition are dealing with the race – are they making a short term all out effort to gain a commanding lead? If so, is it time for an earlier than planned spurt to hold them and therefore unsettle them? Alternatively, it may be that you have settled to a good rhythm and stride, with a conservative rating, and the knowledge that you can steadily pull back a half length or even three quarter length lead. Similarly, if the cox can see signs of distress in the opposing crew, it may be the opportunity to put in a big effort to break them.

We operated before the days of 'cox boxes' so the cox's signals to the crew were also audible to the opposition. We would use code words and innocent sounding phrases to disguise our intentions; but it was also an opportunity to mislead the other crew into a reaction at the wrong moment.

There is not very much opportunity for 'clever' steering on the boomed Henley course and anyway we operated by and large before the days of coxes heading inexorably towards each other with an intention to ram. However, wise coxing could mean, for example, a careful course adjustment just before reaching the top of the Island when there was a strong 'bushes' side wind from the Buckingham shore, so that a severe jink and subsequent heavy rudder application could be avoided.

A couple of other thoughts from my experience of rowing at Henley. The best place to stroke an eight from is the number six seat – not in terms of the basic rhythm setting, but as a place where it is most effective to drive an extra effort from. Doubtless there will be a number of successful strokes who will dispute this, but they will also probably admit that without a responsive and alert number six their crew will struggle to win races. The other thought is that the best seat to steer a four at Henley is from stroke. The straight, boomed course will give side guidance, and the ability to keep your stern lined up with the triangular field on the hills above Remenham without anyone's head getting in the way means that you can go from start to finish without having to look round.

1960–1969

1960

IN EIGHTS WEEK THE HOUSE HELD ON TO 2ND PLACE.

An Eight was entered for the Ladies':

		st. lb.
Bow	J.C.Walton	11. 8
2	N.G. Mills	12. 8
3	R.V. Parker	13. 9
4	M. Aikin-Sneath	12. 12
5	J.Y. Scarlett	13. 2
6	S.G. Sandford	11. 13
7	J.C.W. Mitchell	12. 7
Str	J.R.H. Lander	13. 8
Cox	D.R. Harrod	8. 12

R.H. Thomas, 2 in the First Eight, dropped out, and Lander, the 1958 Head of the River Stroke and 1959 Blue, came in at stroke, the rest of the crew being shuffled around.

Christ Church was 1 of 6 Oxford colleges (as opposed to 11 Cambridge colleges) entered for the event. On the first day the House met Christ's, Cambridge, in a heat. The race was close-fought. Christ's led by ¼ of a length at the Barrier, and by ½ a length at the ½ mile, but could gain no more; both crews *'spurted frequently, but Christ's held on to their small lead.' (Henley Royal Regatta 1939-1968, Volume II, 1959-1968.)* Christ's themselves were beaten by Jesus, Cambridge, in their next heat. Jesus lost the Final to Eton. All 4

Oxford colleges which survived to the first heat were then beaten; 2 had lost in the Eliminating races.

1961

The House continued in 2nd place in Eights Week. As might be expected, the decision was made to enter again for the Ladies, and an entry was also registered for the Visitors. D.C.R. Edwards was member, at 6, of the Leander Eight in the Grand. The Christ Church crews were as follows:

LADIES'

		st. lb.
Bow	J.C.Walton	11. 9
2	D.C. Selley	10. 4
3	A.M. Loukes	11. 7
4	A.J. Boyce	11. 4
5	J.Y. Scarlett	13. 0
6	P. Henry	14. 1
7	D. Hankey	11. 8
Str	J.F. Gladstone	12. 6
Cox	D.R. Harrod	8. 8

VISITORS'

		st. lb.
Bow	D. Hankey	11. 8
2	P. Henry	14. 1
3	J.Y. Scarlett *(steers)*	13. 0
Str	J.F. Gladstone	12. 6

The Ladies' crew was the same as the First Eight, save for Boyce replacing A.D.P. Clover. Harrod had coxed the Isis boat (against Cambridge), in which Clover had rowed until forced to withdraw through illness. The Four had won at Marlow Regatta.

The first race in the Ladies' was against Jesus, Cambridge, the 1960 finalists, as noted. The House had a ¼ length lead at the ¼ mile, which increased to ¾ of a length at the ½ mile. Striking a higher rate, Jesus reduced this lead to ½ a length at Fawley, but Christ Church held on, maintained this lead to the Mile, and won by ⅔ of a length. *The Times* (Thursday, 6 July) commented that

> '. . . *Christ Church, though they were always just about safe, had a hard race against Jesus II who were within a third of a length at the mile post.*'

(Jesus I were entered for the Thames, where they lost the final to the University of London.) The following day the House met SEH, still Head of the River in Eights. This was yet another hard-fought battle:

> *They were level to the ¼ mile. St. Edmund Hall led by a canvas at the Barrier and by ⅔ length at Fawley. Christ Church closed the gap to ½ length at the Mile and ⅓ length at the 1½ mile, but St. Edmund Hall drew away again.*
>
> (*Henley Royal Regatta 1939-1968*)

SEH won by ⅔ of a length. They were beaten in their next heat by Eton, who were again finalists.

The Four fared better in the Visitors'. Their first race was against Christ's, Cambridge. Christ's gained an early lead of ½ a length, and still held it at the Mile. But a spurt by the House gained them a lead of ⅔ of a length at 1⅛ miles, and they won by 1⅔ lengths, in the fastest time (7min, 29sec.) recorded for the Visitors' that day.

In their next race their opponents were Pembroke, Cambridge, who had earlier defeated the London Hospital. The House took an early lead, ½ a length at the Barrier and Fawley, but Pembroke reduced this to ⅓ of a length at the Mile. Christ Church opened up the distance to ¾ of a length in the next 200 yards, but Pembroke again attacked, and reduced the House's lead to again ⅓ of a length at the finish.

The House were now in the semi-finals. Here they met St. Catharine's, Cambridge.

> *St Catharine's led by ¼ length at the ¼ mile and by a ½ length from the Barrier to the ¾ mile. Christ Church made good spurts at 36, but St. Catharine's at 32 led by 1¼ lengths at the Mile and by a length at the 1⅛ mile.*
>
> (*Henley Royal Regatta 1939-1968*)

St. Catharine's won by 1¾ lengths, and went on to be beaten in the Final by SEH.

Leander were 1 of 5 entries in the Grand, which included a foreign crew, that of the Central Sport Club of the USSR Navy. Leander beat Molesey in their heat, and then Thames, which put them into the Final against the

Russians, who had beaten London R.C. The USSR Navy led by a canvas at the end of the Island, and gradually increased this to ¾ of a length. They then held off a Leander spurt to win by 1 length. But, as *The Times* stated on Monday, 10 July, *'though Leander did indeed go down, they did so gloriously.'* They were at a disadvantage of 10 pounds a man against a crew which '*had been rowing together, more or less, for as many years as Leander had weeks.'*

1962

This year the House regained the Headship of the River, bumping SEH on the first day. Earlier, Scarlett had won his Blue in the Boat Race. J.F. (Francis) Gladstone was President of the Boat Club 1962-63. Once again, it was decided to enter for the Ladies' and the Visitors', the crews being:

LADIES'

		st. lb.
Bow	D. Hankey	12. 0
2	A.J. Boyce	11. 10
3	A.M. Loukes	11. 13
4	A.J. Saunders	13. 7
5	J.Y. Scarlett	13. 10
6	P. Henry	13 11
7	P.J.H. Arkell	11 10
Str	J.F. Gladstone	12 12
Cox	D.R. Harrod	8 9

VISITORS'

		st. lb.
Bow	D. Hankey	12. 0
2	P. Henry	13. 11
3	J.Y. Scarlett, *(steers)*	13. 10
Str	J.F. Gladstone	12. 12

The First Eight was unchanged for Henley, and the Visitors' crew was the same as in 1961.

In addition, no fewer than 3 Christ Church men were members of the Leander crew in the Grand, namely, J.H.M. Edwards at bow, F.D.M. Badcock at 5 and D.C.R. Edwards at 6.

In the Ladies', the House first took on Eton, gained an early lead, built on it, and won by 1¾ lengths. As *The Times* (5 July) put it:

Christ Church First Eight and Henley Eight, 1958. Head of the River; semi-finalists in the Ladies'. George Harris is seated on the left. Will Watson

---

> *Nor was there any doubt about the result between Eton and Christ Church. Christ Church led by half a length at the first signal and continued to gain all the way, in sprit of spirited but rather ragged spurts by Eton.*

The next crew met was Pembroke, Cambridge, the House's opponents from the previous year. This was to be no close race, though. While striking a slower rate, Christ Church established a length's lead at Fawley, increased this to 1½ lengths at the Mile and won by 2½ lengths.

This put the House into the semi-finals, the only Oxford crew remaining, along with 3 Cambridge college boats. The opponents now were First and Third, Trinity:

> *Christ Church led by ½ length at the ¼ mile and by ¼ length at the Barrier. The crews were level at Fawley, but Christ Church led by ¼ length at the ¾ mile. First and Third Trinity then put in good spurts and led by ¼ length at the Mile. They gained fast after the 1½ mile and won a good race by ¾ length.*
>
> (*Henley Royal Regatta 1939–1968*)

The Times called this '*a hard race.*' First and Third Trinity were beaten in the Final by Queens', Cambridge.

In the Visitors' the Four again met First and Third, whose crew also consisted of men from their Ladies' boat. The House took a small early lead, and saw it reduced to ¼ of a length at Fawley, but they were 1 length up at the Mile, winning by a comfortable 1¾ lengths. St. Catharine's, Cambridge, opponents from the year before, were the next obstacle.

> *St. Catharine's hit the buoys and went off course in the first half minute, and Christ Church led by 1½ lengths at the ¼ mile. Christ Church although at a low rate of striking, were 3 lengths ahead at the ¾ mile and won by over 5 lengths.*

Buoys, instead of piles and booms, marked the course for the first quarter mile.

Now, in the semi-finals, there were 2 Oxford Colleges left, Christ Church and Keble, plus Chelsea College and Imperial College from London; 8 Cambridge colleges had fallen by the wayside during the heats. Keble and Christ Church raced each other. Keble were ⅓ of a length up at the ¼ mile, and ½ a length or so at the Mile. They won by 1 length. In the Final Keble lost to Chelsea College.

There were 4 foreign entries, out of 9, in the Grand. Leander met Molesey in the second heat.

> *Molesey were taking no chances on a repetition of their experience last year when they let Leander slip them at the start, never to recover. Leander, at 39 to Molesey's 41, gained a canvas in the first quarter-mile but as soon as Leander dropped to 36 Molesey, still striking 41, were able to hold them. The barrier time of 1 min. 51 sec. equalled the record. Near Remenham Club Molesey drew level then opened a lead of three-quarters of a length, never dropping below 41.*
>
> (*The Times,* Friday 6 July, 1962).

It was, however, Leander who had equalled the Barrier record. The USSR Navy crew again entered, and beat Molesey in the next round. They then met Canottieri Moto Guzzi (who had beaten London R.C. and the University of Pennsylvania) in the Final; the Russians prevailed, by the slender margin of ⅓ of a length. The Russians' time to the Barrier, 1 min. 9 sec., set a new course record.

Only very rarely indeed, does the smooth running of Henley Regatta get ruffled, but this year an unhappy incident occurred which provoked something more than a ruffling, and which is worth noting. It arose in the semi-final of the Diamonds, when a Pole, Kubiak, met S.A. Mackenzie, who had won the event for each of the previous 5 years. Let *The Times* (7 July, 1962) give its version:

> *Mackenzie led by a length at the barrier and by the same distance at the half-mile, where he was warned for straying into Kubiak's water. He still led by a length at Fawley, again well over on the Pole's side of the course. He was, in fact, warned at least three times during this unhappy race.*
>
> *Above Fawley Kubiak began a series of spurts which gradually pulled Mackenzie back until at the mile Kubiak led by 3ft. Then Mackenzie seemed to slow down, or perhaps falter. but as soon as the Pole had drawn ahead he spurted after him. The umpire then warned Kubiak for infringing Mackenzie's water, but before the Pole could give way Mackenzie's left scull hit, or at least went into, the puddle made by Kublak's right scull and Mackenzie caught a crab. The scullers went on to the finish, Kubiak now several lengths ahead, where Mackenzie claimed a foul and was awarded the race.*
>
> *In an incident such as this there is roorn for many varying opinions. One may think that the scullers were in neutral water, in the centre of the course, or that the clash was caused by Mackenzie's own bad steering, and even that the umpire might have been justified in taking no action.*
>
> *In short, one may think that justice demanded that if there was any disqualifying to be done Mackenzie rather that Kubiak was to blame. But in the final analysis the umpire is the sole judge of a boat's proper course, and there is no appeal from his decision. This is not a matter of opinion but is clearly stated in the rules of Henley, of the A.R.A., and of the International Federation. Every oarsman knows it.*

Much sympathy lay with Kubiak, especially as, as recounted by Burnell,

> *Passing the press box the Australian called out 'If you can't beat them, fool them', thus clearly proclaiming that he had deliberately engineered the foul.*
>
> (*Henley Royal Regatta. A Celebration . . .*)

But the goodwill evaporated when the Polish team manager withdrew his pair from the Goblets in protest:

> *. . . the decision of disqualifying Kubiak has made us change our opinion about the fairness of the British umpires.*
>
> (*The Times,* Saturday, 7 July).

Mackenzie went on to secure his sixth successive win.

1963

In Eights Week Keble pulled off a bump on the last day which gave them Headship of the River, and put the House into 2nd place. A new arrival on the House (and Oxford) rowing scene this academic year was the American, D.C. Spencer, from Yale University. Duncan Spencer was made stroke of the 1963 Oxford Boat Race crew, which won by 5 lengths. *'He was'*, as the 1963 Christ Church Report stated, *'the hero of the Boat Race'. OUBC News Summary No. 16* spoke of him as *'outstanding for his coolness and power'.*

Duncan stroked Oxford again the next year, without success, but in 1965 he rowed for the third time in the Blue Boat, at 7, and won again. He was elected Secretary of the OUBC in 1963, and was President of the Christ Church Boat Club in 1964.

In 1963 he stroked the First Eight. With E.M.W. Robson coming into the crew for P. Henry, and with some seating adjustments, an Eight was entered for the Ladies':

		st. lb.
Bow	P.J.H. Arkell	10. 4
2	W.M. Watson	12. 8
3	J.D. Orme	12. 6
4	E.M.W. Robson	11. 4
5	A.J. Saunders	13. 3
6	J.F. Gladstone	12. 11
7	C.E. Garton	13. 2
Str	D.C. Spencer	12. 6
Cox	C.E.M. Tucker	9. 3

The crew was drawn against Jesus, Cambridge, who led at the ¼ mile by ¾ of a length, at the ¾ mile by 1½ lengths, and won by 1 ⅓ lengths. *The Times* commented (Thursday 4 July) that:

> *Jesus led Christ Church all the way, but could never really get away from them, and while they must be expected to beat Sandhurst, it is by no means a foregone conclusion.*

The Times' caution was well judged. Jesus lost to Sandhurst, who went on to beat SEH in the Final.

1964

One bump being suffered in Eights Week, at the hands of SEH, who went Head, the House ended 3rd on the River. It was planned to send a Four to Henley, but, because of illness, this did not happen. Christ Church men were, however, busily engaged in the Regatta proceedings. Spencer and D.C.R. Edwards were members of the Leander crew in the Grand, at 3 and 6. Edwards stroked the Leander Stewards' Four, and Spencer the club's Wyfolds entry.

In the Grand, Leander, one of 5 domestic entries in a field of 7, met Thames R.C.. Leander were 1¼ lengths ahead at Fawley, and ¾ of a length at the Mile. But Thames, increasing their rate to 42, began to close the gap and, still ¼ of a length behind at the 1⅛ miles mark, forced their way past to win by ⅔ of a length. The Final was won by Club Zgalghiris Viljnjus, USSR, who set new records at the Barrier and at Fawley.

In the Stewards' Edwards' crew first defeated Molesey (who had comfortably beaten Thames) and met Tideway Scullers School in the Final. The latter built a lead of a few feet at the ¼ mile into a 3 length lead at the Mile, and won easily. Spencer's crew did not fare well in their heat of the Wyfolds, being beaten by Leeds University in a field of 35 entries. Leeds in turn were beaten in their second race by Sons of the Thames Rowing Club, who went on to win the Final.

An article by Duncan Spencer, which originally appeared in *Crew Composition and Racing Results 1946-1993*, is included at the end of this section. It describes his experience of rowing at Oxford during his Christ Church years.

This year was the 125th anniversary of the founding of the Regatta. The initial 7 entries of 1834 had grown to 187, involving 88 Eights, 73 Fours and 26 other entries. A total of 119 races took place on the first 2 days. The victorious Harvard 1914 Grand crew made an outing in an eight on the afternoon of the last day. Queen Elizabeth the Queen Mother, and Princess Margaret and the Earl of Snowdon, the winning Cambridge cox of 1950, also attended the last day.

1965

The First Eight, caught by Oriel, lost 1 place in Eights Week. No crew was entered for Henley, but D.C. Spencer was again invited to row for Leander, this time as bow in a coxed Four in the Prince Philip Challenge Cup, inaugurated 2 years earlier. Leander first met Tabor Academy, U.S.A. whom they beat by 4 lengths. Next came Hollingworth Lake Rowing Club, defeated *"easily"*. Leander's third race was against Thames R.C., won by 1¾ lengths in a time (7 min. 16 sec.) which equalled the record set the previous day by Tideway Scullers School, who themselves had beaten a record time set 30 minutes previously by Thames. Leander were now in the Final against Tideway Scullers. The lead changed 3 times to the Mile, but Leander won by ½ a length. Leander's times at the Barrier, Fawley, and the Finish (7 min, 3 sec.) all set new records. (On the final day of the Regatta new records were set in all but 1 of 11 events.)

1966

Eights Week gave the House great cause for celebration, for the First Eight, stroked by G.B. Chichester, Boat Club President, not only bumped Keble on the second day, but SEH on the last day, to end up in 2nd place. An entry was duly made for the Ladies' Plate at Henley. The make-up of the crew is not recorded, but 2 First Eight members, Lovett and Stewart, were invited to join the Isis Eight entered for the Thames Challenge Cup.

Christ Church were obliged to row in an Eliminating race of the Ladies' against Corpus Christi, Cambridge. They lost. Cambridge crews again dominated the event. Oriel, the only other Oxford college which entered, lost their first heat. The semi-finalists were all Cambridge colleges, Lady Margaret winning the Final.

The Isis crew fared much better. With Lovett at 2, and Stewart at 4 (and with Dan Topolski of New College at bow) they met Kingston R.C. in their first heat, and won easily. They then met Quintin. Rowing at 38 or more all the way, Isis had a lead of ⅓ of a length at the ¼ mile, managed to hold on to it, and won by ½ a length. This put them into the semi-finals, where their opponents were Nautilus (Midlands) Club, whom Isis defeated by 1⅓ lengths. The Final was against Harvard University. This was a close race, with first Isis and then Harvard in the lead by a margin of no more than a canvas. Harvard then increased their advantage slightly, and won by ¾ of a length.

1967

This was not a good year for the Christ Church Boat Club. The First Eight came badly unstuck, being bumped on each of the first three days by SEH, Keble and Merton. Not surprisingly, a trip to Henley was not contemplated.

1968

One of the places lost in 1967 was regained by a bump on Merton in Eights Week. The House had an unprecedented 6 boats on the river, the Third (Schools) Eight, which included 7 members of the Third (Schools) Torpid (gainers of 11 places) and which had made 2 modest bumps on the first 3 days, gaining 6 places on the last day of racing, including the first double over-bump in 12 years.

Once again, no crew was entered for Henley. (*Henley Records 1939-1968* points out that with no Oxford college, and only 6 Cambridge colleges, competing in the Ladies' out of 20 entries, *'the days of dominance by Oxford and Cambridge Colleges seem to be over.'*) The OUBC, however, had entered crews in the 7 main events of the B.U.S.F. Rowing Championships held at Pagbourne in June, and H. von Harrach and N.J. Wakefield (both members of the House First Eight) had rowed at 5 and 6 in the OUBC's Cherwell B.C. Eight, which came third in the Eights event. This crew was then entered for the Ladies'. It won its first heat against Aberdeen U., and its semi-final race against R.M.A. Sandhurst, to get to the Final against First and Third Trinity.

Due to heavy rain starting on the first day (Wednesday) and affecting the upper reaches of the Thames, the flood-stream current at Henley produced a severe disadvantage for crews on the Bucks Station. By lunch time on Friday

The Times (Saturday 13 July) reported,

> *. . . all the regatta boat rafts were submerged and the downstream raft had been swept off its piles . . . The river level was approximately 15 inches above normal . . . It was clear that in the last quarter mile of* [the] *course the Berkshire station had an advantage of something like two lengths.*

Cherwell had the Berks station in the Ladies' Final. First and Third led (by no more than ½ a length) to the ¾ mile. Cherwell then took the lead, a canvas at the Mile. First and Third led once more at the 1⅛ mile, but *'Cherwell then gained fast and won by a length.' (Henley Records 1939-1968.)* Whether or not Cherwell's station favoured the outcome, win they did, and, from the House's point of view, the 2 Christ Church members had participated in the first Ladies' victory in which the College was represented, since 1920.

As noted earlier, in 1968 a second event for coxed Fours was instituted as the "Henley Prize". The trophy was donated the following year by Nottingham Britannia Rowing Club, and the name of the event changed to The Britannia Challenge Cup. It was restricted to crews from the U.K. and the Republic of Ireland.

1969

The decade of the Sixties ended on an encouraging note for the House. Bumps were made on each of the first 2 days (on Oriel and SEH), thus restoring the Eight to 2nd place on the River. Two Christ Church men, C.R.W. Parish and J.K.G. Dart, were in the Isis boat which lost to Goldie. The House won the First Division of the OUBC Fours. Dart, teamed with a Keble man, won the OUBC Pairs. Five Christ Church men had participated in the Trial Eights race.

An entry was put in for the Ladies'. After surviving an Eliminating race against R.M.A. Sandhurst, the crew met Durham University in their first heat, but lost by 1½ lengths. The crew (in no particular order of seating) was:

M.W. Grove	S.E. Wilmer	J.F. Best
M.H. Ashton	C.A.H.J. Scheybeler	S.L. Griffith
F.C.C. Finch	M.W. Wiseman (cox)	C.W. Parish

Burnell (p.33) offers interesting comments on a new arrangement which took effect this year.

> *The desirability of seeding the draw had often been discussed, and rejected on the grounds that there was no reliable way of picking out the fastest crews. Nevertheless a 'selective draw' system was introduced in 1969. Henley insisted that 'selection' is not the same as 'seeding', but the result is similar. The main difference is that there is no 'rank order' as is usually the case, for example, in a tennis tournament. Often there are no 'selections' at all. But if it is apparent that there are a number of outstanding crews, they will be selected and drawn separately from the rest of the entries, to occupy pre-determined positions in the draw chart.*

It will have been noted that in the 1960s the number of appearances of Christ Church crews declined. For example, a crew was entered for the Ladies' each year from 1960 to 1963, but from 1964 to 1969 the House entered only twice. The same trend can be observed in entries by other Oxford colleges. The number of colleges in the final 16 of the event proper, (after the Eliminating races had taken place), gradually dwindled from 5 in 1959 to 1 in each year 1966 and 1967, and to none in 1968. Cambridge colleges, on the other hand, while entering slightly less frequently as the decade progressed, still had 10 "last 16" entries in 1966, 8 in 1967, and 6 in 1968. While still being limited to student crews, the Ladies' was no longer the preserve of Oxbridge and Eton. R.M.A. Sandhurst, Trinity College, Dublin, and Imperial College, London, were regular competitors during this period, and from the mid-1960s they were joined by crews from English and Scottish universities, and schools such as Hampton and Emanuel, as well as by entries from the U.S. and Holland.

It will be seen that the slowing down in Christ Church representation at Henley was to continue.

Henley Records 1939-1968 has had – to date – to the knowledge of this author, no successor. Therefore, instead of being able to look up, year by year, event by event, and race by race, the performances of the College's crews going back to 1839, from now on it is necessary to search for information where it may be found. Even *The Times*, which of course, continues with its daily reports and lists of results, no longer, as it once did, provides a brief commentary on every race, and journals such as *Bell's Life* have long since ceased publication. From 1969 onwards, therefore, the information given about Christ Church crews, while it is hoped it will continue to be complete and accurate in its essentials, will not – in most cases – have the additional "colour" which it has been possible to provide on a goodly scale heretofore.

RECOLLECTIONS OF A YANK AT OXFORD – 1964

by D.C. SPENCER
former President, Christ Church Boat Club

I succeeded to the Presidency of the Ch.Ch. B.C. in 1964, but my influence on the course of affairs at the Club was minimal, as I had pressing duties as Hon. Sec. of the OUBC that year. Our problems, on the two Clubs, were the same however – damage control.

Christ Church was hotly threatened in its place as second in Division I. At the OUBC, an upset win in 1963 had produced those most dangerous of all conditions for Oxford – we were favourites and the Etonians were in firm control.

At Christ Church we were faced with increasingly powerful (and to us at least) unfairly stacked crews both behind and ahead in the premier division from St. Edmund Hall and Keble. Both institutions had let into their corridors a flood of literate athletes with the express intent of becoming Head of the River. The House, as ever, approached sport as an interesting prospect among many such prospects, never as a profession or obsession.

But the philosophy of win at any cost was sweeping the top division; against it, the House had only the slender but flexible reed of George Harris' daily coaching cunning and the input of such old members as were willing to mount a bike and wheel the bumpy clay path to Iffley Lock.

To an American at Oxford who had come from a well-financed and highly organized rowing programme at Yale University, the organization and operation of the Ch.Ch. B.C. seemed miraculous. No one at the undergraduate level, at least, knew how the programme ran, or even where the keys were. There was no textbook on the Christ Church style, though most knew that a firm finish was involved. A few members of the Club – W. Watson, M. Baker, C. Garton, and G. Kinsolving among them – took a strong interest in initiating newcomers. Likely candidates would be trudged down through the Meadow to a rotting "fixed" tub in the weeds beside the prim brick club building, and instructed to heave at the murky waters. This was the first cut.

Yet there was an attitude of unquenchable antique pride about the Boat Club. Was it the 1908 Grand crew that won at Henley? Was it the steady succession of great OUBC Blues – consider father and son Olympians 'Jumbo' and David Edwards that the Club had supplied? Or was it just the fact that our boathouse, made of brick and placed furthest downstream on boathouse row, faced away from the others at an angle of about 20 degrees, like a man forced to talk to unpleasant companions at a cocktail parly? Or was it that our boatman, George, was one of England's finest boatbuilders, while the rest of the college boatmen were competent to make repairs, not much more than that?

Whatever the source, the result was an attitude – the House had not been out of the First Division in recent memory, and that could not happen during our tenure.

George Harris simply nudged the river arrivals along and the rigid structure of river fixtures took care of the rest; that was the organization. In those fond far-off days tlere were no squabbles over places in the Eight or the Four. The President, leaning heavily on George Harris' advice, made the selections, which usually stuck.

My one innovation during my Presidency may have actually hurt the Club. I intervened with OUBC President David Strickland-Skailes to ask George to coach the Blue Boat for some period. Skailes, a Keble stalwart and one of the strongest men rowing at Oxford that year, agreed, and George was duly asked and did assist in coaching the Blue Boat during winter training. It was the first time that a "boatman", a professional and a workingman, had been in charge of a University crew in the modern era, though of course now things have come full circle; none but professionals are sought to coach the University crews these days.

But the experiment was not a success. Harris' methods worked best in small groups and singly with well known men he could mutter to man and man. His well known diffidence – especially to the Etonian gentry – took the fire out of his negatives and therefore bowdlerized much he had to say. He was intensely relieved when his responsiblities to the OUBC ended.

An unexpected case of mumps wiped out my winter rowing that year and almost cost me my place in the Blue Boat. During the bitter months of that cold winter and through a frustrating and leaden struggle on the tideway and a five length loss to Cambridge that early spring, my thoughts were far from the Isis. But as always, a decent Ch. Ch. B.C. Eight was boated and a respectable finish achieved during Eights Week. Though we were bumped by SEH, we finished third on the river.

1970–1979

1970

J.K.G. DART AND S.E. WILMER ROWED AT 2 AND 4 IN THE BOAT RACE, C.R.W. Parish having had the bad luck to be dropped from the Blue Boat following the final course a week before the race.

In Eights Week the Eight rowed over in 2nd place. No entry was made for Henley, but Dart stroked the winning London R.C. Four in the Britannia Challenge Cup.

This year the rules for the open events of the Regatta were amended, permitting composite crews to enter, provided all individuals were members of established rowing clubs. Schools were permitted to enter composite crews in the Ladies'. The Visitors' was opened to foreign crews, as was the Ladies' already.

1971

This year the House had 4 men in the Blue Boat, K. Bolshaw at 2, S.D. Nevin at 3, Parish (who had done well in Trial Eights) at 4, and M.T. Eastman at cox. Cambridge won for the fourth year in a row.

The First Eight – its stern four, and the cox, all Blues – bumped Keble on the first day of Eights Week, and finished the week Head of the River, for the first time since 1962. Entry for the Ladies' followed, as might be expected. The Eight may be taken as comprising the Henley crew:

Bow	P.D.E.M. Moncreiffe
2	E.R. Savage
3	D.F. Mayhew
4	G.I. Reid
5	C.R.W. Parish
6	K. Bolshaw
7	S.D. Nevin
Str	J.K.G. Dart
Cox	M.T. Eastman

The House met Keble in the first round, and must have derived much additional satisfaction from their 1¾ length win. In their second heat they were up against First and Third Trinity, who succeeded in winning by ¾ of a length.

Henley had, in June, suffered a double repeat of the floods of 1968:

> '*the flow of water down the course was reckoned to be ten times the normal*'.
> (Burnell, *A Celebration . . .*)

In other OUBC events on the Isis the House did well, Nevin winning the Silver Sculls, Parish and N.D.C. Tee the Double Sculls, and the First Four the First Division of the Fours.

1972

The House had 2 men in this year's Boat Race, Bolshaw (now Secretary of the OUBC) at 2, and Moncreiffe at 7. The race was again lost, but the Oxford crew participated against American universities in a regatta held in Miami. Oxford won against 4 opponents.

Keble got their revenge in Eights Week for their 1971 defeats at Christ Church's hands; they bumped the First Eight on the final day. A Four was entered for the Wyfolds, as follows:

Bow	P.D.E.M. Moncreiffe *(steers)*
2	Viscount Quenington
3	D.F. Mayhew
Str	K. Bolshaw

The Four beat King's, Cambridge, by 2½ lengths in their first heat on the first day of the Regatta. The following day they met London R.C. and were beaten by the same distance.

Nevin, stroke of the First Eight, and of Isis before that, and winner (with Bolshaw) of the OUBC Double Sculls, was in the OUBC Four entered for the Prince Philip Challenge Cup. They beat Hereford by 1¼ lengths, and then took on a composite crew representing the LSE and Marlow R.C., whom they beat easily. They then met St. Catharine's R.C., Canada, in the Final, which they lost by 5 lengths.

1973

Blues were won by R.G.A. Westlake at bow, and D.R. Sawyier at stroke, in the Boat Race, where Oxford shipped a good deal of water and lost by 48 seconds. Dave Sawyier had rowed 3 years for Harvard, and had stroked the winning U.S. Coxed Four in the 1972 Olympics before coming up to the House.

With Nevin at stroke, Sawyier at 6, Bolshaw at 5, and Westlake at 5, it took the House Eight just 2 minutes to reclaim the Headship of the River from Keble. For reasons unknown, an Eight was not entered in the Ladies', but Sawyier and D.R. Payne of Balliol (another member of the Blue Boat) represented Leander in the Goblets, and Sawyier was a member of the Isis Four in the Britannia Cup.

The 2 Isis crews entered won their opening heats. The Eight beat Queen's University, Belfast by 1⅓ lengths, and the Four beat Crowland by 3¼ lengths.

> *This was a race controlled by 2 Olympic strokes. But Sawyier, who had stroked the United States Olympic coxed fours in the final, had the upper hand over Smallburn, stroke of Britain's Olympic four.*
>
> (*The Times,* Thursday, 5 July, 1973).

On the second day, in the Ladies' Isis met University College, Dublin, and lost by a canvas.

The Oxford crew pushed University College Dublin through the record barriers.
(*The Times*)

University College set a record in this race, their time of 6 min. 37 sec. for the course beating by 5 seconds that set three years before by G.S.R. Aegir of The Netherlands.

The Four met Tideway Scullers in the Britannia Cup, and beat them by ¾ of a length. This was then followed up with a win, by 1⅔ lengths, over Vesta, to put the crew into the Final against London University. Isis won by a commanding 3¼ lengths, their time of 7 min. 15 sec. lowering the record the 7 min. 22 sec. set by London University, earlier in the week, by 7 seconds.

Sawyier had as stated fitted in his stroking of the Isis Four with rowing in the Goblets. The first heat which he and Payne rowed in was against the British National training team members Pemberton and Summers, also rowing for Leander.

With a comfortable lead of three lengths along the enclosures, Sawyier began to pull his partner around and they hit the booms just short of the finish. For a moment the Oxford oarsmen seemed to freeze while their opponents rapidly closed the gap, but not in time. Payne and Sawyier collected themselves together to scramble home a length and a quarter clear.
(*The Times,* Thursday, 5 July, 1973).

Sawyier and Payne next faced Machado and Albero from Santa Clara University, U.S.A., and achieved an *'easily'* verdict in their win. They next faced another pair of U.S. opponents, Borchelt and Adams, representing Potomac B.C., in the semi-final. Borchelt and Adams had beaten a second British national winning team Pair on the first day. *The Times* predicted that the Potomac crew would win, and this they did, winning *'easily'* and then proceeding to the Final against Belgian opponents.

7 of 12 events at Henley this year were won by foreign competitors.

1974

This year Nevin (4) and Sawyier (stroke) again rowed for Oxford in the Boat Race, which was won most convincingly by 5½ lengths in a time which bettered by 15 seconds a record which had stood for 26 years. Sawyier was President of the OUBC, only the second American to hold that office. (The first had been Bockstoce, of Yale and SEH in 1968).

The House remained Head of the River. '*Few crews can have retained the Headship with greater authority than Christ Church*', stated the OUBC News Summary. The crew were never less than 4 lengths clear, and on the last day led by at least 6 lengths. Crews were duly entered for the Ladies' and the Visitors', as follows:

LADIES'		VISITORS'	
Bow	M.P. Berry	*Bow*	J.K.G. Dart
2	A. McDougall	*2*	J.D. Lever
3	P.R. Butler	*3*	D.R. Sawyier
4	J.E. Hutchings	*Str*	S.D. Nevin
5	A. Baird		
6	J.D. Lever		
7	D.R. Sawyier		
Str	S.D. Nevin		
Cox	N.O. Huxtable		

(It is assumed that the First Eight was also the Henley Eight.)

This year the Regatta started on Thursday, and finished on Sunday, a change which continued to apply in subsequent years.

In the Ladies' the House met London University on the second day, and lost by 1 length. This race was described, ahead of time, by *The Times* as

> *'a key race . . . with the American Olympic oarsman, Sawyier, in the unfamiliar seven seat'.*

London University progressed to the Final, where they were beaten by University College, Dublin.

The Four first met First and Third Trinity in the Visitors', and beat them '*easily*'. They then beat London University '*not rowed out*' – the circumstances surrounding this verdict are not known. This paved the way for a semi-final encounter with Reading University, which produced another win, this time by 3¾ lengths. The Final was rowed against Pembroke, Cambridge, who had beaten Selwyn, Cambridge in the other semi-final. Pembroke won by ½ a length. The Pembroke Four was composed entirely of 1974 Blues. The House was the only Oxford college crew in the event proper (that is, following the Eliminating Race(s), if any).

This year members of the House had won both the OUBC Double Sculls and the OUBC Sculls, while the Second Four, in Michaelmas Term, had, once again, won the Pazolt Cup.

Christ Church in the Final of the Visitors', 1974. Henley Royal Regatta

1975

This was the last year in the decade in which a Christ Church crew was entered for Henley, the chosen event being the Visitors'.

A.G.H. Baird and J.E. Hutchins had rowed bow and 5 for Oxford against Cambridge. Cambridge won, but the Isis/Goldie race, with D.J. Newman at bow for Isis, was won by Isis by 9½ lengths.

The First Eight retained the Headship of the River *'with real authority'* in the words of the OUBC News Letter.

The House Four, entered for the Visitors', was as follows:

Bow J.S. Wikramaratna *(steers)*
2 D.B. Law
3 J.E. Hutchings
Str. P.R. Butler

The crew met First and Third Trinity in their heat of the Visitors' on the first day, and lost by 2 ¼ lengths.

Baird stroked the Isis crew in the Ladies'. Isis beat Emmanuel, Cambridge '*easily*' in this first heat, in the process setting a new record to the Barrier of 1 min. 48 sec. They then took on a crew from Harvard, and beat them by 1½ lengths. Next they met Durham University, and proceeded to the Final against London University. London won in a time of 6 min. 31 sec., 1 second outside the course record they had set earlier in the Regatta.

1975 was the last year in which a Pineapple Cup was made for the Diamonds. Burnell explains the circumstances:

Unfortunately inflation in the 1970s made the cost prohibitive. The last Pineapple Cup was made in 1975 and donated to the Regatta by De Beers Industrial Diamond Division Ltd as a permanent addition to the Challenge Trophy. De Beers also donate a miniature replica of the silver sculls which are presented to the winner instead of the cup.

This year also saw a call for a revision of the selective draw system initiated in 1969. Thus *The Times,* 3 July, 1975:

> *It is certainly time Henley thought in terms of seeding crews in a range order and scattering them because more productive finals would result. This could have been achieved this year by holding back the Henley draw until after the Nottinghamshire regatta last weekend, where so many crews revealed their hand.*

1975 saw the retirement of George Harris, the Christ Church boatman, for decades a much-loved and much-respected cornerstone of House rowing. The sum of £2,000 was raised for a farewell present, and a slightly smaller sum for the Boat Club endowment. George's service to the College is well recalled in Francis Gladstone's *'A Tribute to George Harris'*, which appears at the end of this 1970-1979 section. (Francis' article originally appeared in *Crew Composition and Racing Results 1946-1993).* Nor should George's contribution to Oxford rowing be overlooked. He was (as Duncan Spencer has earlier noted) first invited to coach the Blue Boat in preparation for the 1973 race – the first professional waterman to be so honoured for well over a century – and continued for several more years.

1976

The First Eight was caught first by Oriel, and then by Keble, so ending in 3rd place in Eights Week.

K.C. Brown, who had come up to the House from Cornell University in the U.S., and who was to row in the U.S. Coxed Fours crew in the Olympics in Montreal that year, and A.G. Baird, rowed at 6 and stroke in the winning Oxford Boat Race crew. S.J. Majd and D.J. Newman rowed for Isis, who beat Goldie. The OUBC Lightweight Eight, with A.N. Haywood-Smith at 3, beat Cambridge over the Henley course, rowed downstream. This Eight, rowing as Isis, lost in the first round of the Ladies'. R.W.D. Staveley rowed in the Cherwell crew which reached the second round of this event. Majd and Newman were members of the Isis Four which had to scratch after the draw was made for the Wyfolds. Later in the year Majd was a member of the Oxford University Eight which *'recorded a remarkable double' (Christ Church Report)* in the Egyptian Rowing Festival.

All the above men, except for Staveley, were members of the First Eight in Eights Week.

1977

The First Eight rowed over in Eights Week. There was no Christ Church representation in the Blue Boat for the first time in 8 years.

K.C. Brown was a member of the OUBC Grand crew which lost in the first round to a composite Leander and Thames Tradesmen crew. *The Times* offered this comment (Saturday, 2 July) on the encounter:

Two of rowing's most famous establishments had their boats rocked when they were dismissed yesterday in the opening rounds of the Grand Challenge Cup. Oxford University's defeat by the new national Eight, Leander/Thames Tradesmen, came as no real surprise. Harvard University fought tooth-and-nail and sold their lives dearly before succumbing to the relentless beat of the Irish Police (Garda Siochana) eight.

Oxford University and Harvard, with traditions reaching back to the last century, both led early in their races. Harvard bowed to an Irish police club who received the key to the door only last year, and Oxford yielded to the national team in their early months of infancy.

Oxford and Leander/Thames Tradesmen rather stupidly risked disqualification yesterday, arriving almost late at the start. Oxford saved an embarrassment by just 30 seconds and was fortunate to find a kind umpire in David Jennens. Oxford looked like a milk train at Nottingham last weekend. Yesterday they went off like an express and for moments there were glimpses of the Boat Race crew, who ruled the roost back in March.

The National eight looked ragged for the first quarter of the course and somewhat surprised at being led by a crew dismissed by four lengths less than a week ago. Oxford's supremacy lasted a fraction over two minutes. After that the National eight switched on, remembered they were a national eight and pushed through a gusty headwind to a 1¾ lengths lead.

Ken Brown, of the United States, and a former world champion was in the engine room of the Oxford boat. He shrugged off defeat: "We are only a part-time crew now with examinations and college rowing having taken their toll." The truth is that Oxford lost their drive after the Boat Race, and there was, perhaps, an air of over-confidence.

1978-9

1978 the First Eight lost 3 places to go to 6th in Eights Week, but in 1979 they regained 1 place by bumping New College (and nearly catching Balliol twice).

No Blues were won in either year, and no entries were made for Henley. Nor did any House men row in crews entered by other Clubs.

The decade ended, then, quietly.

A TRIBUTE TO GEORGE HARRIS

by **J.F. Gladstone**
former President, Christ Church Boat Club

I rowed in the Christ Church VIII in '61, '62, and '63. I think that I was President in '63 when we were bumped, and stroke in '62 when we went Head of the River. This was a particular triumph because Oxford rowing was rather dominated at the time by the Keble heavies, many of whom were imported from Eton by Vere Davidge. The House had not been head for some time and we had a crew that was a crew rather than a crew of talents. Jonathan Scarlett may have been a Blue, but he was the only one. He and I and Dominick Harrod, the cox, were instrumental in bringing George into being the key figure in House coaching and we also commissioned a new boat from him. I think this may have been the first eight he built. I am not sure where we got the money from but I think Nono Rathbone may have been important in helping us. This boat was extremely lightweight, a wonderful piece of boat building, but possibly too flexible for its own good in bad water. On the Isis in summer, however, it sang when the crew worked as a crew, and gave me a sensation of speed and control in a boat that I had never really had before. It was a case of a very good tool being able to help pretty good appliers of the tool. One had the sense that one could wind up that boat as one has that sense in a very powerful car. George built a Porsche among boats and we took advantage of it in going Head and doing reasonably well at Henley -- I think we reached two semi-finals, Visitors' and Ladies'. And lost them both.

I found George Harris a deeply affectionate human being. There was always some sense of his being deferential to "young gentlemen" and I hope we tried to stop that. He was, as I remember, wonderful in any boat and could manipulate a big punt across the river in full winter flood and full of lumbering undergraduates as if with the flick of a wrist, often smoking his pipe and generally chatting as he did so. I think that that was the only boat I ever saw him control. But it was quite clear that he had an extraordinary sense of how to move something solid in water. I had been coached in my time by good and eloquent coaches, a bit by Jumbo Edwards in Trial Eights, by Bobby Bourne at Eton, but being coached by George seemed to have that sense of a master class, that sense one gets occasionally when one is good at something but good enough to recognize a real master. I was not small, but I was probably a stone and a bit under Boat Race weight and apart from Patrick Henry and Jonathan Scarlett and, perhaps one other, A.J. Saunders, we were not a big crew, so that George's sense that the application of strength is more important than strength, and that so much depends on rhythm and togetherness, was particularly important. He was also a great psychological coach, and knew all about when to strain a crew and when to rest one. Being on the stake boat at Henley was a far less nerve-wracking experience than usual with George on the bank on his old black bike and wearing his green tweed suit, regardless of the heat.

I have a hunch he was about as unskillful with a bike as he was skillful with a boat. Even a small-framed bike seemed slightly outsize for his small, hunched frame, particularly as he would, on occasion, take to smoking his pipe even on the bike. This pipe I remember vividly. It never seemed to be alight when he wanted to smoke it, but certainly on one occasion set a brand new tweed coat on fire, fanned by the breeze as he rode the towpath. Tobacco, pipe and matches always seemed to be lost or scattered, and we gave him a small silver tobacco holder as a present when we went Head. Like all people endowed with the gift of true concentration, like the artist-boat-builder-coach that he was, George had a wonderful habit of forgetting certain things, and the winning humanity that tended to depreciate his great talents.

One final note: My uncle, A.C. Gladstone and my father C.A. Gladstone both rowed for Ch.Ch. early in the century. My uncle went on to win a Gold Medal in the 1908 Olympics; if not rowing under 10 stone, certainly not far off it. My father never rowed for Oxford as my uncle did, but he was also small and represented the school of non-thug rowing which George embodied (and which is a wonderful amateur tradition in which rowing rather than other exercise is at the center of the enterprise). My father went on to coach Eton in the 1920s and, somewhat at George's suggestion, we asked him to coach the House VIII He did this in both 1962 and 1963, riding a bicycle up that pot-holed and hazardous tow path. He would have been 73 in 1962. Like George he smoked a pipe, but not on his bicycle.

I owe to George many of the happiest days of my life. That is high praise. But it is true.

(There are many references in the year-by-year reports to the contribution George made as coach. One of the nicest, found in Cherwell's Eight Week report, and not quoted for the year 1959, speaks of the traditional run on the 1st VIII boat coming from a "Jumbo- polished George Harris -Finish". In the material I looked through in doing my research I never came across any reference to George Harris' death. Through the helpfulness of Mr Cox, Clerk of Works at Christ Church, I got into contact with George's son, who continues to operate the firm George Harris Racing Boats at Iffley. From the son I was able to learn that George died, very suddenly, in 1987, aged 77. GCP – 1993).

1980–1988

1980

R.P. EMERTON ROWED 6 FOR ISIS, WHO WON AGAINST GOLDIE. The First Eight bumped Balliol and SEH to rise to 3rd place on the River. An entry was made for the Ladies', the crew being (it is assumed) the First Eight:

Bow	P.M. Robinson
2	R.J.B. Jakeman
3	C.A. Rumbold
4	L.J. Scrine
5	N.R.S. Watson
6	R.P. Emerton
7	H.K.N. von Schweinitz
Str	M.E. Davies
Cox	D.M. Freud

In their heat (one of an unprecedented 100 races taking place on the first day at 5 minute intervals, with the first race taking place at 8 a.m.) the House met Imperial College, London, who won *'easily'*. On that day 28 crews competed in the Ladies' Of these 9 were Cambridge colleges, 6 were from abroad, 10 from U.K. and Ireland universities, colleges and hospitals, and 3 only (of which 1 was an Isis crew), from Oxford, Christ Church being one of the 2 colleges entered.

1981

R.P. Emerton rowed 4 in the Boat Race crew. Oxford's winning margin was 8 lengths. In Eights Week the First Eight rowed over in third place. There was no Christ Church representation of any kind at Henley this year.

1982

P.M.R. Buchanan stroked Isis to a win against Goldie. The First Eight again rowed over in 3rd place. Buchanan, the First Eight stroke, again stroked Isis at Henley in the Ladies' Having beaten Harvard University in the semi-final, Isis met the University of London in the Final, and lost by ¼ of a length.

1983

C.L.Richmond (OUBC Secretary 1983-1984) rowed 2, and Buchanan 7, for Isis, who beat Goldie for the fourth year in a row. P.D.P. Castle rowed for the Oxford University Lightweights against Cambridge.

In Eights Week the First Eight, with C.K. King at stroke for the first 2 days, bumped Keble, and went (and stayed) 2nd on the River. Buchanan returned to the boat for the final 2 days.

There was again no Christ Church representation at Henley.

1984

Richmond was now President of the OUBC, but rowed, not in the Boat Race, but in the Isis crew.

The First Eight *'made a determined assault on Oriel's seven-year reign at the head of the river' OUBC News Summary No. 37),* but to no avail, rowing over in 2nd place.

Christ Church and Oriel combined to make up a composite Four, entered for the Visitors'. R.J.B. Jakeman was at bow, and Richmond at stroke. The Four won their first heat, against University College and Hospital, London, by 2 lengths, but lost the second to another composite crew representing Shiplake College and Sir William Borlase's School, who won the Final against Reading University.

1985

Richmond won a place in the Blue Boat, rowing at 2. Oxford recorded their tenth win in a row, the longest sequence since Cambridge's run of victories ended in 1937. The First Eight bumped Oriel on the first day of Eights Week, and held on to the Headship. This was the first time the House had been Head of the River since 1975.

It was decided to enter for Henley with D. Aeron-Thomas substituting for W.T. Pattisson (who had been a member of the Eight for 3 years) at 5. The crew was:

Bow	D.S. Joyner
2	C.P. Eastwood
3	D.G. Gentle
4	T.J. Adams
5	D. Aeron-Thomas
6	T.J. Jenkinson
7	C.L. Richmond
Str	R.J.B. Jakeman
Cox	A.S. Green

This year the qualification for the Thames Challenge Cup was

> *'radically changed . . . to ensure a standard below that of the Ladies' Plate'.* Including further modification in 1987, *'recent Henley winners and internationals are excluded, as also are crews, other than school crews, rated on the Amateur Rowing Association points system above the equivalent of Senior II . . .'.* The Ladies' Plate, in turn, was opened to all clubs, except that *'. . . as the sole concession to students, combined entries are accepted from schools or from college boat clubs within the same university, but not from clubs.'*
>
> (These quotations are from Burnell).

As a consequence of these changes, the House crew was entered for the Thames. They were defeated in their first heat by London Rowing Club.

1986

A.S. Green, who had coxed the First Eight the 2 preceding years, was chosen to cox the (losing) Blue Boat against Cambridge. H.M. Pelham rowed 3 for Isis, who beat Goldie.

The First Eight were bumped by New College on the first day of Eights Week, regained the Headship on the second day, were bumped again by New College on the third day, and by Oriel on the last day.

There was no Christ Church representation at Henley this year.

1987

This was the year of the Oxford Boat Race "Mutiny". Pelham was Secretary of the OUBC, so played a significant part in the re-constitution of the Oxford crew. He rowed bow in the race itself, in which, as is well known, Oxford, against all expectations, beat Cambridge by 12 seconds.

The First Eight was bumped by Univ. in Eights Week, and so ended 4th. An Eight was entered for the Thames at Henley, but did not survive its Elimination race. The First Eight this year (and likely Henley crew) was:

Bow	M.W.A. Nixon
2	J. Spicer
3	T.M.J. Butterfield
4	A. Turberfield
5	H.M. Pelham
6	C.P. Eastwood
7	A.J. Veal
Str	T.H.R. Roberts
Cox	Tracy Bettridge

This was the first year the Eight had had a woman cox. (The first Christ Church Women's Eight had been formed in 1981, and a Ladies' Captain – later Women's Captain – appointed the following year. Elizabeth Chick coxed the Oxford boat in 1992).

1988

The House had 2 men in the Blue Boat this year; Pelham rowed bow, and J.W.C. Searle 7. Cambridge were again beaten. Jonny Searle had only come up to the House in Michaelmas Term 1987, but in that first term had won a place in Trial Eights. For a Freshman to win a rowing Blue was almost unprecedented, (see the reference to Gavin Sorrell's selection in 1955) but Jonny Searle already had an impeccable pedigree. He had taken up rowing at Hampton School, and was a member of the Hampton Eight which, in both 1985 and 1986, had won the Schools' Head of the River Race, the Schools' National Regatta, and the Princess Elizabeth Cup at Henley. In 1987 he was in the first British crew to win gold at the Junior World Championships. In 1988 he won the Wyfolds with the Nottinghamshire County RA crew.

The House First Eight (with Searle – President of the Boat Club – at 5 and Pelham at 7) rowed over in 4th place in Eights Week. A crew was not entered for Henley.

Technically, the story of Christ Church's involvement with Henley Regatta over the first 150 years of the Regatta's existence should end here, in 1988. However, because of the continued participation of individuals already named, this account will be extended to cover a little more time.

Searle rowed for Oxford a second time in 1989, and Oxford won again. In October he was elected President of the OUBC. No Christ Church crew was entered for Henley, but House men were active in 2 events. Pelham was a member of the Isis "A" Four, entered for the Visitors', and Searle joined with his former Hampton schoolmate, Rupert Obholzer, new of St. Cath's, and 2 London University oarsmen, to form a "University of London and Oxford University" Four which entered for the Stewards'.

Isis "A" first met Isis "B", whom they beat by 5 lengths, and then went on to beat Durham University "A" and the University of London, to face Durham University "B" in the Final. They won, again by 5 lengths, setting a new course record of 6 min. 50 sec.

The Stewards' Four beat Heeressportverein Linz (Austria) to meet Nautilus in the Final. This was a closely-fought race, with the London/Oxford composite crew winning by ⅔ of a length in 6 min. 28 sec., another course record.

Jonny Searle's further rowing successes also deserve mention. In 1990 he rowed for Oxford for the third year running and brought his number of wins to 3, giving him a 100% record. In 1991, rowing for Molesey, he won the Grand. In 1992, partnered by his brother Greg (a frequent crew co-member) he won a gold medal in the Coxed Pairs at the Barcelona Olympics. This victory, over the Abbagnale brothers of Italy – Olympic champions in 1984 and 1988 – has been described as *'one of the greatest in Olympic history'.* (Richard Burnell and Geoffrey Page *The Brilliants – A History of the Leander Club,* 1977, p. 183).

Jonny had won bronze medals rowing in the British National Eight in the World Championships in 1989 and 1991; in 1990 the crew earned fourth place. In 1993 he won gold in the Coxed Pairs World Championship event; this was followed by bronze in the Coxless Fours in 1994, and silver in the same event the following year. In 1996, at the Atlanta Olympics, he again won bronze in the Coxless Fours; in 1999 in a Coxed Four, he won silver again in the World Championships.

A truly remarkable record, amply justifying for him the title of the greatest Christ Church oarsman of the second half of the 20th century. A digest of Jonny's reflections on the factors influencing his record of personal rowing triumphs will be found at the end of this section.

The decline in Christ Church crews' representation at Henley from the 1960s onwards has been alluded to in earlier pages. It is appropriate to consider the reasons underlying this trend, and it is important to note that these were not ones affecting Christ Church alone, but all Oxford University colleges as a whole, and to a lesser extent, Cambridge colleges.

The House's years of entries declined, decade by decade, from 6 in the 1950s, to 5, then to 4, and to 3 years only in the 1980s. Yet the College was never out of the top 4 in Division 1 in Eights Week between 1970 and 1989. In 1959 Oxford and Cambridge entries for Henley events had totalled 44 combined (Oxford 18, Cambridge 26). In 1968 this had reduced to 19 (Oxford 2, Cambridge 17). In 1988 the total was 18 (Oxford 8, Cambridge 10). So both Universities' number of entries declined. If Cambridge had an edge, it was not on account of any Boat Race superiority. In the 1960s and 1970s combined, each University won 10 times. In the 1980s Oxford had 9 wins to Cambridge's 1.

Finding an explanation for the decline in Christ Church participation in Henley events proved to be a difficult challenge. Clearly, as suggested, the situation was not unique to the House, and several possible factors, common to all Oxford colleges, could be pre-supposed, but difficult to express with any real authority. Fortunately, however, more than to-be-imagined help came from two sources. Daniel Grist, Secretary of Henley Royal Regatta, offered, on behalf of himself and Mike Sweeney, Chairman of the Committee of Management, the following reasons for the fall in Oxbridge entries:

1. The rising academic standards required of applicants to the Colleges and the Admission Tutors' definite 'anti-sports' attitude.

2. The pressure on the students to study, study, study.

3. The admittance of women to the Colleges in the 1970s and 1980s effectively halved the male undergraduate population of the two Universities.

(Daniel Grist's letter to the author, 25 July, 2012).

In addition, *Well-rowed Magdalen! A History of Magdalen College Boat Club 1859-1993,* includes a chapter by Richard Burnell, himself – like his father, and his son – an old Magdalen man. The chapter's title is *Why Magdalen have not been Head of the River since 1954; changes in post-war college rowing.* (Pages 64 to 67). Burnell's authoritative views are equally relevant to the House or to any Oxford college at the time of writing in the early 1990s. Moreover, his commentary goes well beyond performance in Eights Week, and relates this aspect to the realistic chances of any college Eight making any impression at Henley.

Here are some of Burnell's thoughts, reproduced by kind permission of Magdalen College. (They do not constitute a continuous narrative).

Rowing can be just a spare time recreation, and it is absolutely right that this should be so for many, perhaps for the majority of those who row. But competition at higher levels is a serious business, demanding dedication and sacrifices. You only get to be Head by finding better oarsmen or women, coaching and equipping them better, and working them harder than their rivals. The college which admits more undergraduate and graduate oarsmen with previous rowing experience, and gives more moral and financial support to the members of its Boat Club, the members of which then devote more time and effort to their training, will surely reap its reward.

Prior to 1939 it can be said in all fairness that rowing in the higher echelons in Britain was based on college rowing; and that meant 'Oxbridge' college rowing. Only the London, Thames and Leander Clubs were significant challengers for the open events at Henley Regatta, and, at least from the closing decade of the nineteenth century, Leander was largely an Oxbridge based club. The college oarsman who rowed near the top of the river in Eights at Oxford, or the May Races at Cambridge, was one of the elite among British oarsmen of the day. The men who were striving to gain the Headship of the Isis, or of the Cam, were the same men who hoped, a few weeks later, to mount the prize giving rostrum at Henley Regatta. And when there were Great Britain national crews in the making, the odds were that most of those selected would hail from Oxford or Cambridge.

College rowing in turn was based on school rowing, and that effectively meant rowing at what used to be described as the 'Henley Schools', those few, generally 'privileged', schools which entered regularly for the Ladies' Plate at Henley Regatta.

During its 'golden era' [c.1880-mid 1920s] *Magdalen stood at or near the top, both of intra-mural rowing on the Isis, and of rowing in the world beyond. The two were effectively self, or mutually supporting, Magdalen's successes at Henley and internationally, and the renown of Magdalen men in coaching and administration, encouraged the supply of oarsmen from Eton and other rowing schools who in turn provided the next generation of star performers.*

Oxford rowing, at university level, languished after 1923, when Cambridge began their sequence of thirteen successive wins in the Boat Race. Despite a revival before and after the war, Oxford remained very much the under dogs until about 1960. Their response was the formation of a 'university squad', system, which meant that the most promising freshmen rarely if ever rowed in Torpids, and in some cases never rowed in college crews at all. At the same time the introduction of sectional boats which could easily be carried on small trailers, enabled the university crews to shift their training to more favourable waters at Radley, Wallingford, and further afield. Increasingly, college rowing became a backwater, and college oarsmen were deprived even of the example of seeing good university crews practising on their home waters. No doubt this was a factor in Oxford regaining the Boat Race initiative; but it was damaging to college rowing.

The nature of the University itself was changing too. I suppose one might say, clumsily if not crudely, that 'nationalized education' took over from 'private enterprise education'. No doubt this was overdue and beneficial. But an inevitable result was that tutors in most colleges, and certainly at Magdalen, became less tolerant of time spent in recreational activities. Indeed that may be an understatement, for Magdalen earned a reputation for being averse to admitting candidates who had rowing aspirations even if their academic standards were satisfactory. The supply of undergraduates with previous rowing experience dried up, and rowing was not encouraged. Two colleges at Oxford bucked this trend. Keble, during the immediate post war period, welcomed oarsmen, particularly from Eton, with quite spectacular results which soon took this hitherto 'unknown' rowing college to the Head of the River, followed by Oriel on a more ongoing basis which continues to this day. [1993]

Not only Magdalen, but college rowing in general, at both Universities, went into decline in the mid-fifties. In part this was due to academic pressures and changing economic and social conditions. Later, the arrival of women at the men's colleges added to the problems. Rowing is a good sport for women, and they have made a considerable contribution to rowing at Oxford. All the same, simple arithmetic tells us that if there are twice as many 'oarspeople' rowing, without a doubling up of finance and equipment, without an influx of additional expert coaches, on a river already overcrowded and now progressively more congested with motor launches, the problem of turning out good crews must inevitably be made harder.

The quality of crews at Oxford, in point of fact, may not have deteriorated much. But the quality of crews elsewhere has improved enormously. This is true of other academic institutions, many of which did not row at all in the past. It is certainly true of clubs. The ever-expanding list of entries at Henley Regatta, and at Head of the River events during the autumn and winter months, bears witness to this.

Extra-mural competition is important to college rowing because it gives experience of racing side-by-side which racing at Oxford does not; because it adds to the interest and fun of the sport, which should never be underestimated; and because it provides a genuine yardstick by which to judge standards. In time past the best college crews regularly competed at Henley, Marlow and Reading Regattas. Today only a handful of Oxbridge college oarsmen get to race in the world outside, and rarely with sufficient success to encourage others to do likewise. This, of cou.se, is not true of oarsmen at other universities, which race regularly at outside events.

It may seem brutal to say so, but over the past thirty years few of the crews which have occupied the top three places in Summer Eights could have reckoned winning even one heat at Henley Regatta. Worse, only a handful have tried to do so. That, I believe, is one of the main reasons for the decline of rowing on the Isis.

A club can achieve success from scratch because it has time and continuity on its side. A complete novice can be recruited and instructed over a period of years. Some may learn quickly, others slowly; but there will always be a range of crews suitable to their abilities, training throughout the year. And, of course, club rowing takes place 'after work', in the evenings and for longer 'free periods' at weekends. The concept of 'after work' and 'free periods' at weekends may not exist for the hard-pressed student. The newcomer at college is often available for only an hour or so, four or five a week, during three short terms with a prolonged gap during the Long Vacation, with a complete turnover of personnel over a three year period.

To produce crews on that basis which are good enough to go Head is a tough assignment. But, the position is improved immeasurably if one or two freshmen arrive each year with a sound background of school rowing. Not only does this mean that the weakest in the group need not be used in the 1st VIII, but the leavening of ready-made oarsmen provides a nucleus on which to build. Secondly, a crew will never achieve its potential if individual crew members are frequently unavailable due to academic commitments. Thirdly, the time available between the beginning of term and the onset of Torpids or Summer Eights is too short to shake a new crew together, and bring it to racing pitch. Nearly all the crews which succeed contrive to start practice before term commences. Finally, however popular and entertaining bumping races may be, they are not conducive to good rowing because of the inevitable emphasis on dashing off the start. Some experience of side by side racing is vital.

To achieve the position which Magdalen enjoyed in the 'golden era', I believe, is no longer possible, for Magdalen or any other college. It is inconceivable that any college could enjoy the crop of ready-made oarsmen, from what, seventy five years ago, was virtually the only source capable of providing such talent. The main events at Henley Regatta . . . are now dominated by internationals who have, sadly perhaps, become full-time, semi-professional gladiators. Coaching at the top level is becoming increasingly a professional preserve.

JONNY SEARLE

What makes an Olympic Oarsman?

Notes from a conversation between Jonny Searle and Simon Offen from the Christ Church Development and Alumni Office

Jonny started rowing at Hampton aged 13, as he searched for a sport at which he could excel. This interest was instilled by his mother, a PE teacher, and his father, both of whom enjoyed watching competitive sport. He had the right physique for a rower, and had a talent for moving the boat efficiently, but above all he had an enormous desire to be a great rower. Rowing is repetitive and physically hard; determination and mental strength are vital. Winning at the National Schools Regatta aged 15 in the same summer that one of his school teachers won an Olympic Gold medal convinced him that he could one day be an Olympic Champion himself.

Jonny's Headmaster had studied at Christ Church and Oxford had a good reputation for both biology and rowing so applying to the House was a natural choice. But what really attracted him to the Isis was that the National Squad trained nearby at Henley. His main aspiration was to be picked to row in the 1988 Seoul Olympics; he even saw the Boat Race as a stepping stone to this. Unusually Jonny won his first Blue as a Freshman. In his first year there were still reverberations from the 1987 mutiny, so he just focussed on gaining his seat and improving. Coach Mike Spracklen was one of the best he ever experienced. By his third year, as President, the pressure had built on Jonny; responsibility was a challenge, selection of the crew difficult, but his competitive streak and desire carried him through. Always in the back of his mind was the goal of one day winning an Olympic Gold Medal.

He enjoyed racing in Summer Eights and rowed for at least a few days in each of the three years that he was at Christ Church. In his second year he travelled from Oxford to Duisburg via overnight ferry to race in an international regatta after racing in Eights on Thursday. In his final year he raced on Saturday evening after his final examination in the hope of moving from second place to Head of the River; realising as he walked to the Boat House from the examination room that it had been the race not his exam that had inspired his nerves all day.

Rowing in the Olympics in 1992 was his rowing high point. He was always nervous and apprehensive when racing; but the feelings were magnified at the Olympics. He slept well the night before the final but the knowledge of the pain to come and of the possibility of losing his opportunity to win a Gold Medal, filled him with apprehension. He wanted to perform at his best and once in the boat he concentrated on "controlling the controllable," focussed on how to get off the start and into race pace.

There is always a race plan, and in the early stages it is more about the feel of the boat and moving efficiently, later you can think more about the opposition and beating them. If the race is close the difference is always in the mind; who is more determined to win? When winning Gold in the 1992 Olympic Pairs he knew that the Italians would go hard from the start, and that his brother and he were fast at the finish of the race, so he just concentrated on his boat at the beginning. In the Boat Race it was always more about finding a good and efficient race pace then breaking clear of the other crew as soon as possible.

Jonny still coaches a little now, and continues to row with a group of rowers who are not quite as good as they used to be, but most of his spare time is spent with his children. His observation is that the coach's role is vital: to inspire, to lead, to help improve; to be calm, confident and build the crews' confidence. He notes that a coach can provide technical input, set a training programme and provide the tactical advice, but the most difficult element to teach is the most important element in developing and winning; the desire and hunger, the mental strength. That is largely down to upbringing, role models and inspiration at the right moments in your life.

Conclusion

IN ITS FIRST 150 YEARS OF EXISTENCE following its inception in 1829, Henley Royal Regatta – as it soon became – took place 139 times, the difference in totals being the years of the two World Wars in the 20th century, during which the Regatta was not held.

From its initial year, where there were 7 entries for the 2 events offered, it grew in size and world renown to – in 2012 – an amazing 499 entries (366 from overseas) competing for some 20 men's and women's events.

From the outset, Christ Church, as has been seen, was a leading participant in the Regatta. In its very first year 5 House men were members of the Oxford Etonian crew entered for the Grand. The first Christ Church entry was made in 1844; only 3 Oxford colleges could claim to have made earlier entries. In the first 10 years of the Regatta the College entered over 5 years, in 9 events, of which 7 were won. House men were, additionally, members of 17 crews of other clubs in 15 events including participation in all 10 years of the opening decade, and in crews which won 10 further trophies. The record of Milman and Haggard in winning 5 events in 1848 (of which 4 were in Christ Church crews) has never been equalled.

In the 1850s a further 12 events were won by Christ Church men in College or other crews and the award (for the second time) of the Wyfold Cup against performance in the Grand brought the total number of trophies won to 13 in that decade alone.

The 1860s and 1870s saw, as it were, a pause for breath after such a tremendous start, with House representation in only 6 of the 20 years (with 4 wins) but in the eighties and nineties 12 of 20 years saw participation of Christ Church crews or crews with House men's membership, with a further 10 event wins being achieved. From the turn of the century until the outbreak of the Great War Christ Church men appeared at the Regatta in no fewer than 12 of 15 years, with 25 House entries and participation in 5 other crews, for a total of 6 wins.

The resumption of the Regatta in 1920 saw the first of 20 consecutive years in which the names of Christ Church men appeared in every programme. Christ Church crews entered for 31 events, and House men appeared in 26 more; between them these crews won 11 Finals.

Following the end of World War II the number of House crew appearances at Henley began to decline. Nevertheless, between 1946 and 1959 entries were made by the College's crews in 17 events covering all but 3 of 14 years, during which a further 6 events saw participation by Christ Church men. And in 21 of the final 29 years – to 1988 – House crews and House men appeared in no fewer than 35 events.

These numbers amount to 100 years of representation (out of 139 years) with 227 crews in 221 events. Christ Church crews achieved 22 event wins, the "jewel in the crown" being the Grand victory in 1908, supported by 4 wins in the Ladies', 6 in the Goblets, 7 in the Visitors', 2 in the Stewards', and 1 each in the Thames and the Wyfolds. Other crews with House members' participation account for no fewer that 21 wins in the Grand, 10 in the Stewards', and 5 in the Goblets, out of a total of 43 event wins, with in addition, 2 awards of the Wyfolds Cup referred to.

While, in the spirit of Henley tradition and Christ Church modesty, it would be invidious to claim for the House any sort of record for number of years of appearances, or events entered for, or wins achieved, (no comparable statistics for Oxford colleges are known to exist), it cannot be disputed that Christ Church's commitment to the Regatta has to be viewed as being of the highest possible quality, one which many others could gladly wish to match.

But the listing of appearances and successes and failures is only part of the story. Interwoven into the threads of the reporting of year-by-year achievements of House crews and men are to be found the tales of moments of great glory, of dogged determination not to give up, of chivalrous response to an opponent's misfortune, and the like. Passing references to the 136 Boat Race Blues won, 13 years of Headship of the River, 3 Olympic victories, and to the outstanding personal successes of a number of outstanding individuals also add colour to the recitation of the basic facts. And as the 150 years of the Regatta have passed, it has been possible to see, in outline, how the Regatta evolved, its scope, its rules and practices, its organization, and how the line of the physical course itself evolved.

As the Christ Church Boat Club nears the start of its third century of existence, it is hoped that this book will be deemed to give reasonable respect and honour to those who have gone before, and in a small way give encouragement to those who now follow to keep the flame of pride in participation at Henley alight and burning brightly.

Course maps

These maps, reproduced by kind permission of Peter Burnell, originally appeared in his father's *Henley Royal Regatta: A Celebration of 150 Years.*

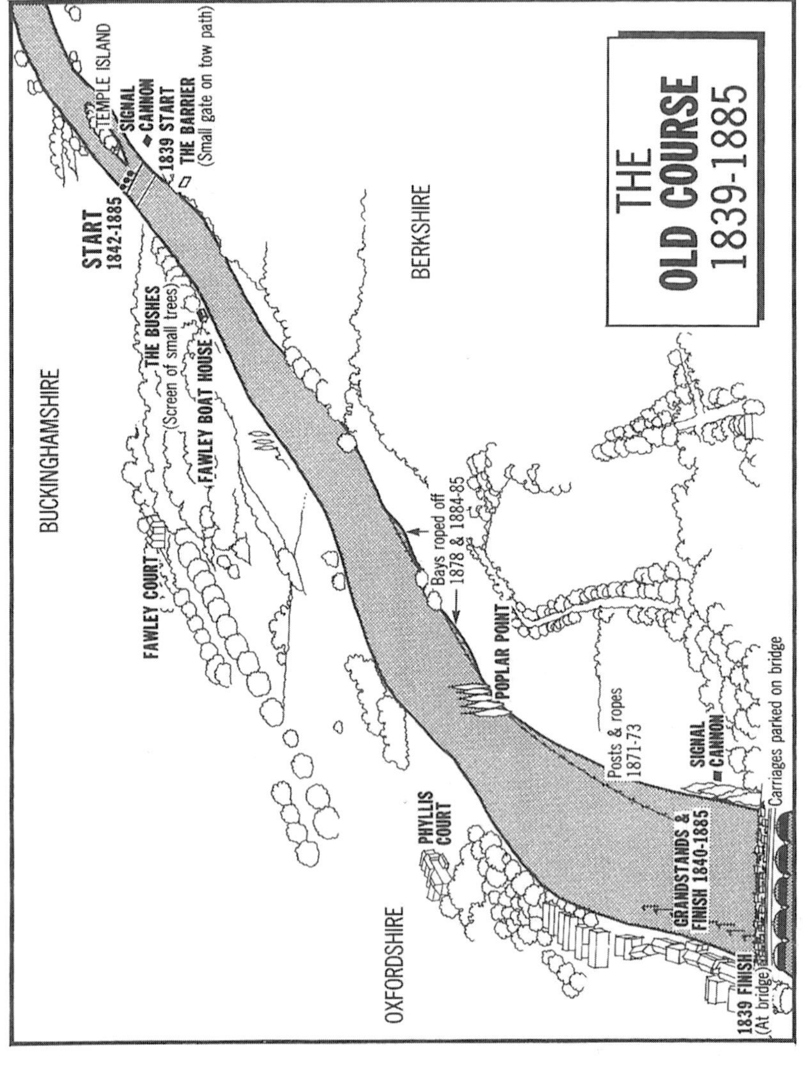

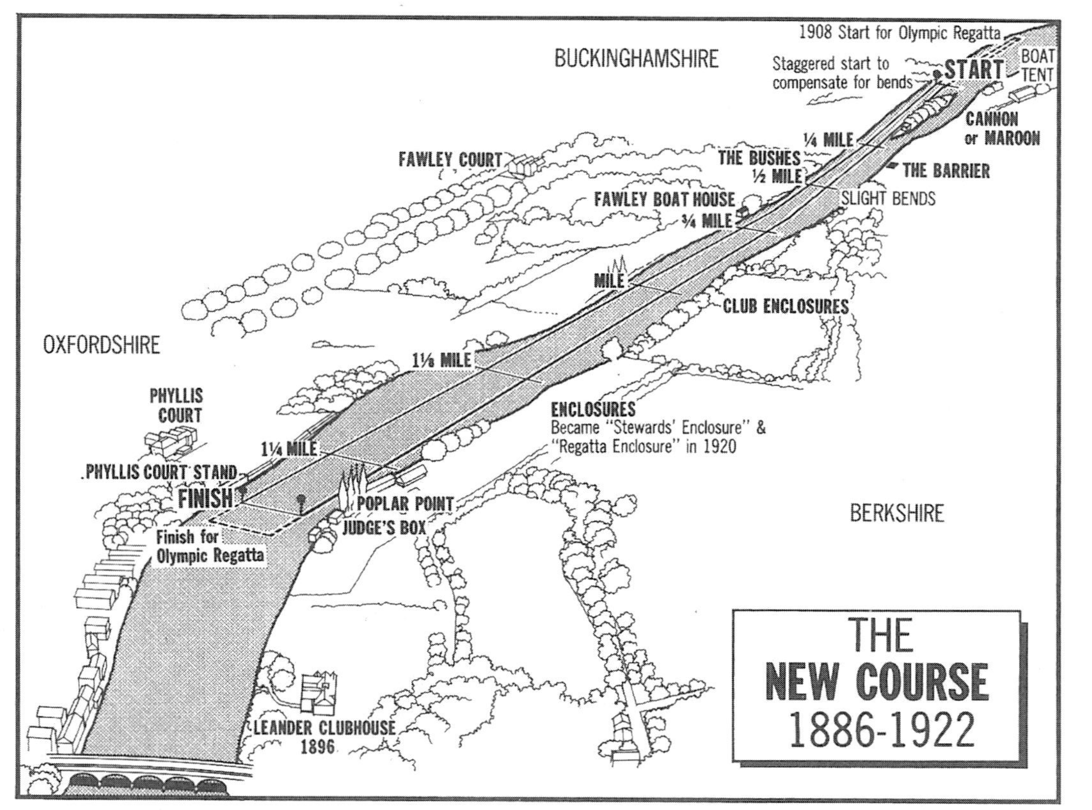
1908 Start for Olympic Regatta
BUCKINGHAMSHIRE
Staggered start to compensate for bends
START
BOAT TENT
CANNON or MAROON
¼ MILE
FAWLEY COURT
THE BUSHES
½ MILE
THE BARRIER
FAWLEY BOAT HOUSE
SLIGHT BENDS
¾ MILE
MILE
CLUB ENCLOSURES
OXFORDSHIRE
1⅛ MILE
PHYLLIS COURT
ENCLOSURES
Became "Stewards' Enclosure" & "Regatta Enclosure" in 1920
1¼ MILE
PHYLLIS COURT STAND
FINISH
POPLAR POINT
BERKSHIRE
JUDGE'S BOX
Finish for Olympic Regatta
THE NEW COURSE 1886-1922
LEANDER CLUBHOUSE 1896

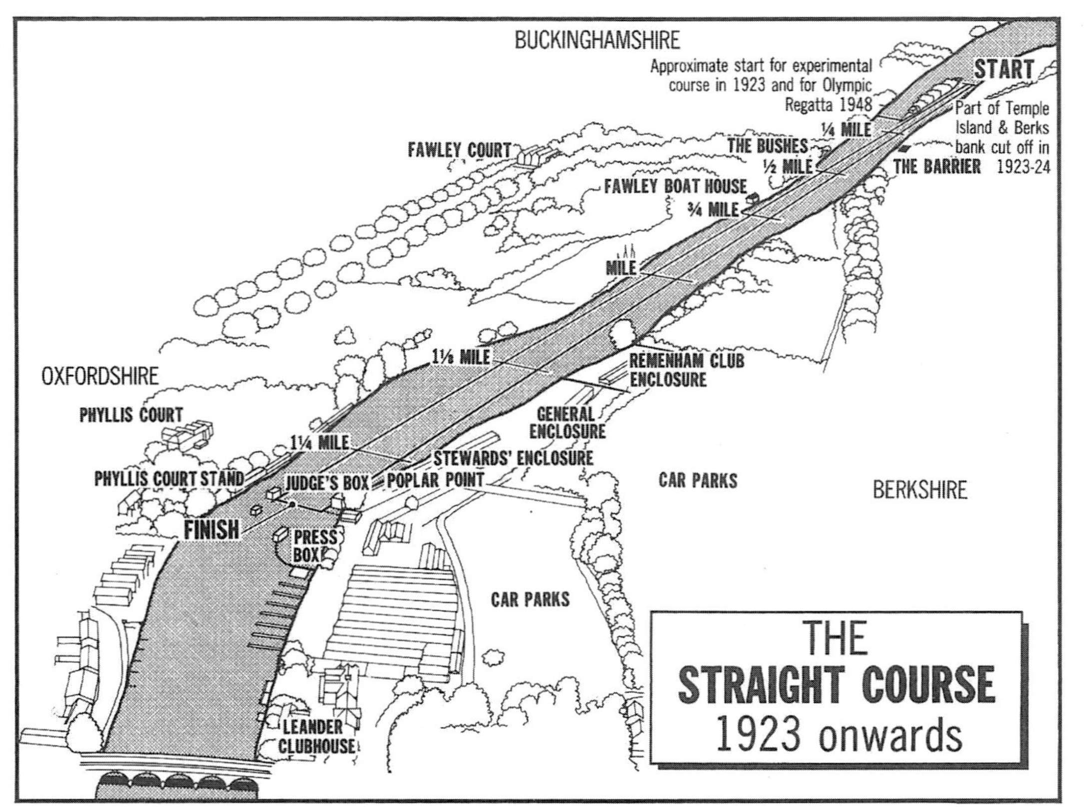
BUCKINGHAMSHIRE
Approximate start for experimental course in 1923 and for Olympic Regatta 1948
START
Part of Temple Island & Berks bank cut off in 1923-24
THE BARRIER
¼ MILE
THE BUSHES
½ MILE
FAWLEY COURT
FAWLEY BOAT HOUSE
¾ MILE
MILE
1⅛ MILE
REMENHAM CLUB ENCLOSURE
OXFORDSHIRE
PHYLLIS COURT
GENERAL ENCLOSURE
1¼ MILE
STEWARDS' ENCLOSURE
PHYLLIS COURT STAND
JUDGE'S BOX
POPLAR POINT
CAR PARKS
BERKSHIRE
FINISH
PRESS BOX
CAR PARKS
LEANDER CLUBHOUSE
THE
STRAIGHT COURSE
1923 onwards